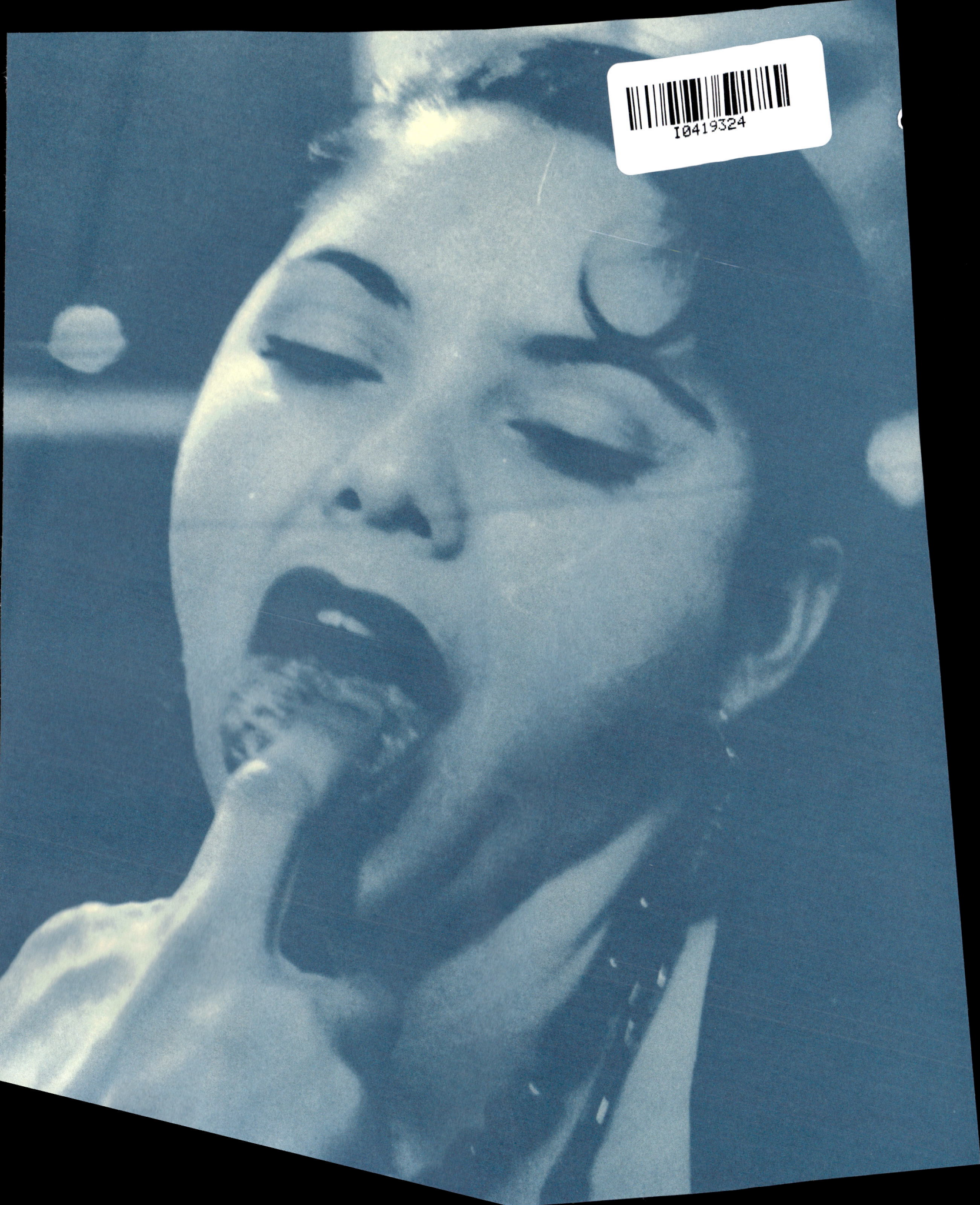
I0419324

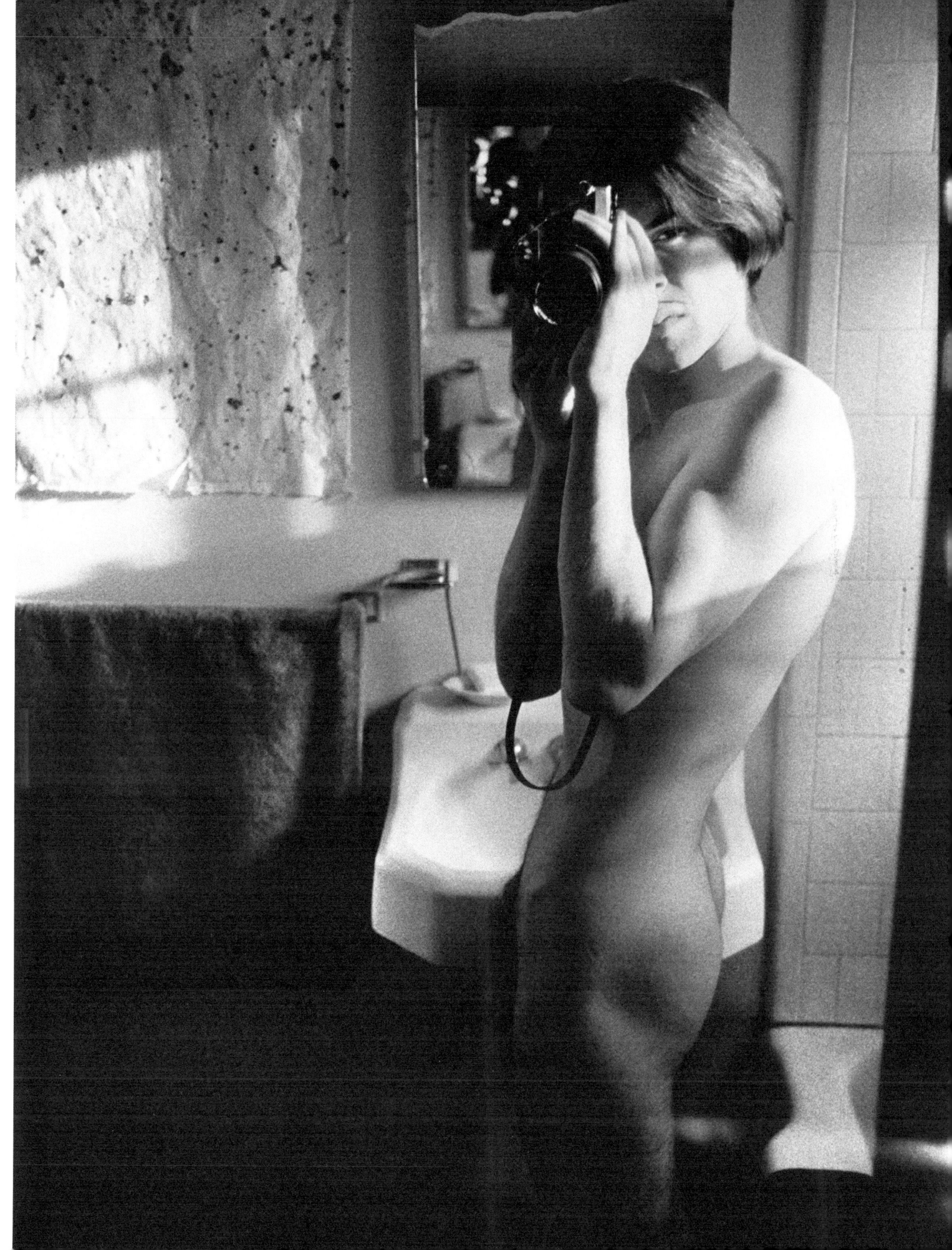

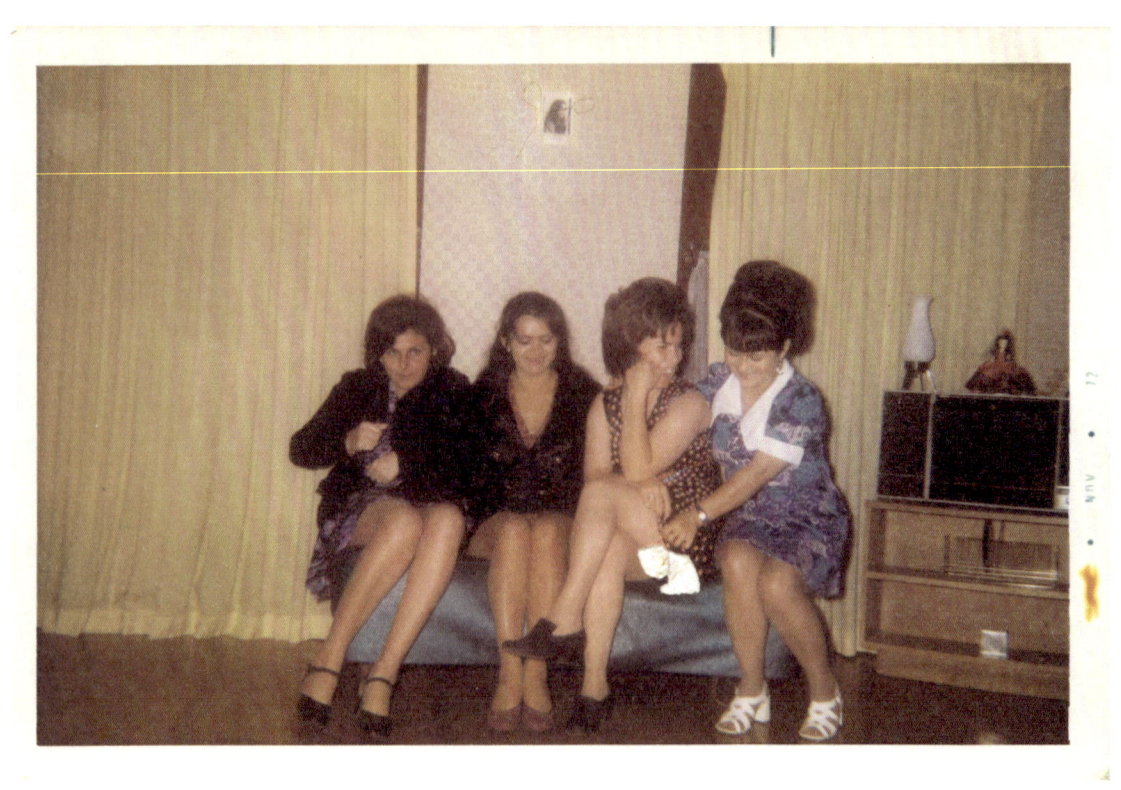

SEMIOTEXT(E)

Reynaldo Rivera Propiedad Privada

Edited by **Hedi El Kholti** & **Lauren Mackler**

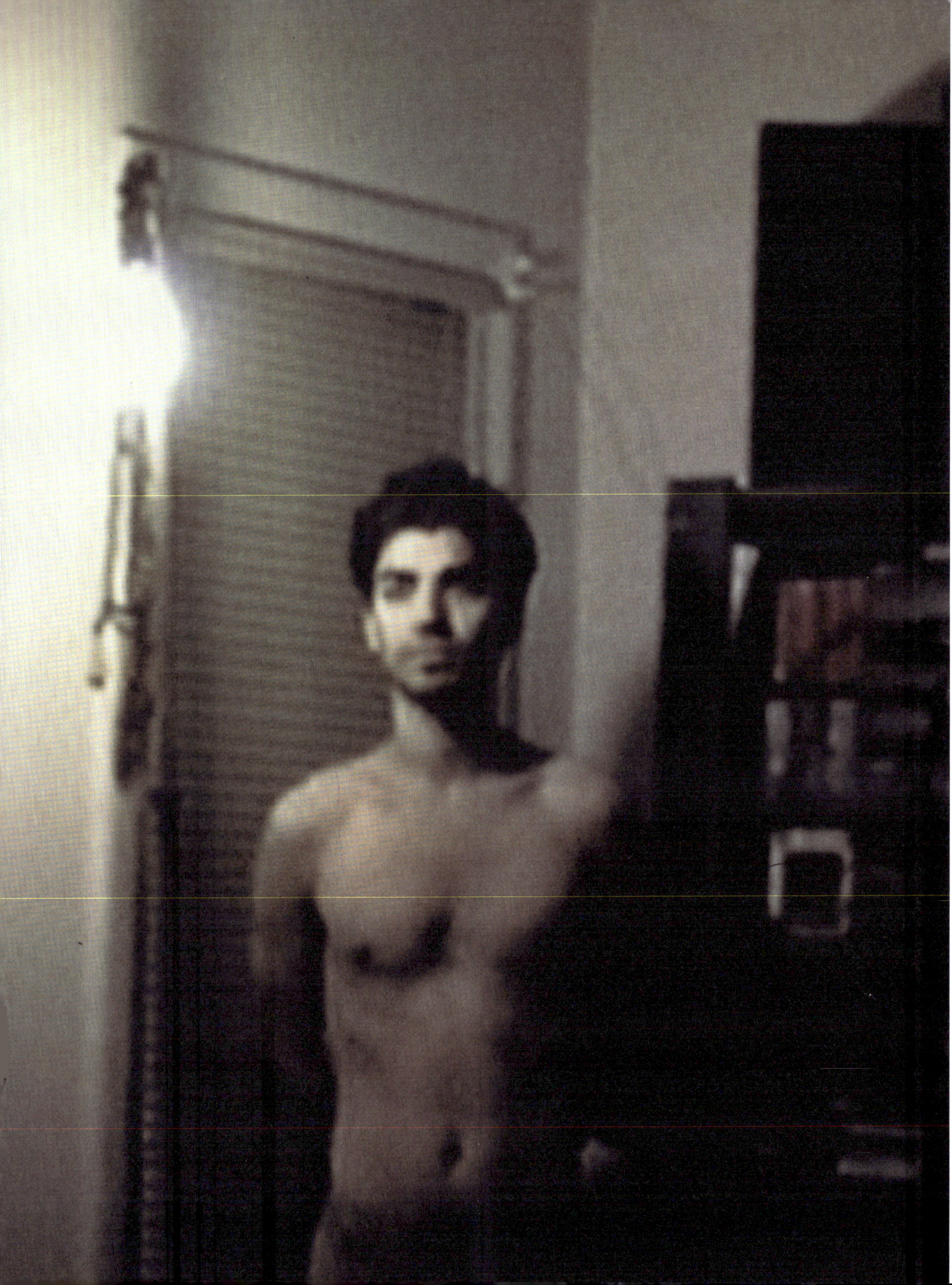

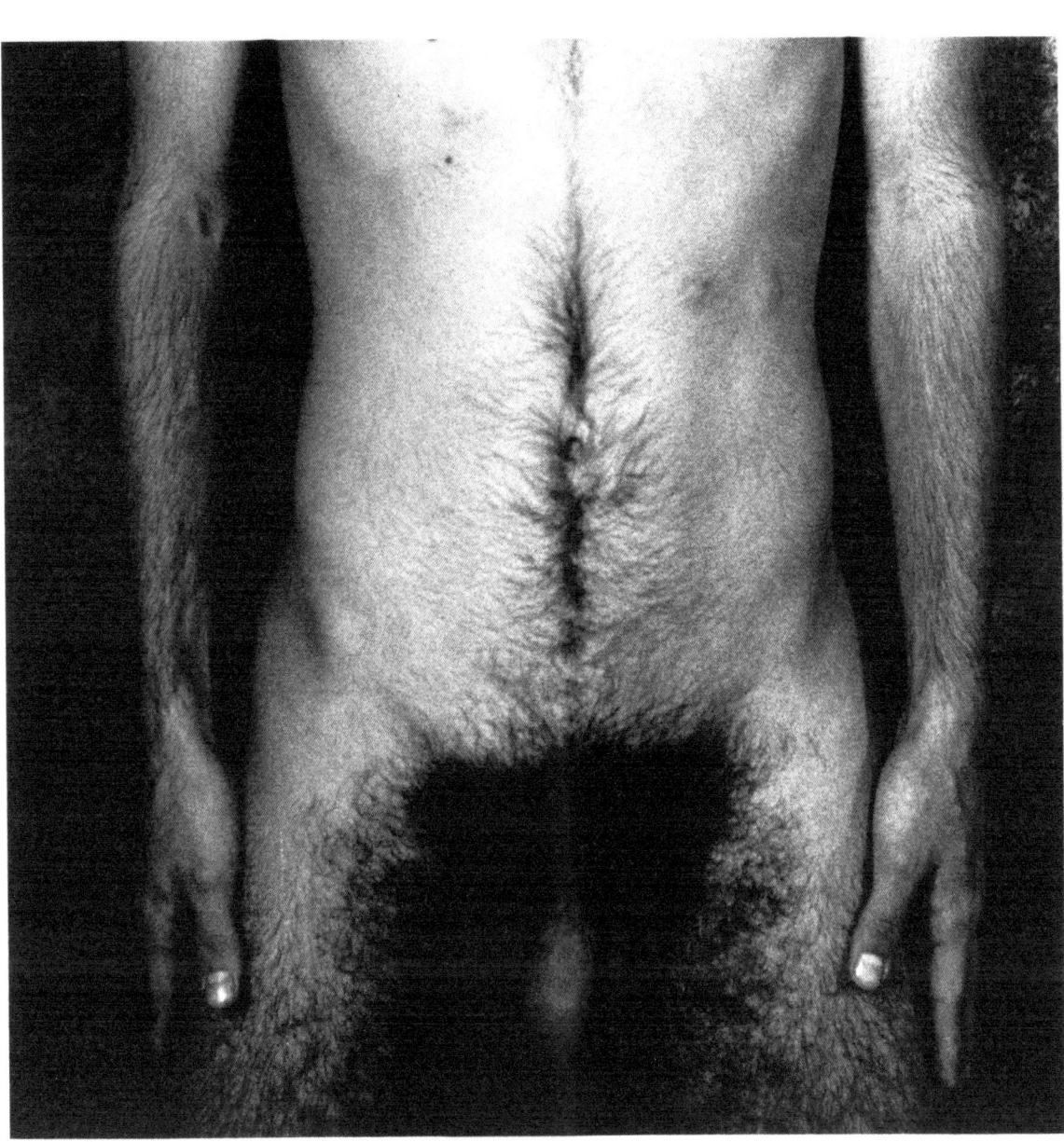

V

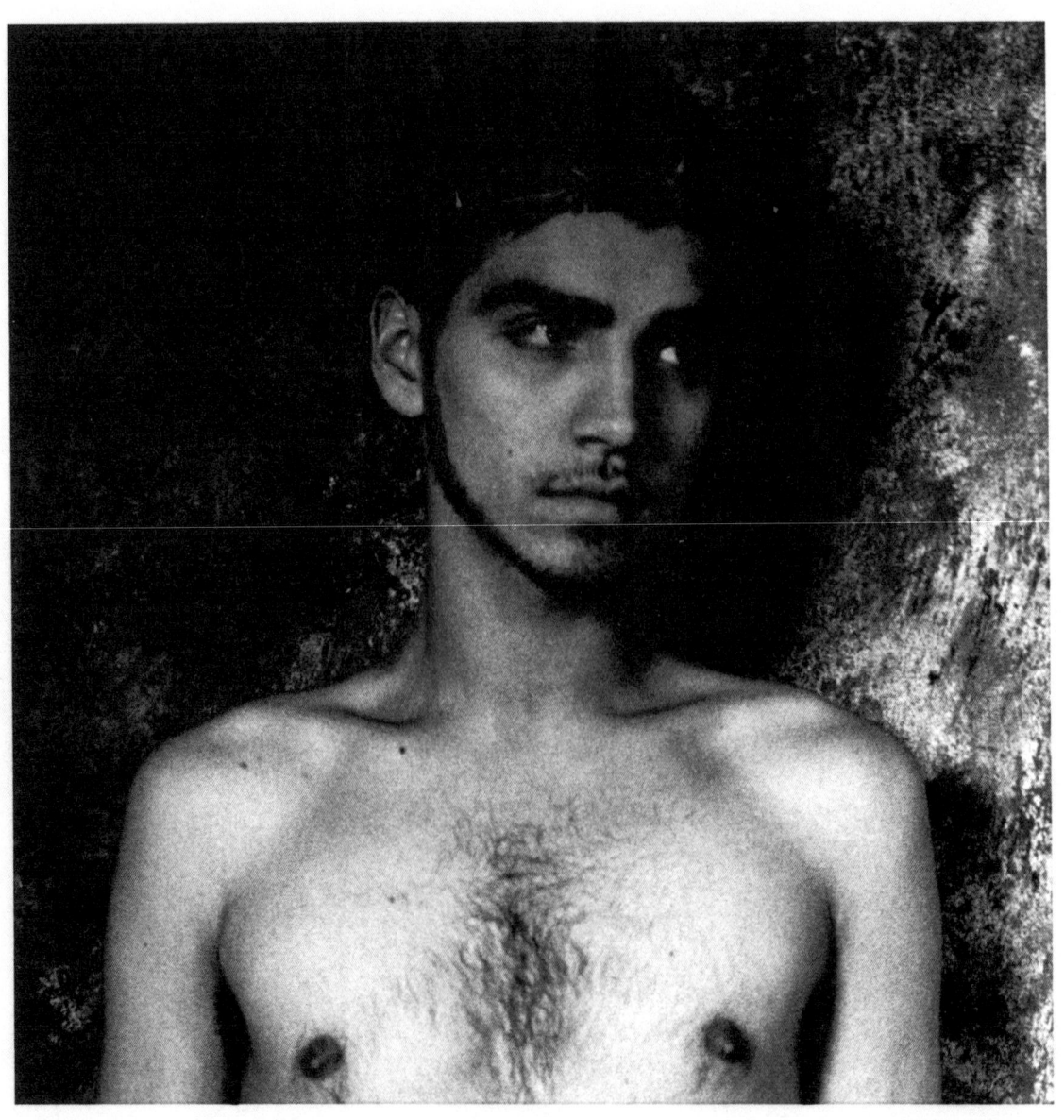

PP. i–vii: *Self-Portrait, Pasadena*, 1985; *Cathy Rivera and Friends*, 1972 (photographer unknown); *Bianco, Echo Park*, video still, 1995; *Bianco, Echo Park*, ca. 1992; *Bianco, Echo Park*, ca. 1992; *Reynaldo,* Polaroid, ca. 1985; *Martine,* Polaroid, ca. 1983

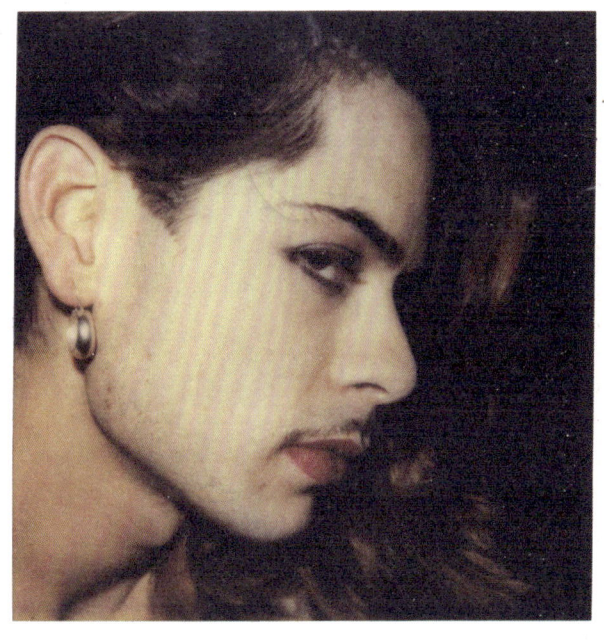

[TEXTS]

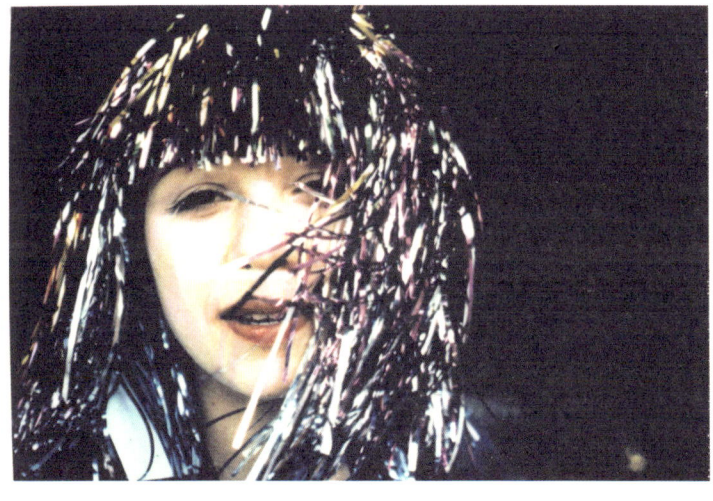

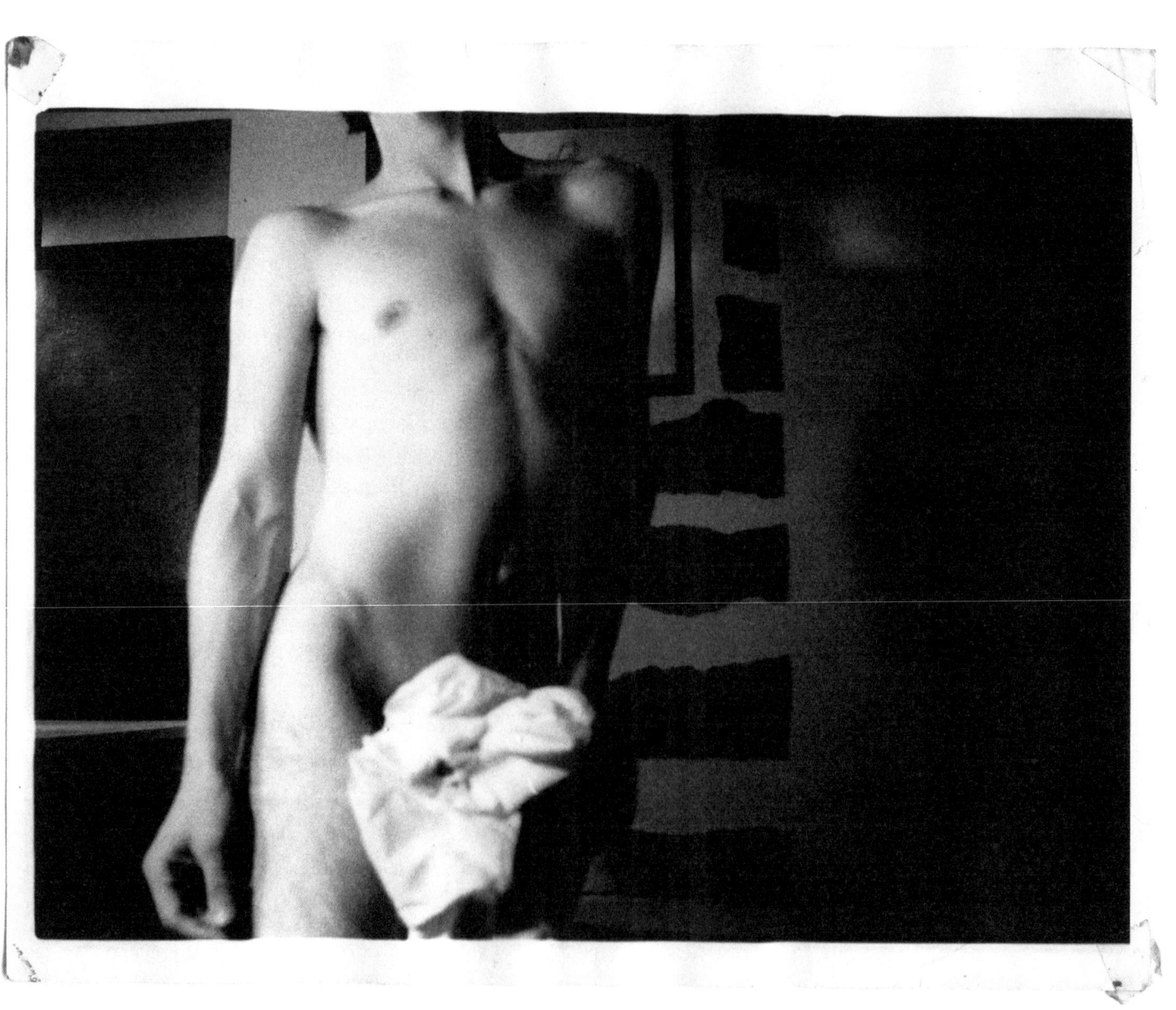

Self-Portrait, Pasadena, ca. 1987

PROPIEDAD PRIVADA
—Reynaldo Rivera

Over time, I've noticed love fizzles into hope. Hope is the drug. Love is the high. The smallest act of kindness can spark hope. It keeps you going. We return, incessantly, for that little hit. At what point are you just in hope?

I have a collection of photos I've taken of my friends and of their exes. Some of them have three or four. With each photo, you can see the hope for the future—like they thought, *This is the one. This is forever.* At the beginning, you have this moment of clarity. Everything feels possible. You feel borderless. And that's when the hope begins. And then, a few months later, there's the next one. That's what interested me: how quickly we jump from hope to hope. But I don't want to be Truman Capote; I don't want to be a pariah. Even though this book includes some exes, this book isn't about them. It's about the nebulous space between desire, love, and hope.

One of my earliest memories of desire is wanting to be a singer. I wanted to be Rocío Dúrcal. I twisted a towel around my head. My mother should've known. There was a movie— *Amor en el aire* (1967)—and it was everything to me. *Amor en el aire. Que nació del aire. Que vive del aire. No puedo olvidarlo, no, no, no.*

I'm a person who cries to song lyrics. I was just listening to David Bowie and Queen's "Under Pressure" and started sobbing. *It's the terror of knowing what this world is about. ... Keep coming up with love, but it's so slashed and torn.* Boo hoo hoo.

My idea of love began accumulating as a child. It started in innocence. A relative lured me in by making me feel special. She turned on me as soon as she thought I was a liability. She told me I would be better off dead. That I was hideous. That everyone hated me. And you know what? I almost did die. Went up to the roof with a note, ready to jump.

That shit—it wasn't traumatic. It was shocking. It set me up to always wait for the bottom to drop out. Always thinking, *When good things happen, something terrible's coming.* It was the first time I learned love equaled death. It wasn't the last.

After I failed to jump off the roof, I ended up living with our neighbor, Toña Ruedas. She had a pharmacy and she loved to play her Toña la Negra 45s while I sat on her lap. She taught me all the lyrics—songs brimming with tormented love. My education. Later, I discovered Lucha Reyes and Bessie Smith. Women singing about messy love—their songs were my road map. I heard them, and I felt like they were preparing me. Telling me what was to come. And that's how I learned about love. It wasn't the happy kind; it was the kind that left you drained but needing more, and thinking you could save someone, thinking that love meant sacrificing everything. Their voices were my Oracle of Delphi. The oracle foretold that I would lose my eyes. *Arráncame la vida con el último beso de amor ay arrancala y toma, toma mi corazon arrancame la vida y si acaso te hiere el dolor a de ser de no verme porque al tus ojos me los llevo yo.* They weren't wrong. All is fair in love and war.

All these women threatening to cut up their lovers, all these women going back to men who hurt them. *Well I'd rather my man would hit me, than to jump right up and quit me. 'Tain't nobody's bizness if I do.*

They made it seem like this is how you're supposed to be. Your man beat you? Well, you shouldn't have done what you did. He loves you. *He hit me and it felt like a kiss.* Hello. How fucked up is that? Songs were teaching me that love isn't clean, that pain and desire are so tangled up that a slap becomes intimacy. And I lived that shit. I kept thinking, *This is what love is.* With the first one—the one who dragged me out of the closet—I hoped he'd never realize he was kissing a frog. With Craig, I hoped I would be safe. With Samir, I hoped he'd never leave. Samir opened the floodgates of vulnerability and love. And with Steven, as with Craig, I hoped I wouldn't end up with AIDS. I hoped that when he sliced my eyeball in half, I wouldn't go blind. By the time I got to the one I'm with, I just hoped I wouldn't end up with a combination of all the others.

I used to think love meant being there for your man, no matter the cost. I was looking for someone to love unconditionally like a dog. *No, por Dios, no te me vayas, te lo ruego, que la vida como un perro pasaré: sin hablarte, sin llorar, sin un reproche, siempre tirado a tus pies, de día y de noche.* I wanted to give love without being judged or punished for it. I wanted to love freely, to pour everything out without fear that it would be used against me.

But the blues singers, the *boleros*, the *rancheras*—they knew before I did. They told me: *You will try everything and you won't give up.* They said: *Love will make you a fool.* They said: *Love makes me do foolish things. Sit alone by the phone, a phone that never rings.*

And I did. I chased love through the bars of Los Angeles. I followed men down streets, through intersections, across red lights—hoping to catch them before they drove drunk, before they died. I searched. I cut myself open. I spent a night locked up next to my man, both of us near death, and saw my soulmate, a grand romance. I did everything there was to do. I gave everything that I had. I came back again and again, a doormat. And I'd do it again.

Now I've been with my partner for thirty years. I thought at this point my libido should have died—but it hasn't. It's more desperate, more confused, more hungry. I always thought the finale would be this coasting into the sunset. But there is no coasting. I'm still full of questions. But I have survived. I made my way through the emotional minefield. And eventually, Bianco and I will walk off into the horizon—slouching, wounded by the journey, still not sure how we made it this far.

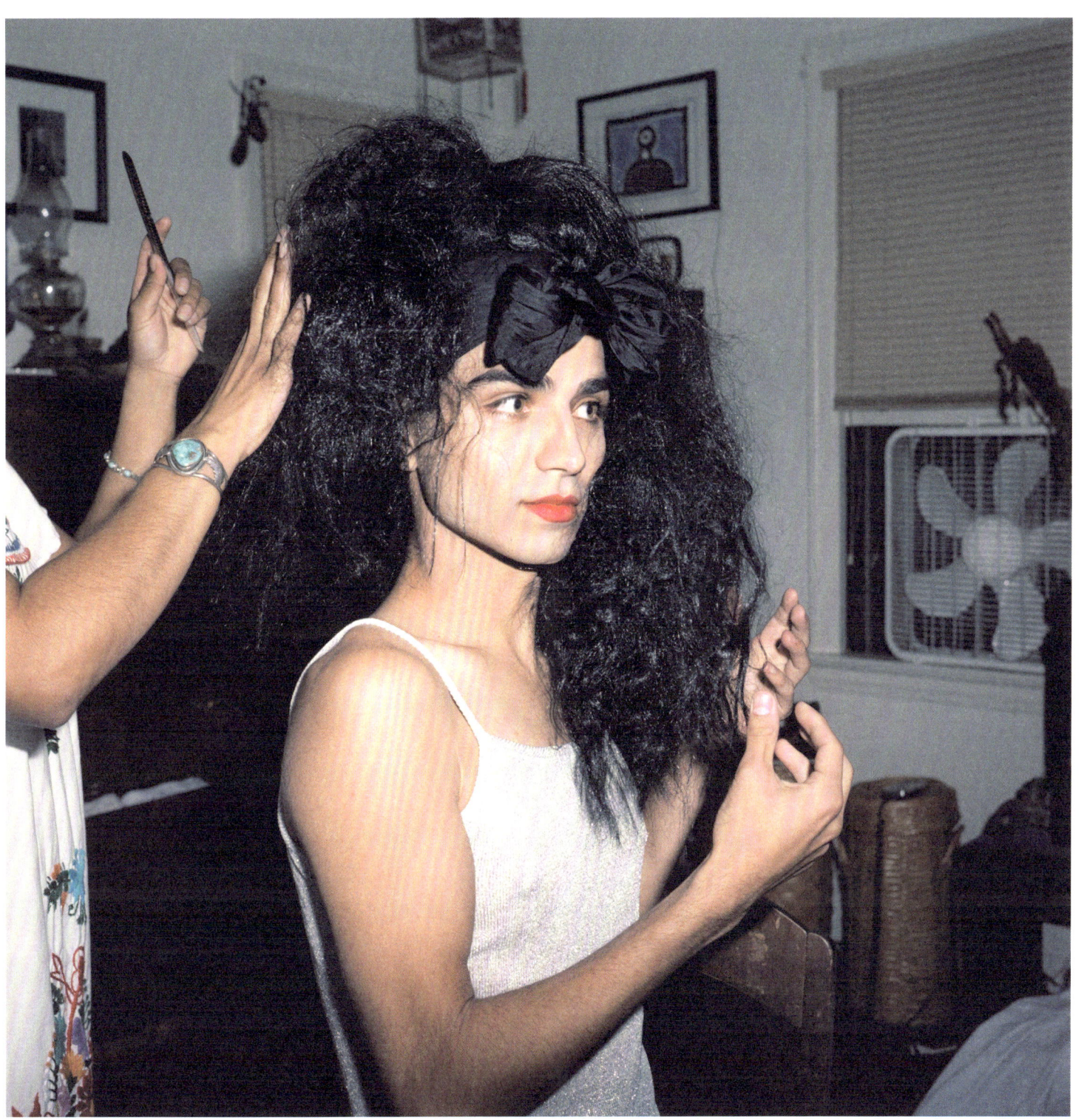

Bianco, Silver Lake, 1994

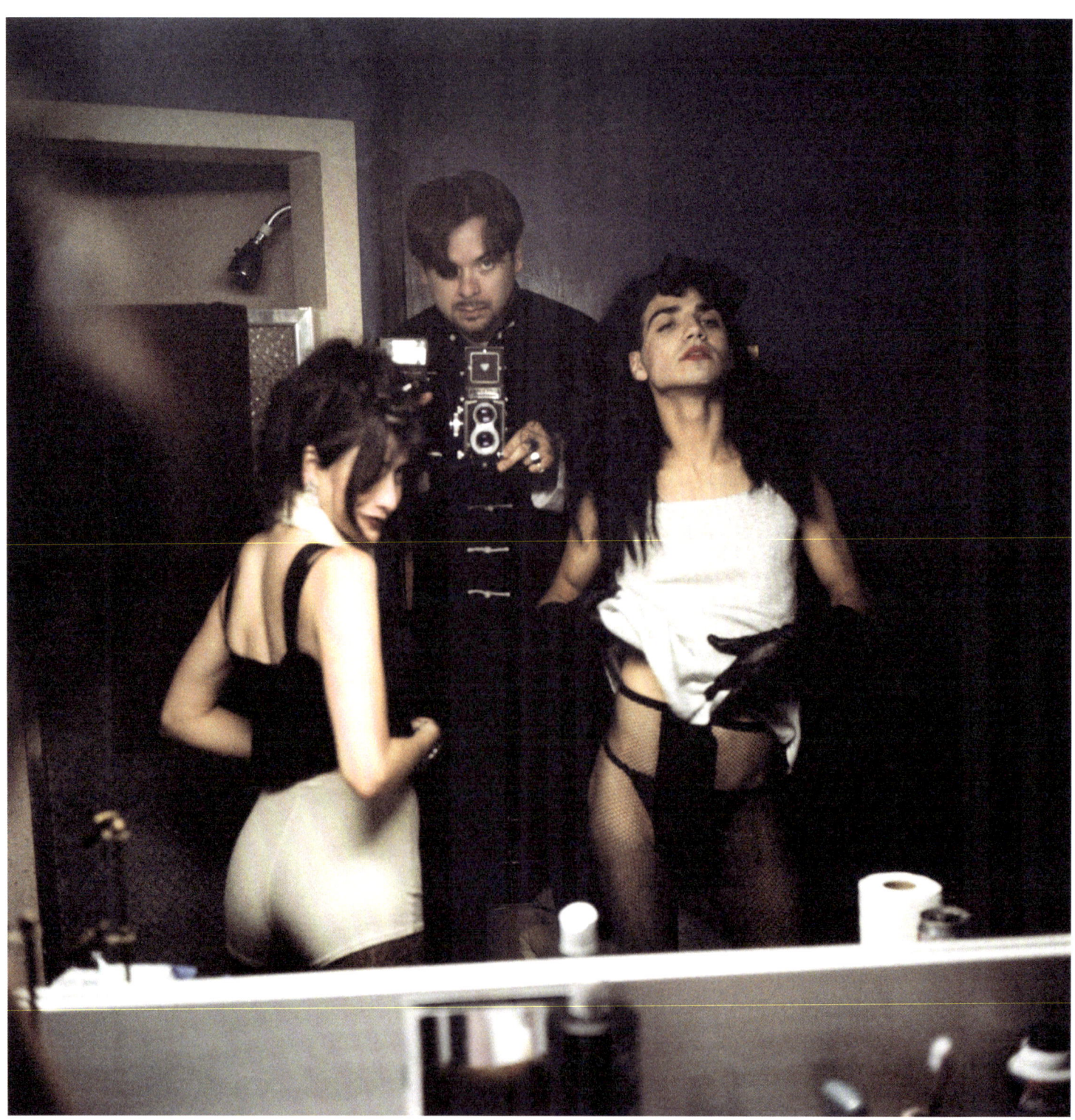

Amy, Reynaldo, Bianco, Silver Lake, 1994

I DREAM OF A LIFE WITH NO LOVER
—Constance Debré

I dream of a life with no lover / Am I too intense, she says sitting naked on me her hands on my shoulders / I think we should fuck, says a woman I don't know / The first time was with a guy in Paris in an apartment under the roof I think we'd watched a James Bond movie before / The last time was yesterday here in Los Angeles with her we saw *The Long Goodbye* after / My sexual life improved when I became a writer / I became a writer when my sexual life improved / The main obstacle to my writing is my sexual life / They're right when they say writing about sex is obscene, not because sex is obscene (it's not anymore) but because of how easy it is that trick / Punishment: to have to read my own books or be this cool writer writing about sex / I never received any dick pic / A woman used to send me nudes I didn't know what to answer I used to "heart" them then I broke up with her / I found her especially hot that week she had lost her voice / First times are the most interesting philosophically speaking / Imagining a world built on the opposite of the unwritten rule as-often-as-possible-with-the-fewest-people—a world where having sex twice with someone would be prohibited / I remember bodies better than faces / I have to talk to her about money I can't go on like this / I remember bodies very precisely—I think I remember each body, something physically specific about each body I had sex with / Paris New York Los Angeles Florence Marseille Naples London Hong Kong Arles Montlouis Corsica Marrakech Rome Madrid / How many naked bodies do we see in a lifetime? / Spank me,

she said and I spanked her, Spank me harder and I spanked harder / Why are you homosexual? / I never think of myself as homosexual / She's shy and trashy all together / Has the technique improved through human history? / The problem when one writes in the first person and one writes about sex is that some people assume you want to have sex with them / talk to them / listen to them / *Certainly Not* (good title) / Are the French good lovers? / Every time I go back to Paris I wonder why the Americans find the French attractive / I'd like to write a book about French ugliness (ten volumes) / My fetishism for Americans meets her fetishism for the French / Do we learn anything from sex? Yes. What? I don't know / Idea of a zero-sum equation / I don't know what I earn, I know what I lose / I'm in favor of celibacy for priests and writers / *Eppure si muove* (And yet it moves) as Galileo used to say / When I was a lawyer: talking about sodomy in the courtroom before the highest judges in the old Paris courthouse that used to be the king's palace / my client the whore who was telling the judge: I, Madame la Juge, I fuck to buy myself purses shoes jewelry, I, Madame la Juge, I could not live like you do with a little paycheck and ugly sweaters (the judge was wearing a pale-blue mohair sweater—pity for the judge, admiration for the whore) / The main inconvenience is work / I say it's always good for my English / The journalist in Copenhagen who asked How to seduce women? / The journalist in LA who asked Who are the ten hottest girls in LA? / The student applying for my class at the Berlin University who wrote I haven't read your books I'm going to tell you how attractive I am / The student who wrote I want to attend your class because you look hot on the cover (of one of my books) / No book no writer ever wrote the truth / The truth is that the truth is impossible to write / I can't have sex with anybody without wondering which one of us will die first / Which one of our bodies will decay first / None of my lovers has died yet (I think) / Every day, no matter the girlfriend, from 4 a.m. to 8 a.m. I plan to break up, then I go swimming and it passes.

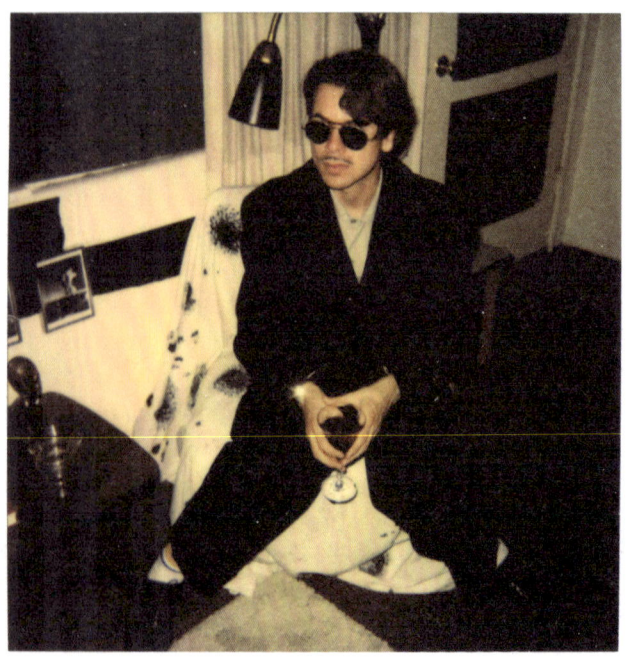

Reynaldo, Polaroid, 1990
RIGHT: *Bianco, Echo Park,* video still, 1995

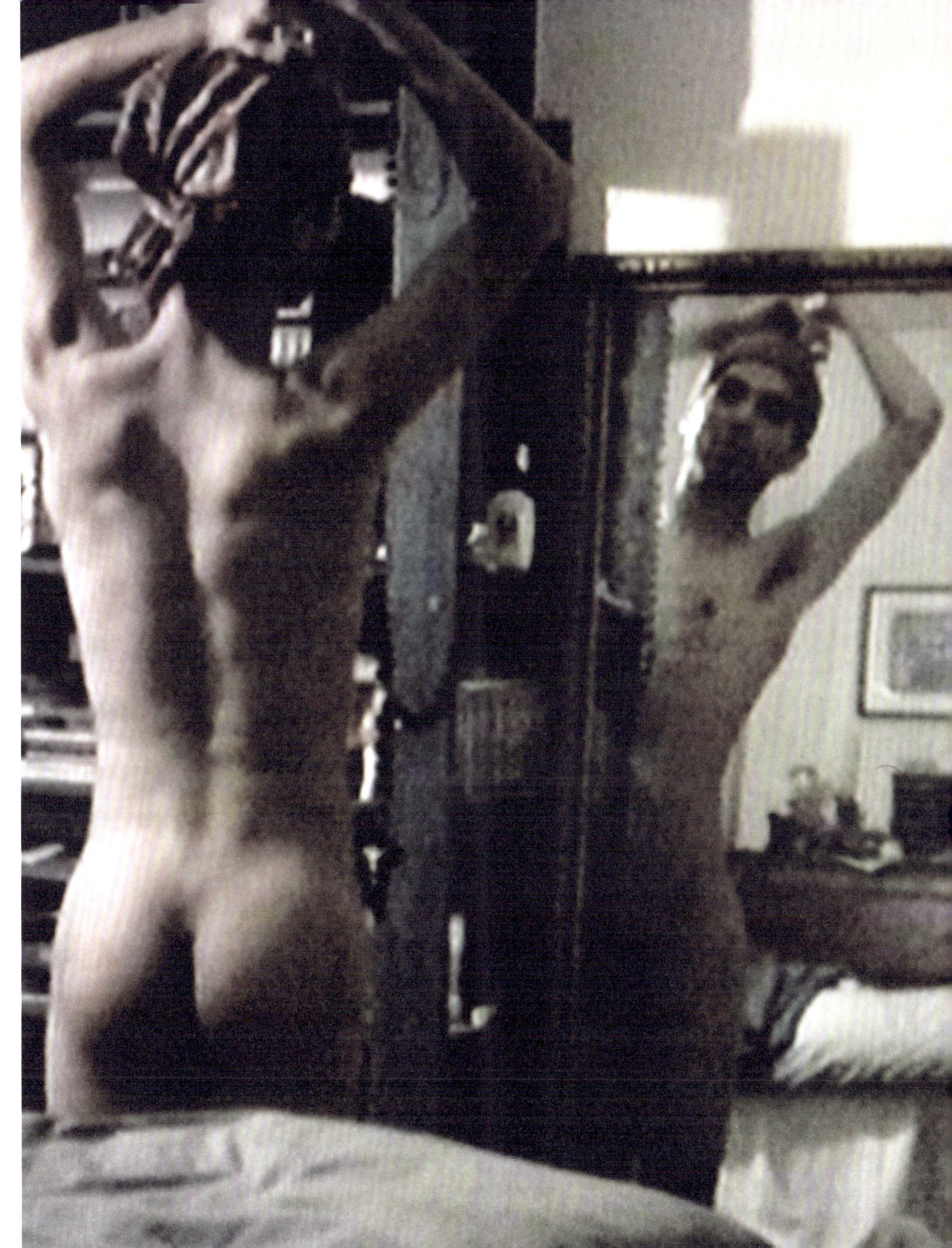

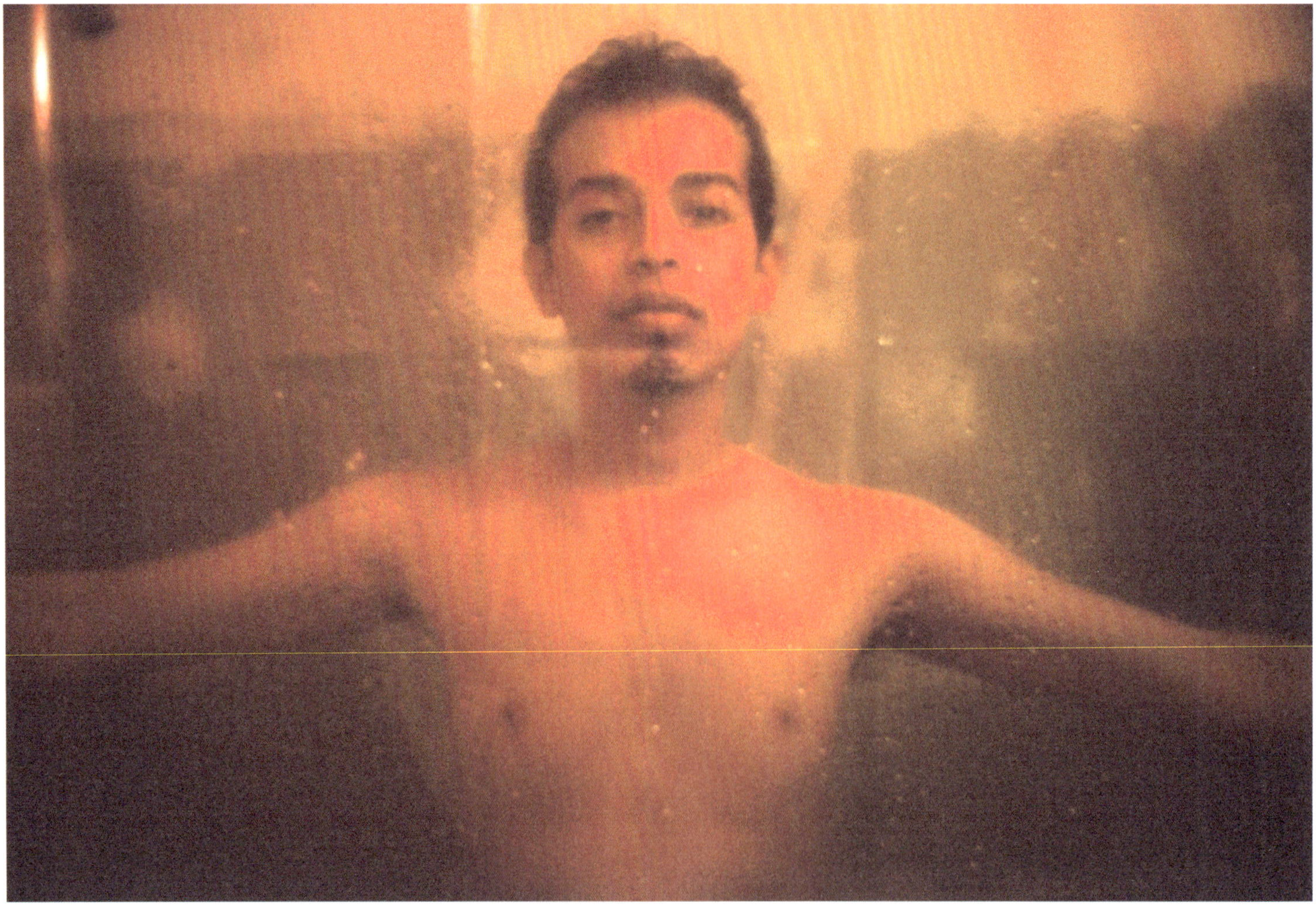

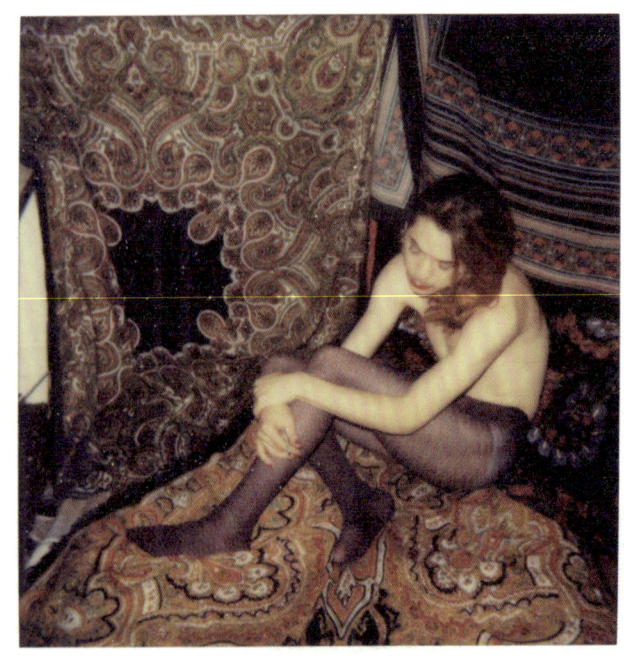

Ceri, Echo Park, ca. 1999
Reynaldo, Polaroid, ca. 1985
RIGHT: *Self-Portrait, Beachwood Canyon*, ca. 1995

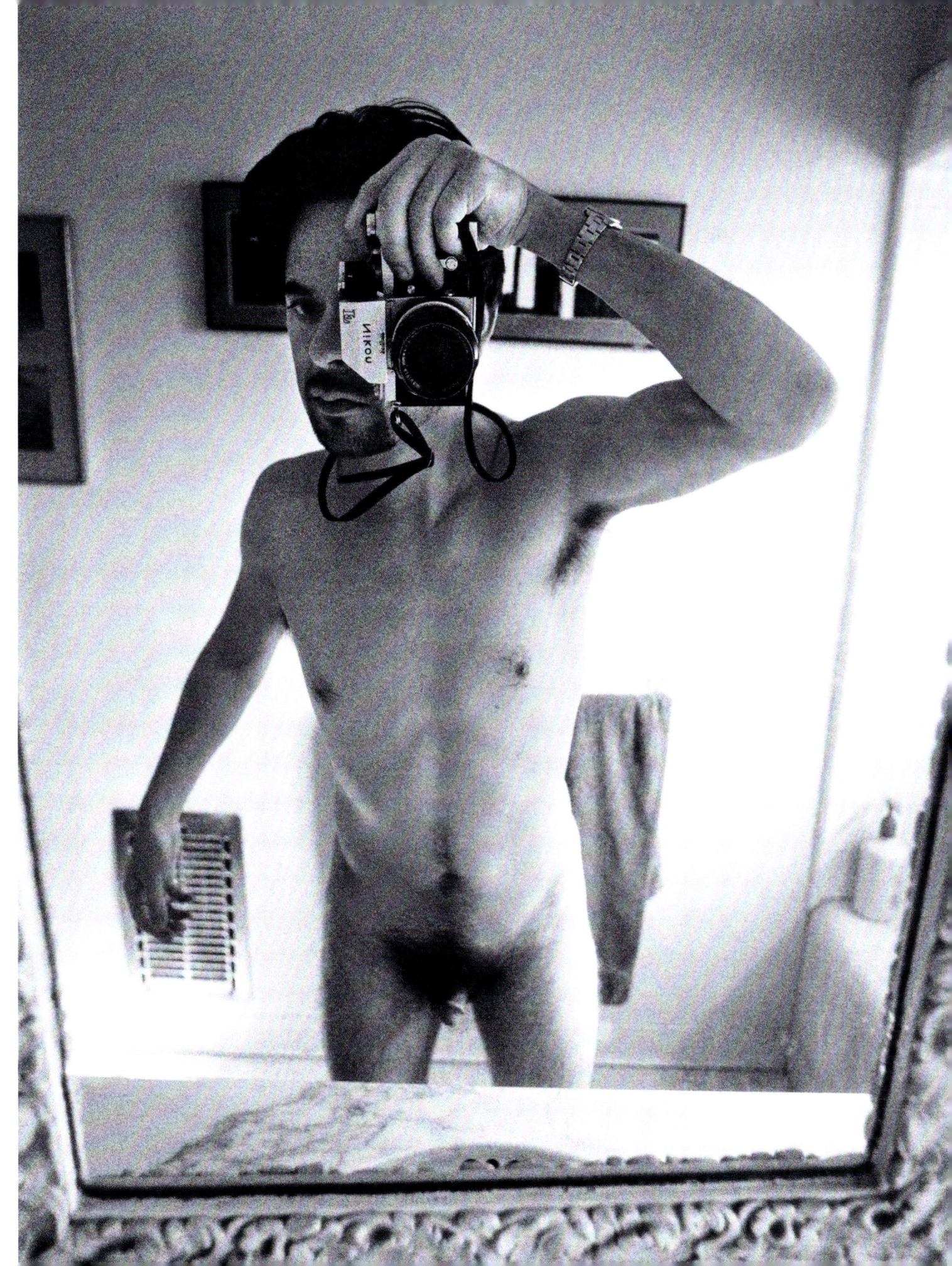

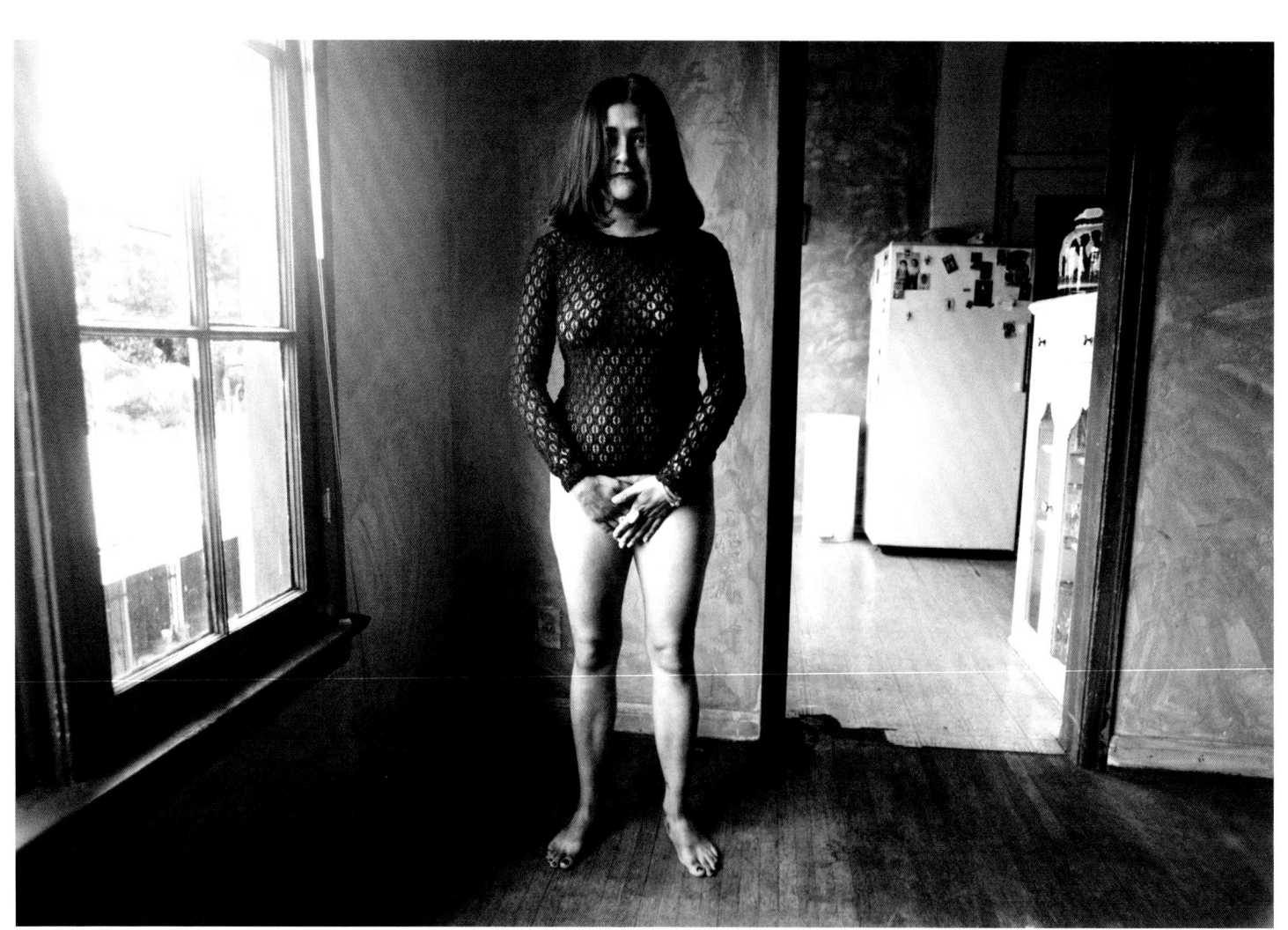

Pamela, Echo Park, ca. 1998

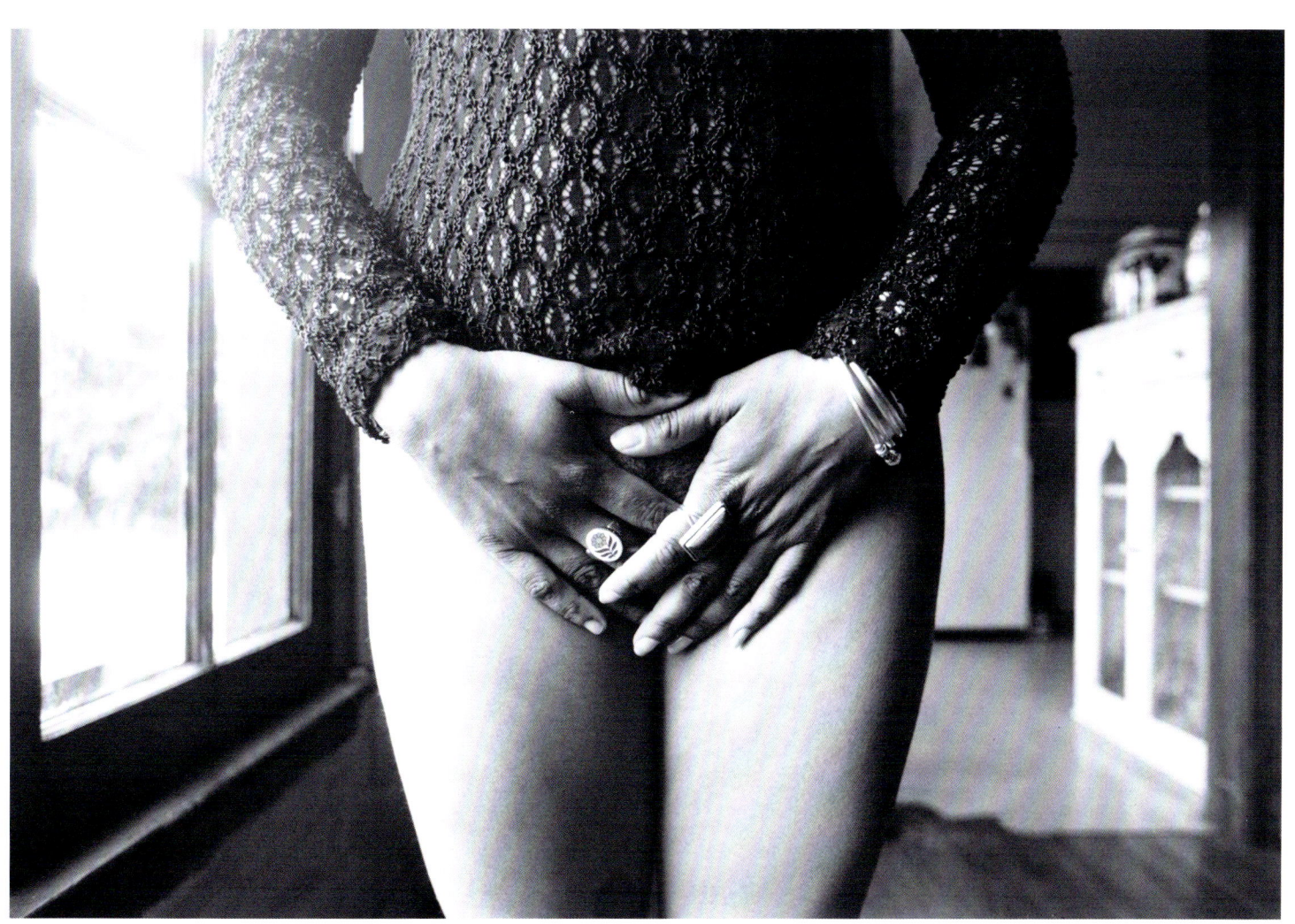

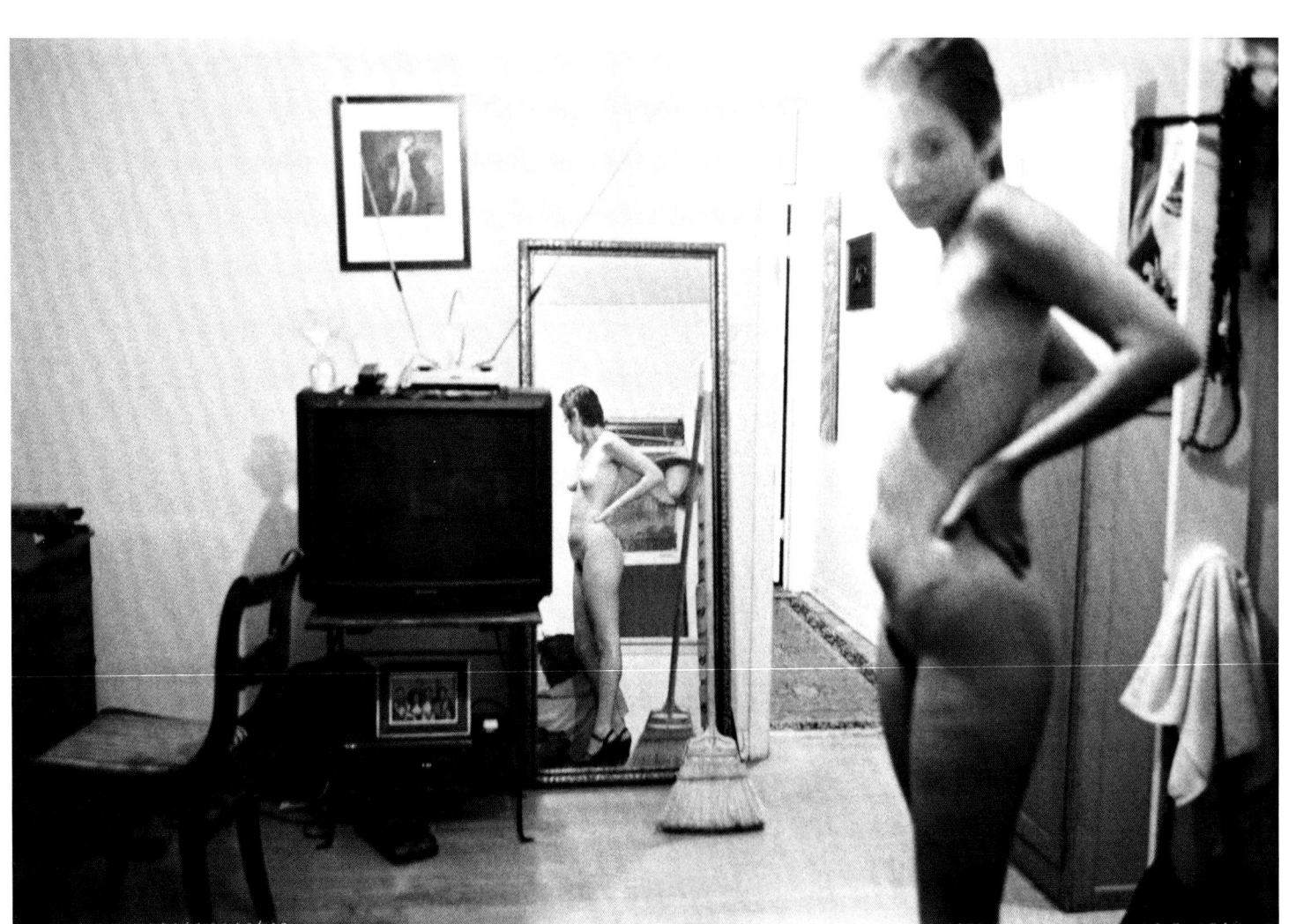

Carla, Echo Park, 1997

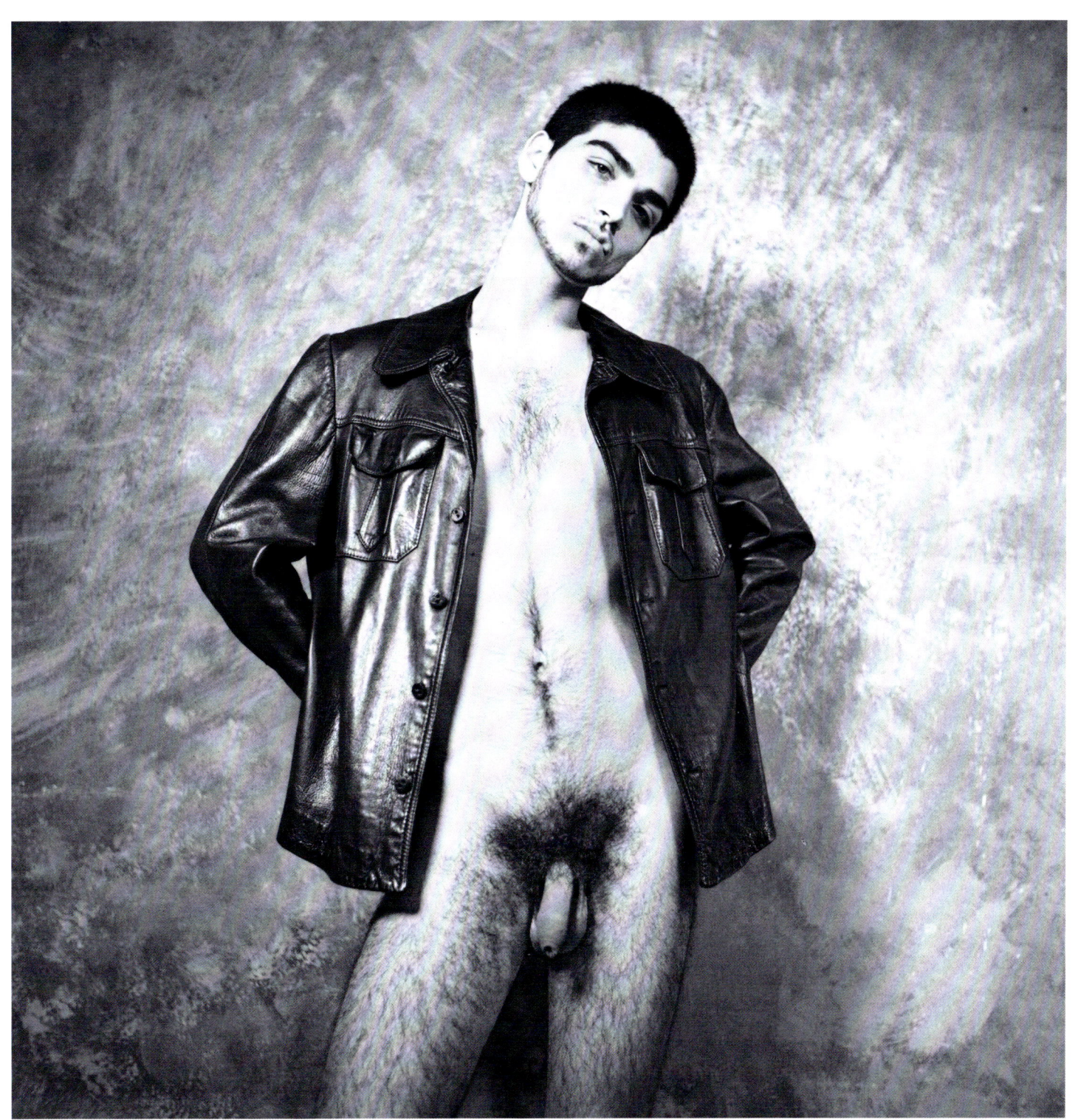

Bianco, Echo Park, ca. 1992

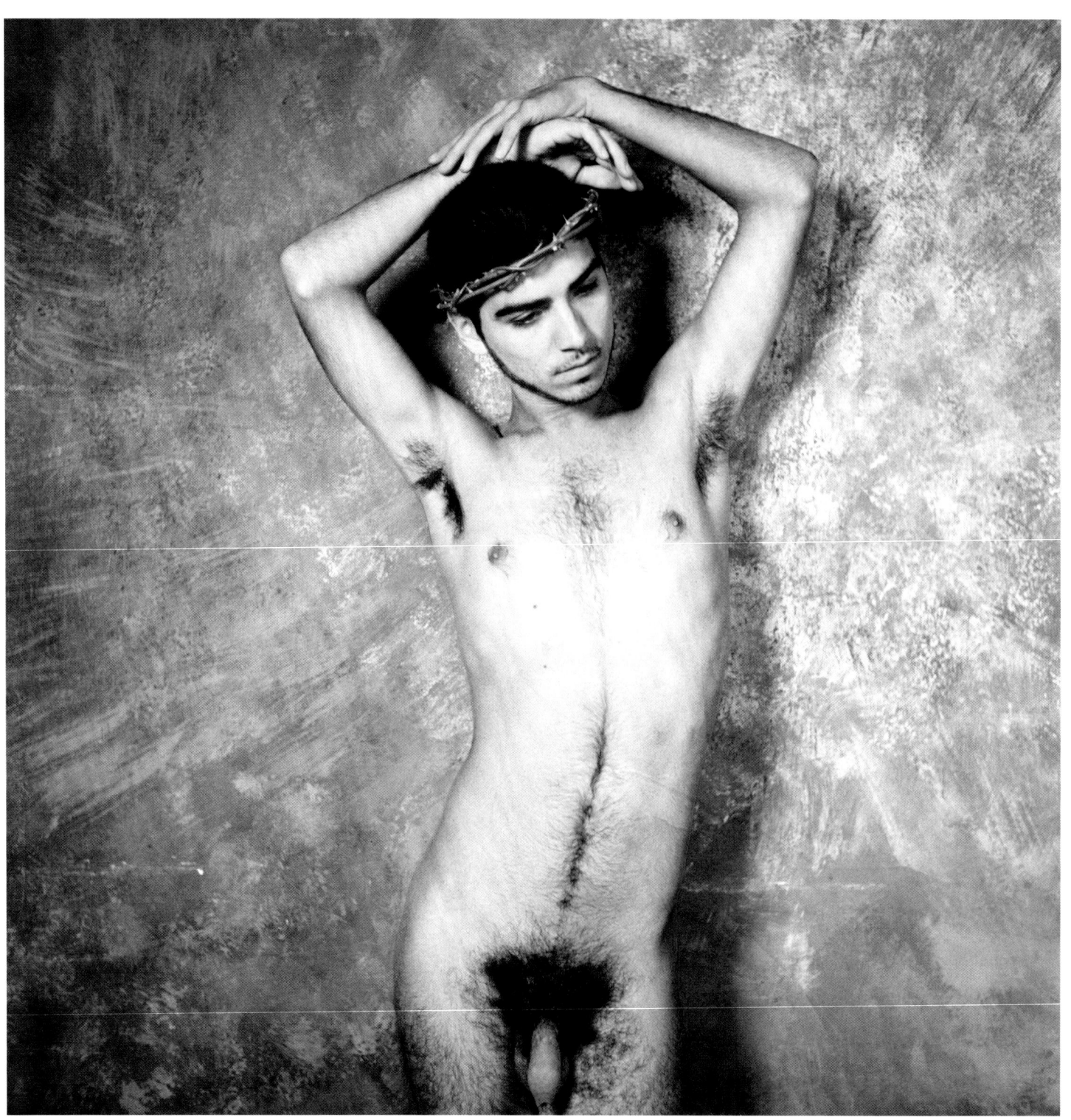

Bianco, Echo Park, ca. 1992

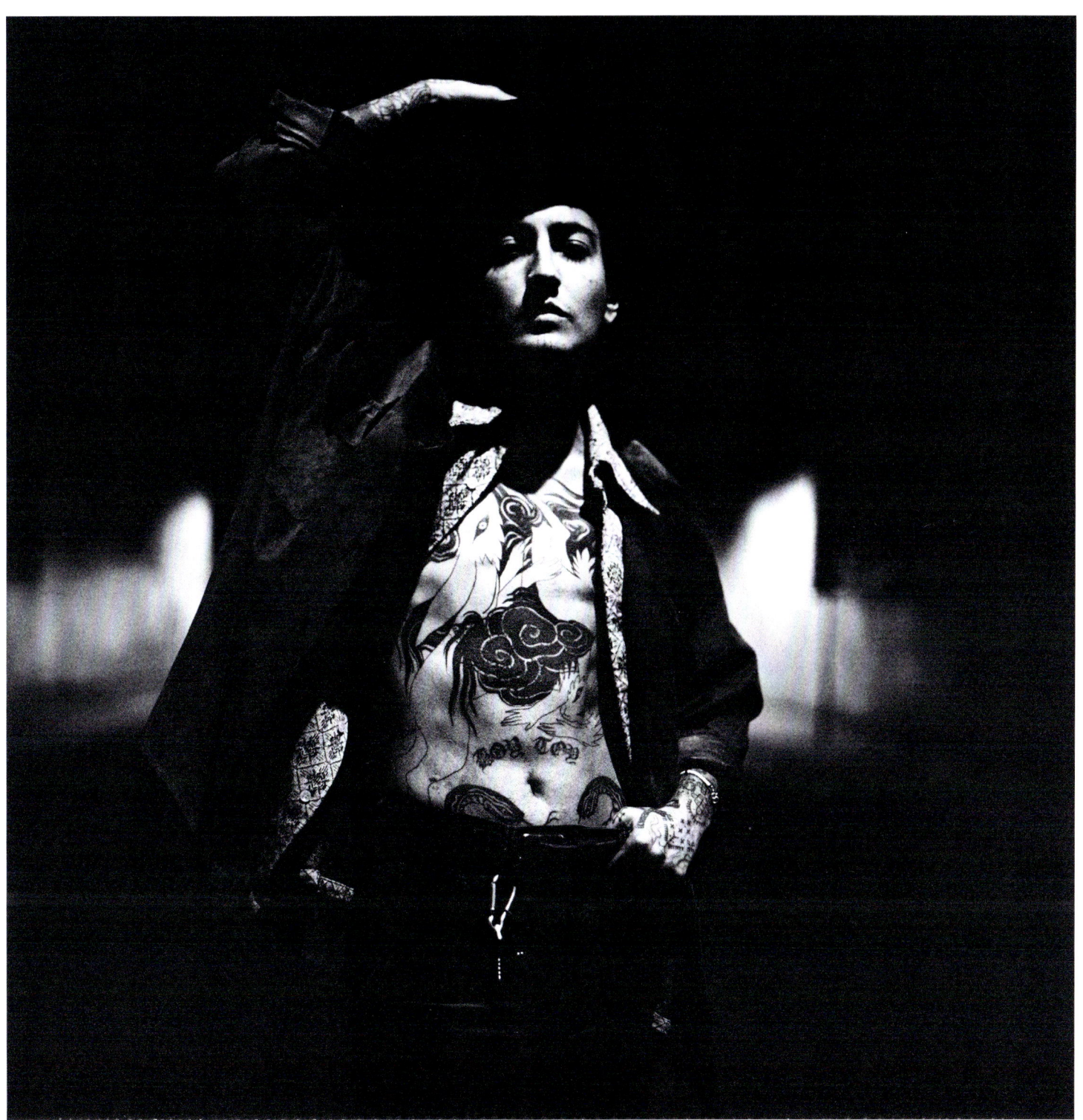

Coyote, Downtown Los Angeles, 2022

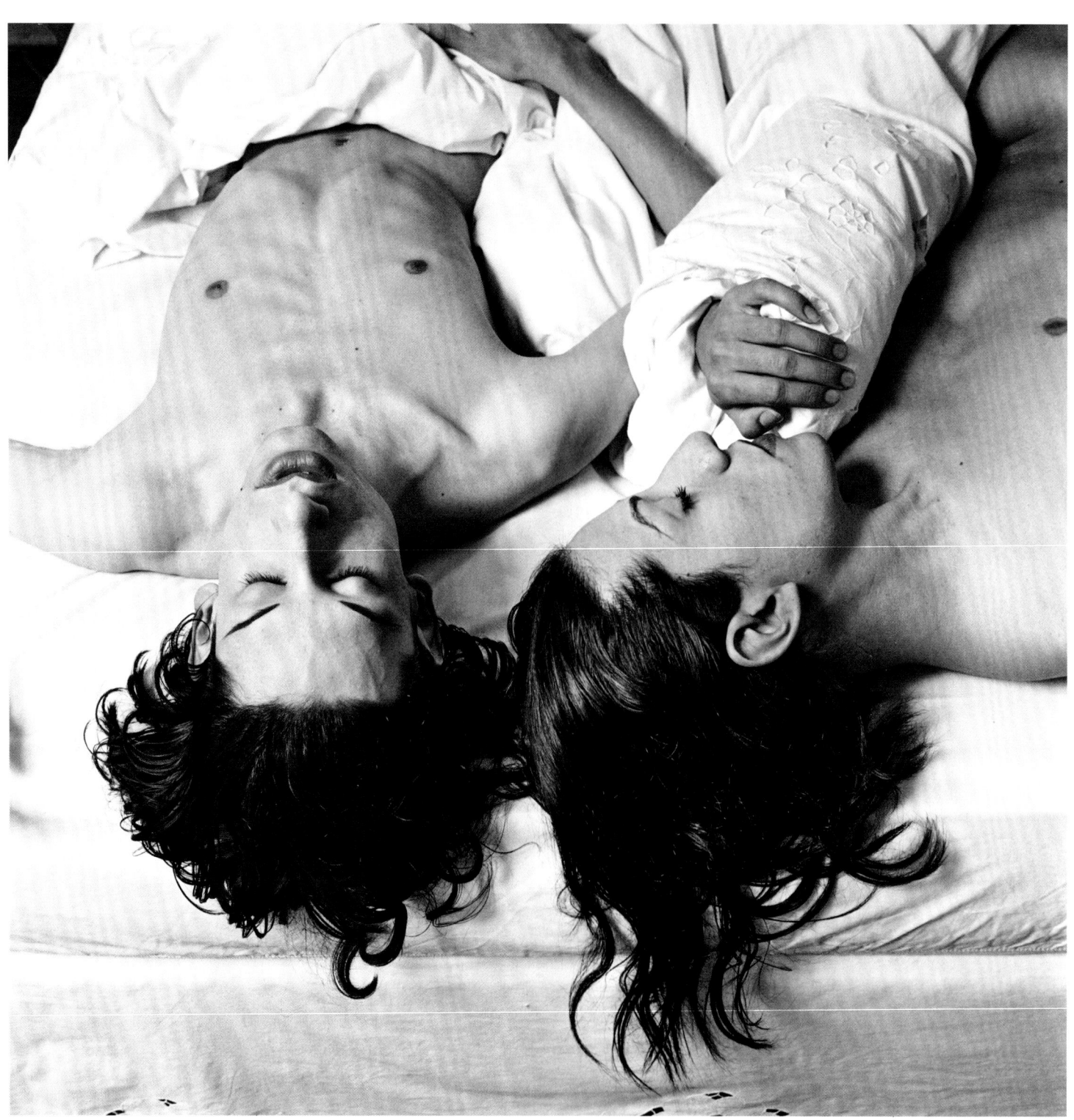

Juan, Javier, Los Angeles, ca. 1991

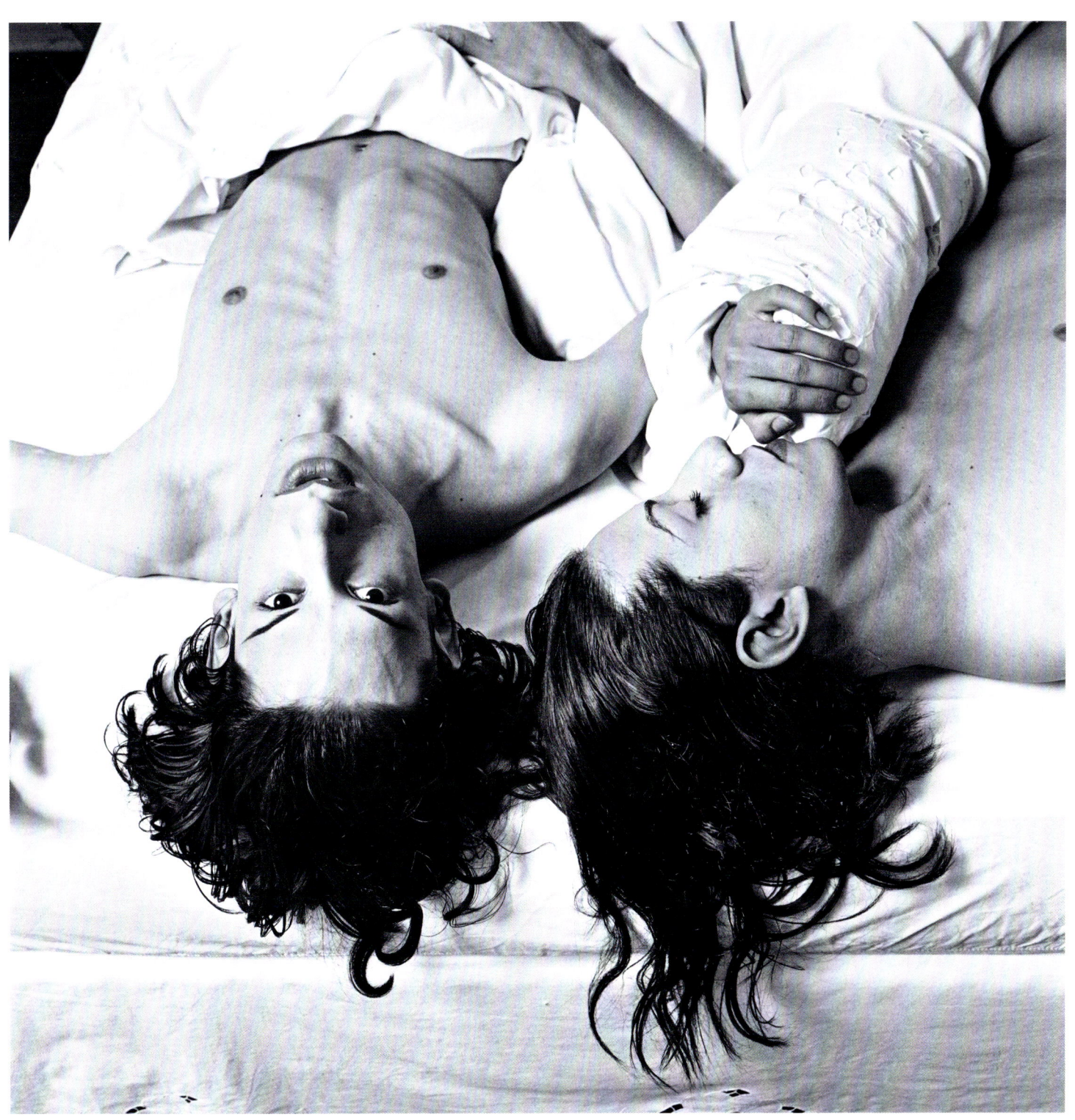

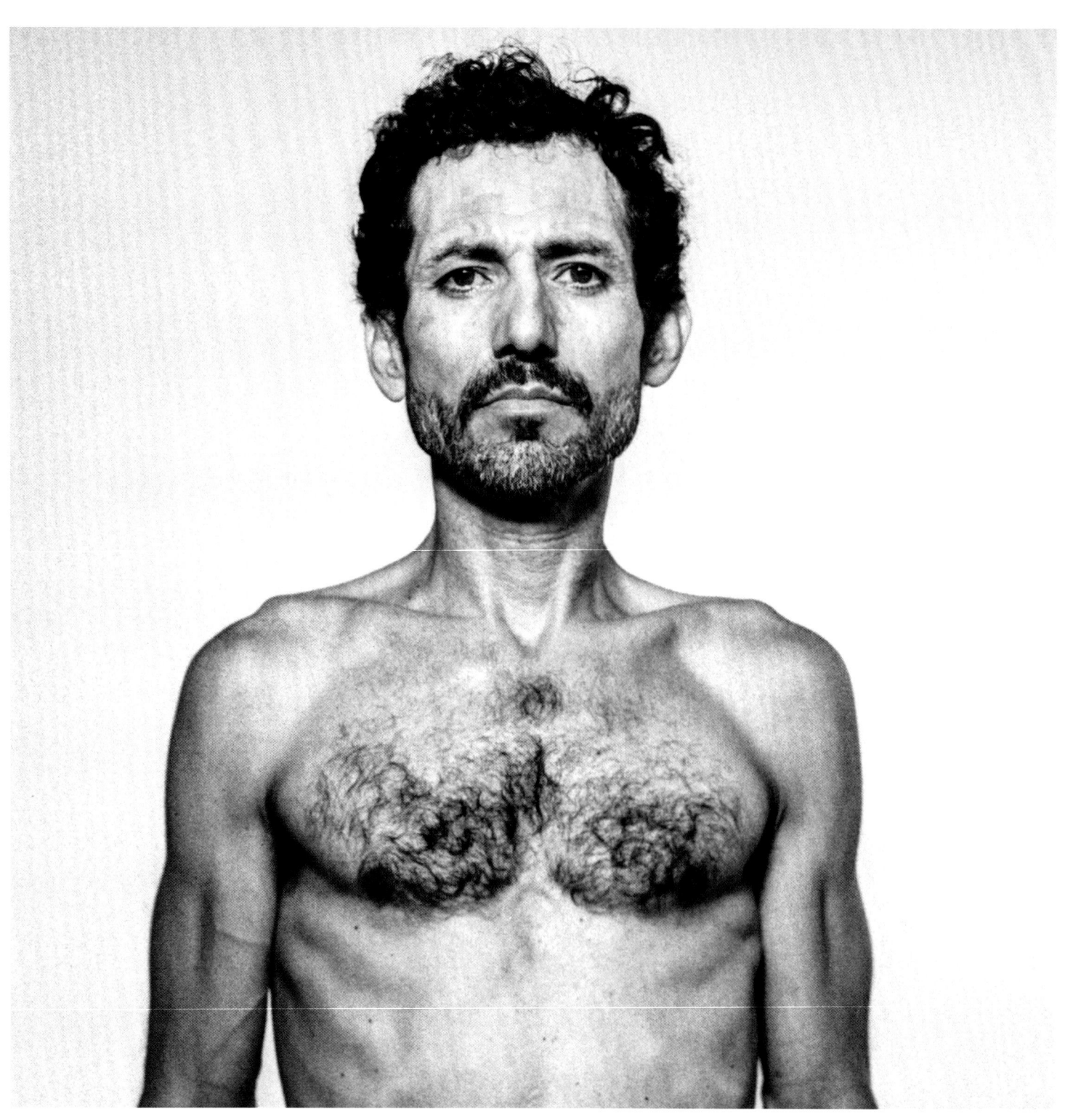

Justo, Lincoln Heights, ca. 2015

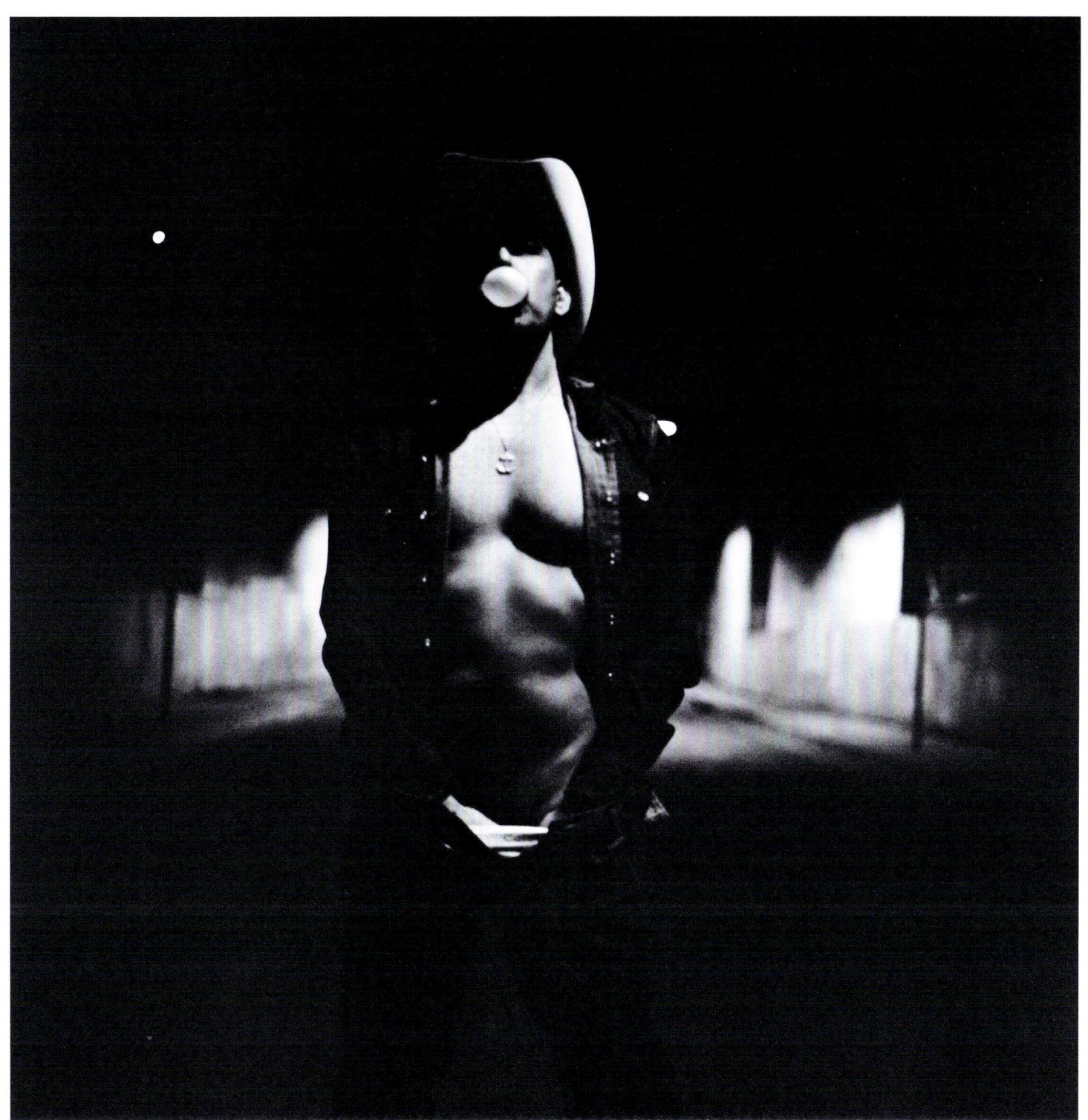

Richard, Downtown Los Angeles, 2023

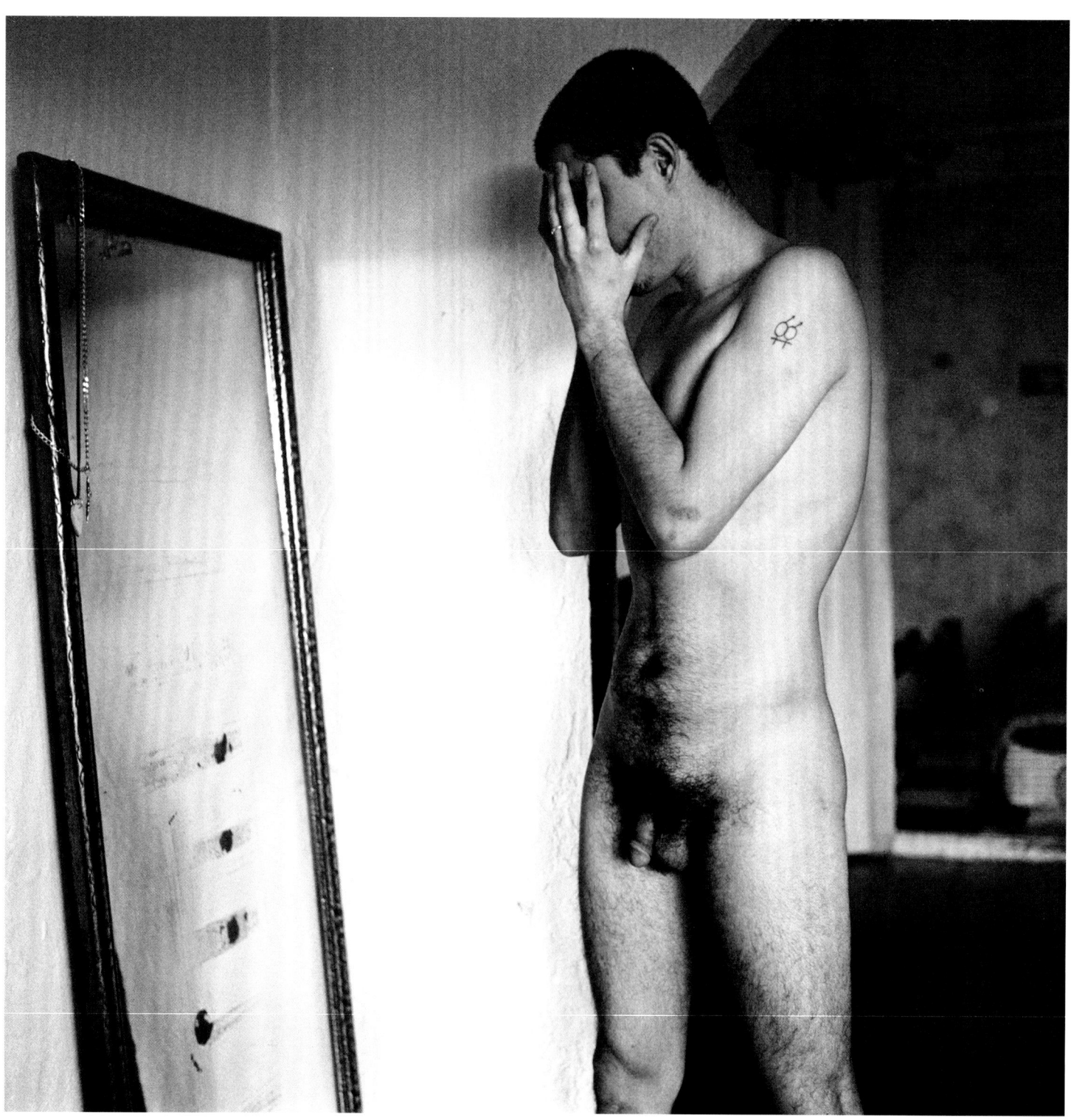

Steven, Downtown Los Angeles, ca. 1990

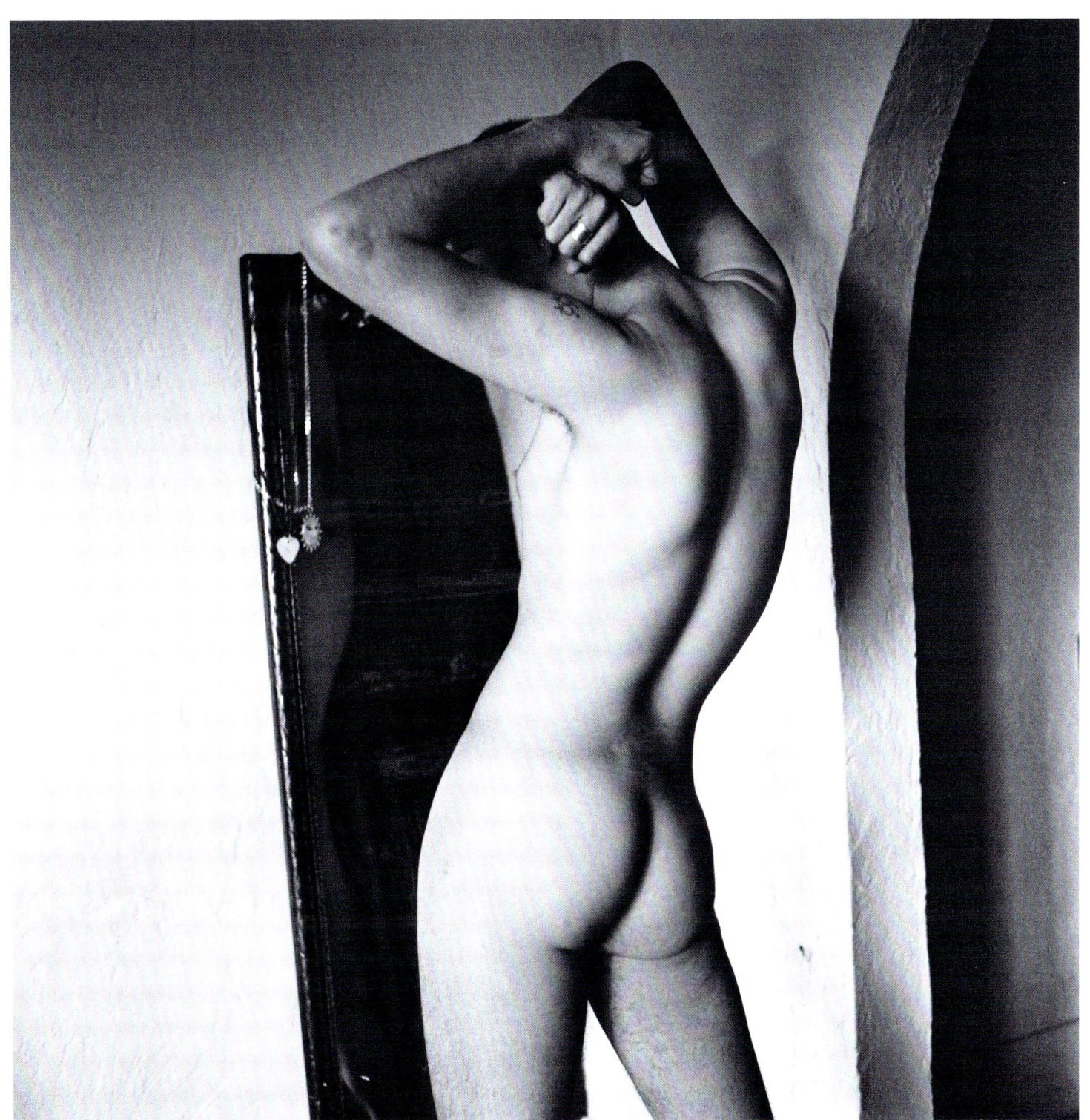

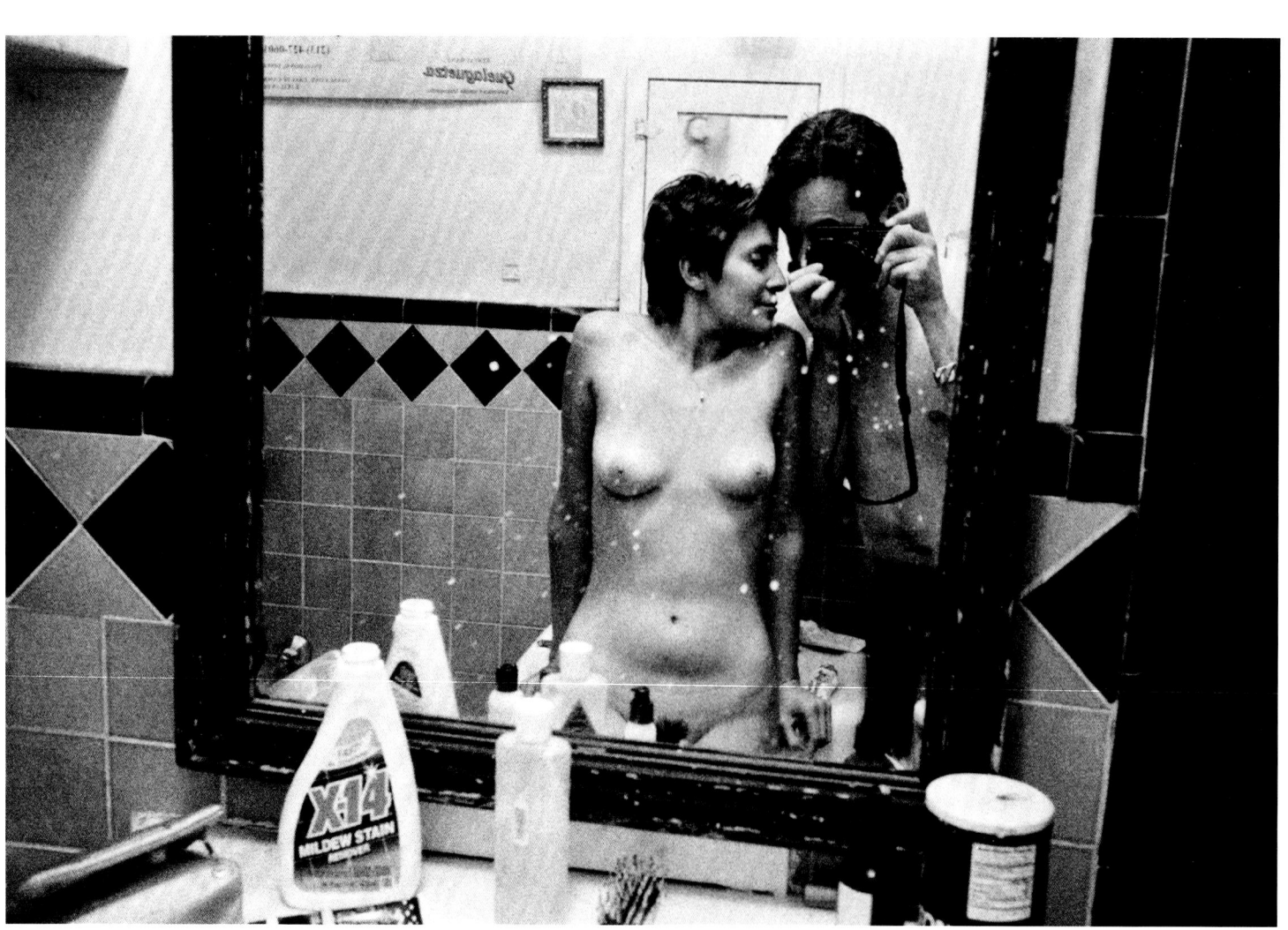

Reynaldo, Carla, Echo Park, 1997

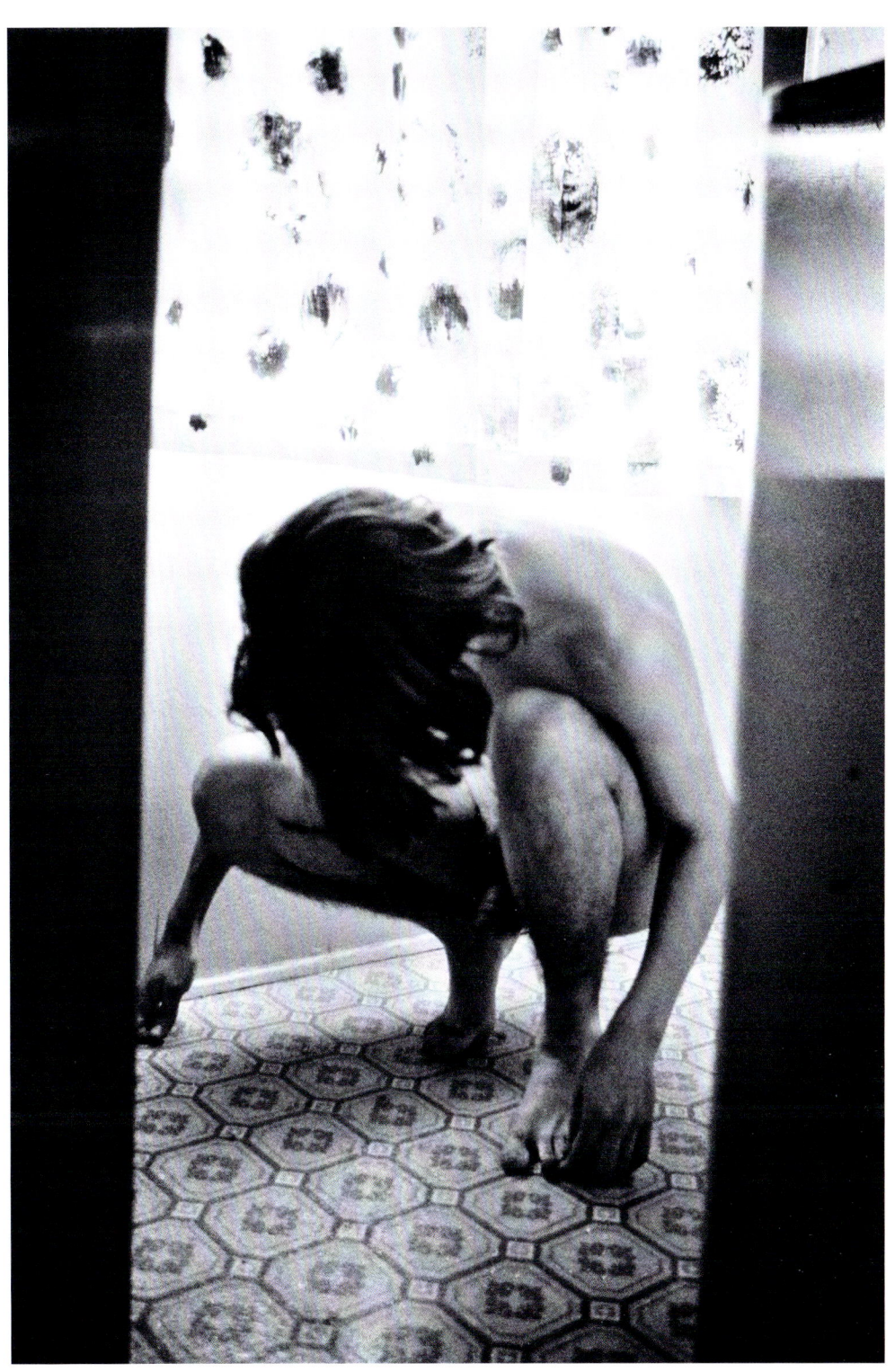

Self-Portrait, Pasadena, 1985

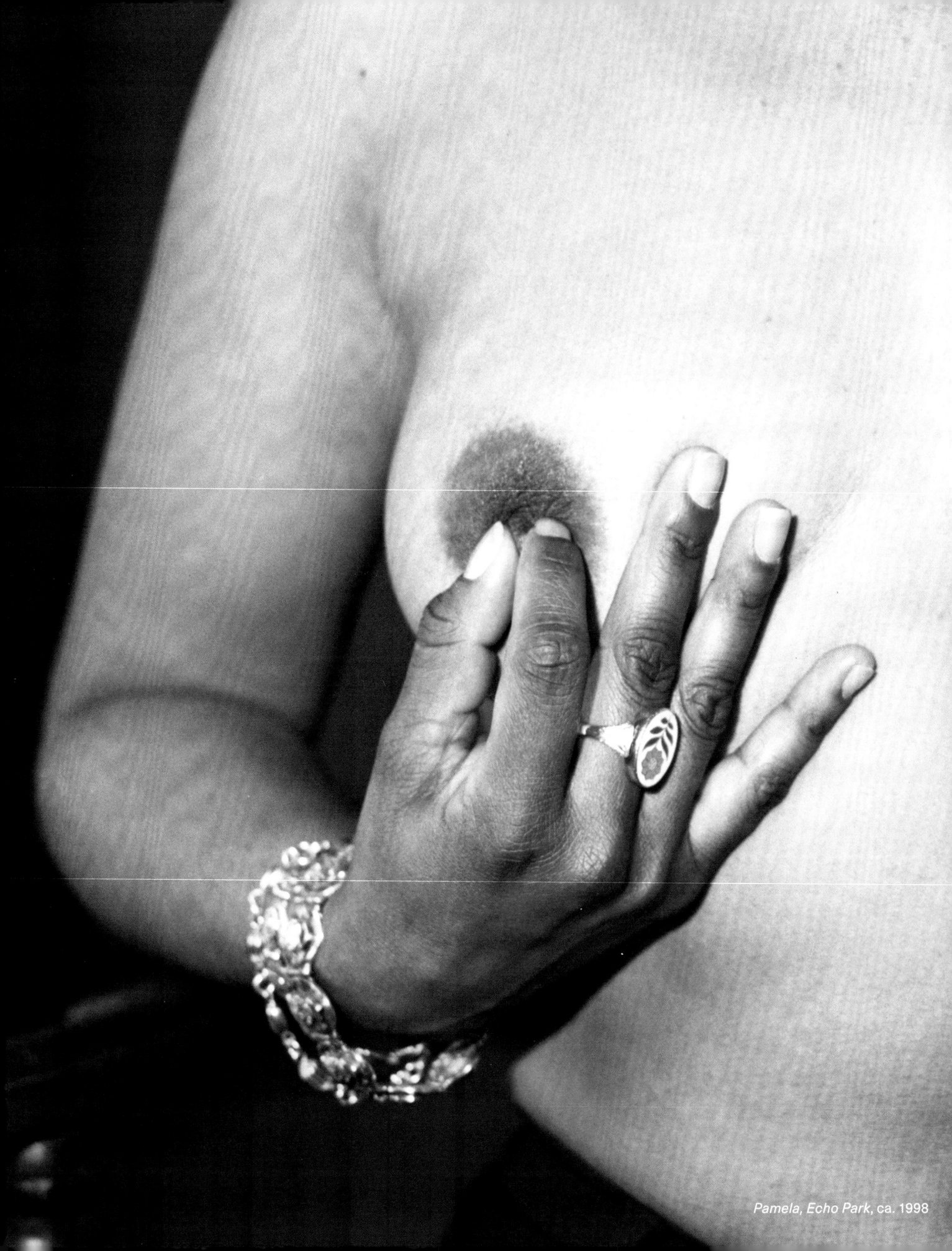

Pamela, Echo Park, ca. 1998

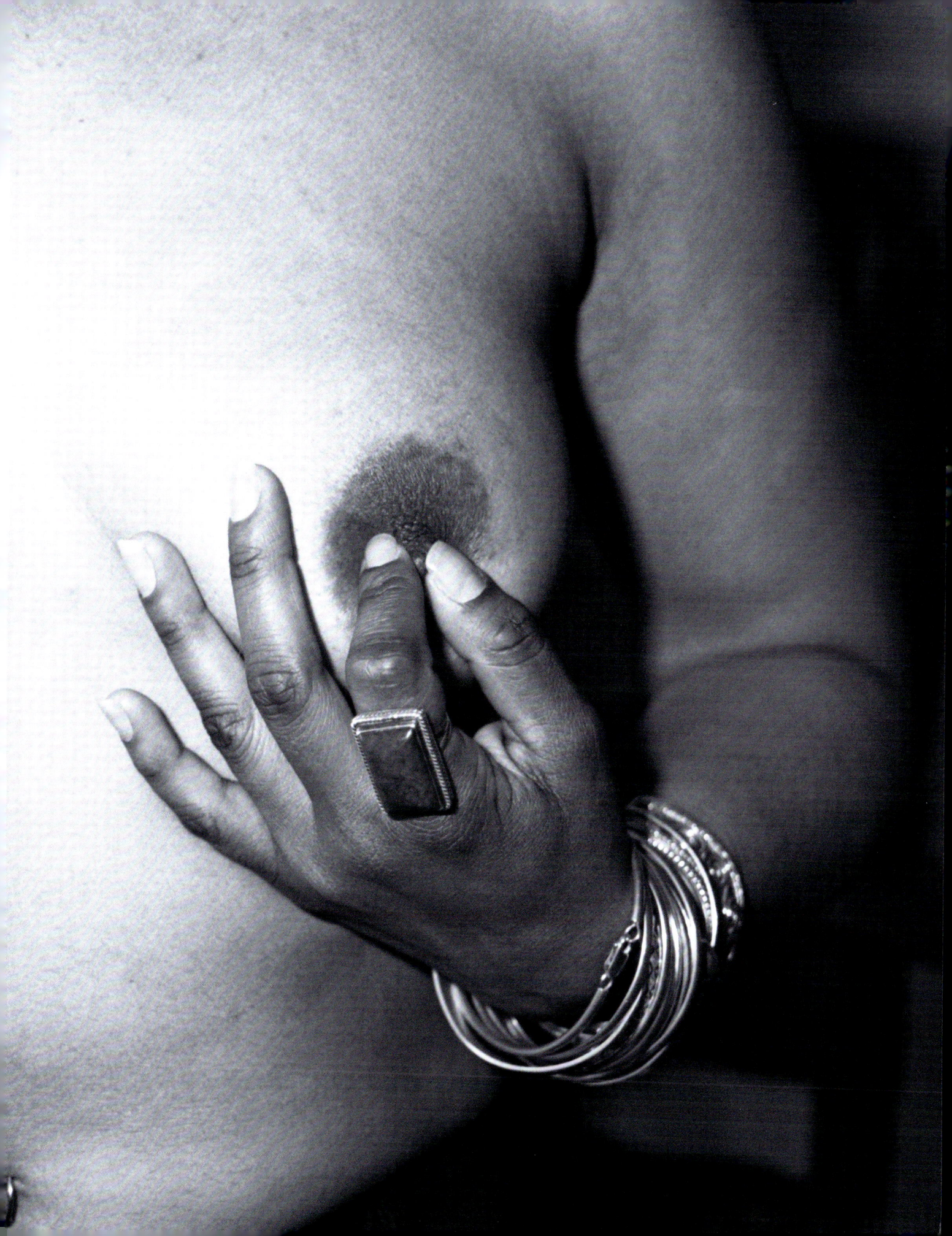

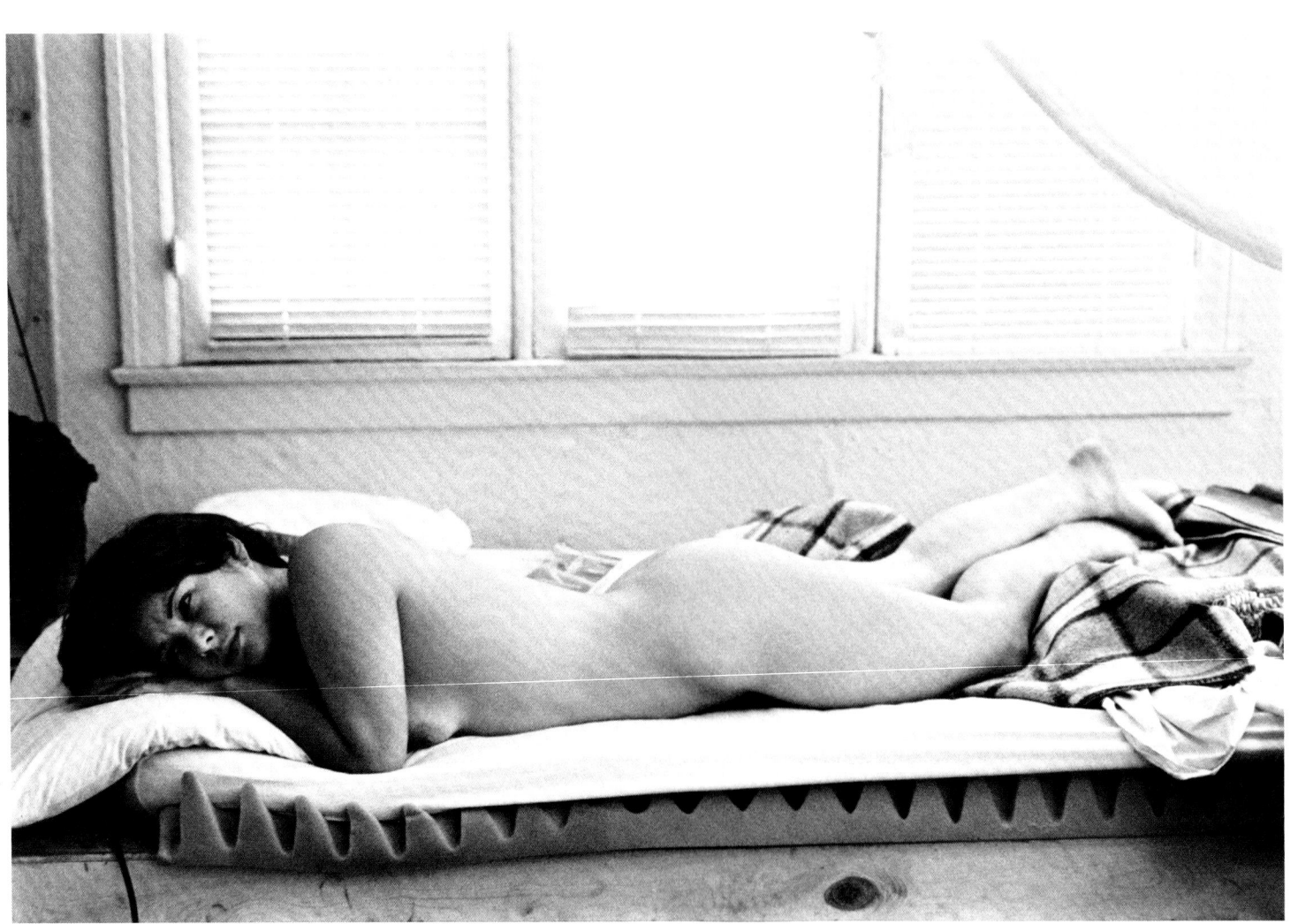

Connie, Echo Park, 1993

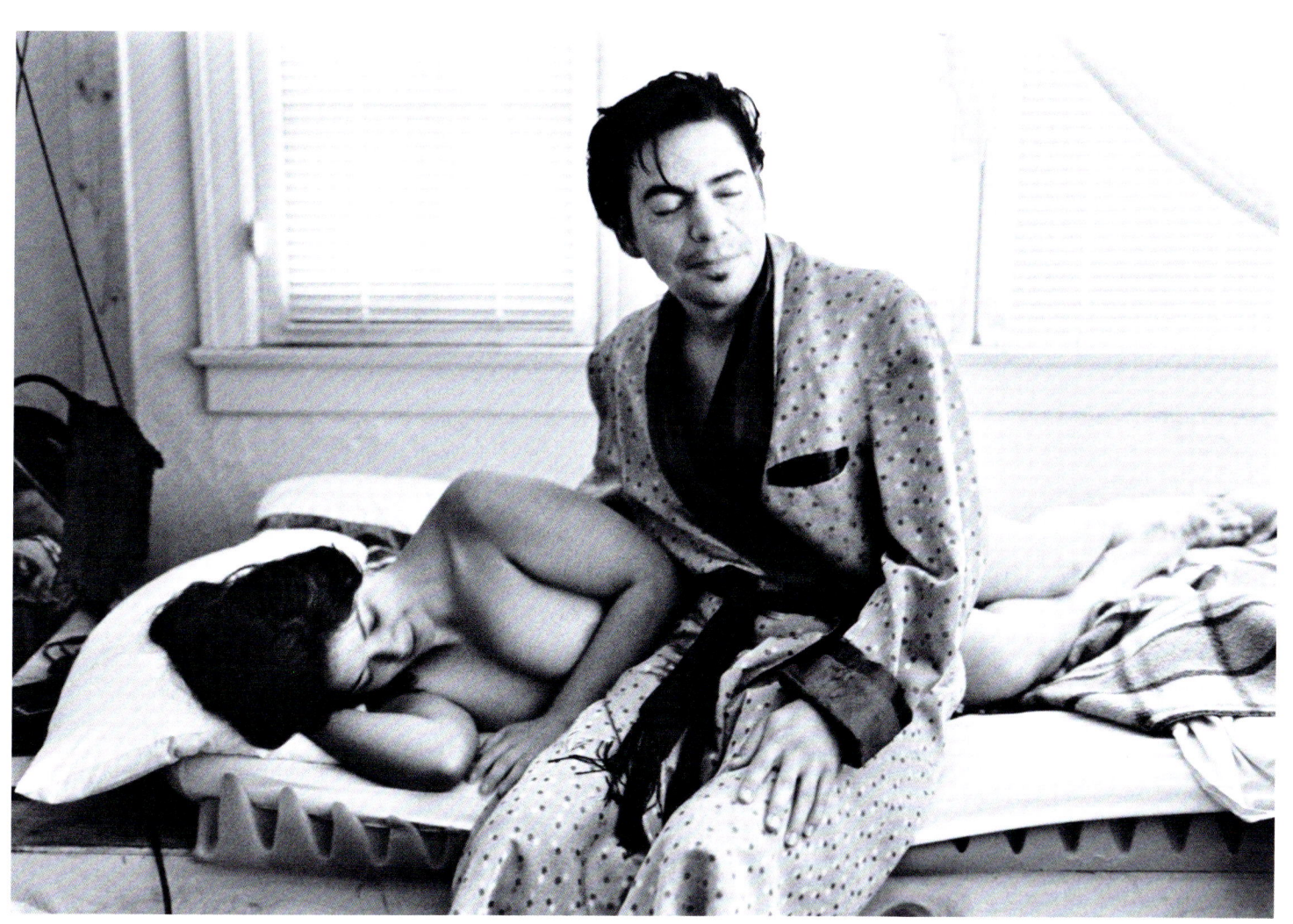

Connie, Boyfriend, Echo Park, 1993

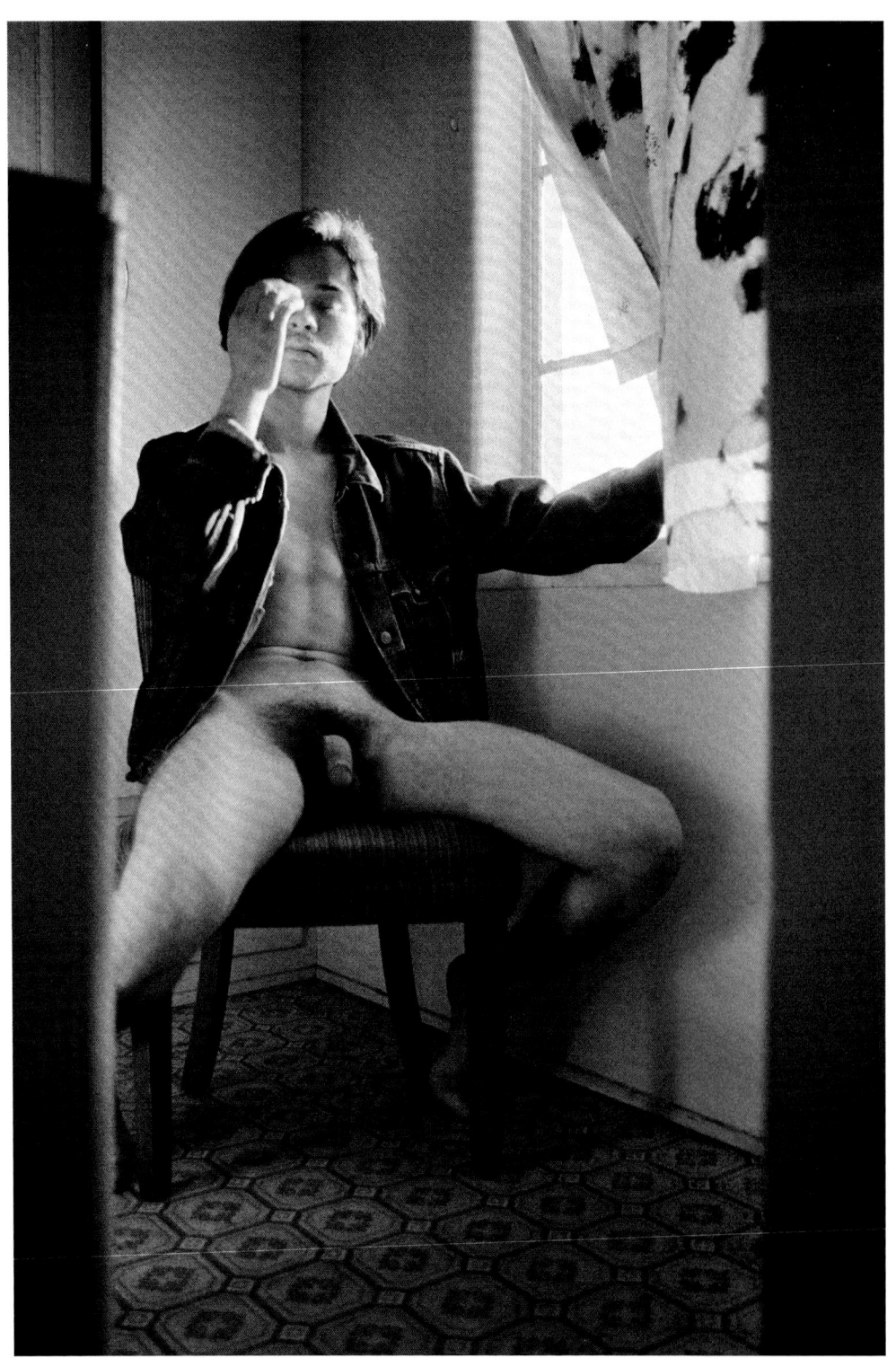

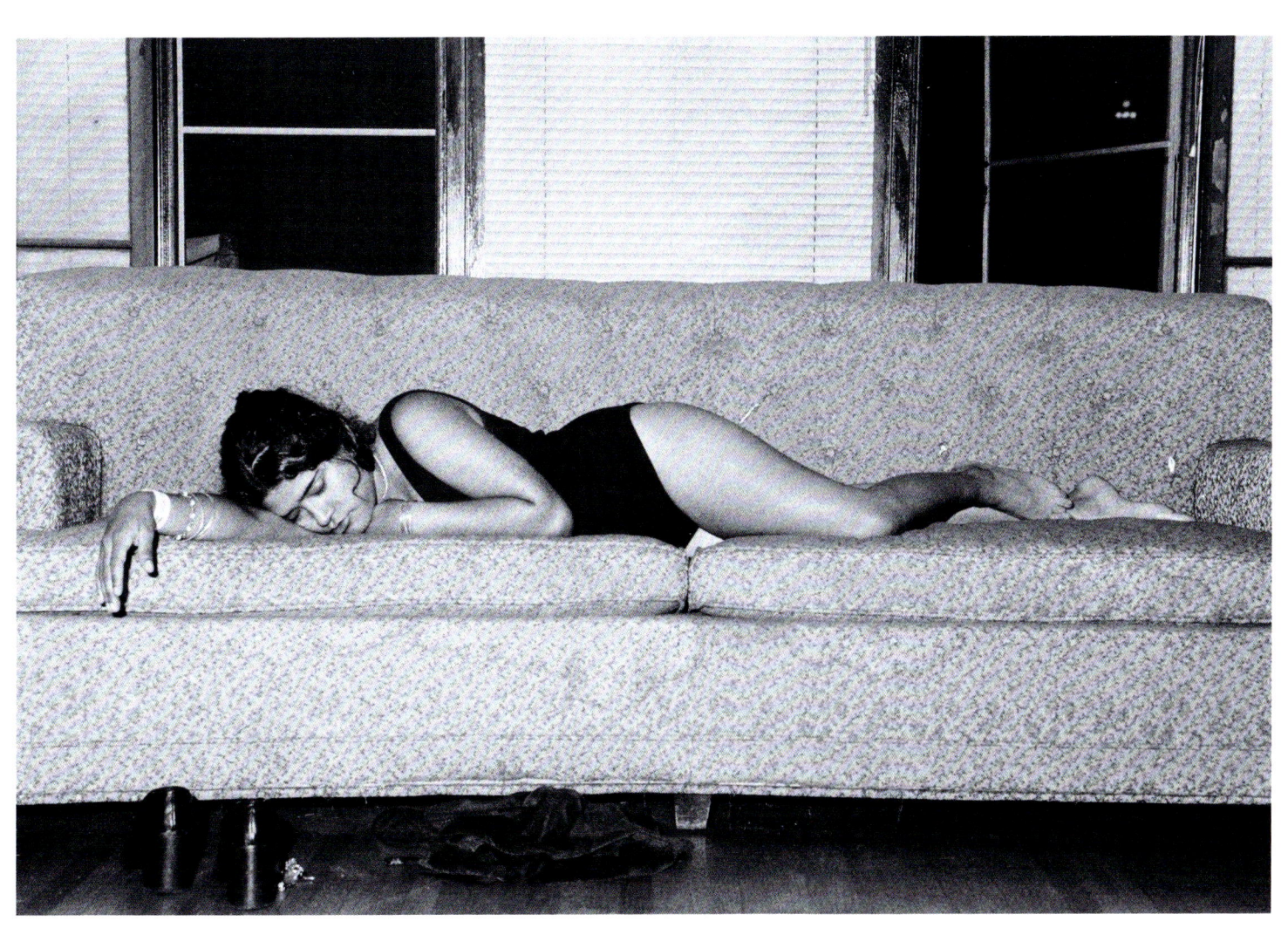

Pamela, Echo Park, 1998

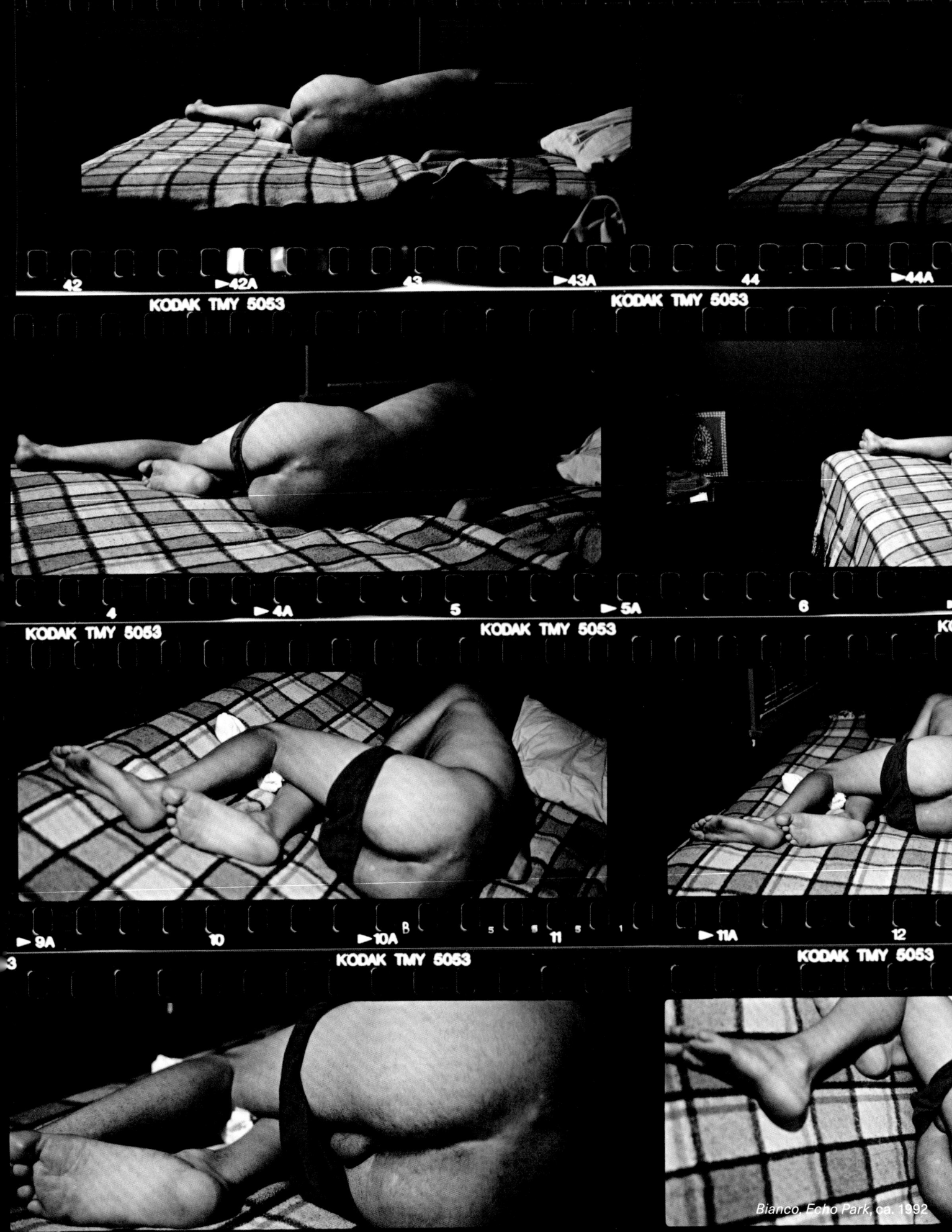

Bianco, Echo Park, ca. 1992

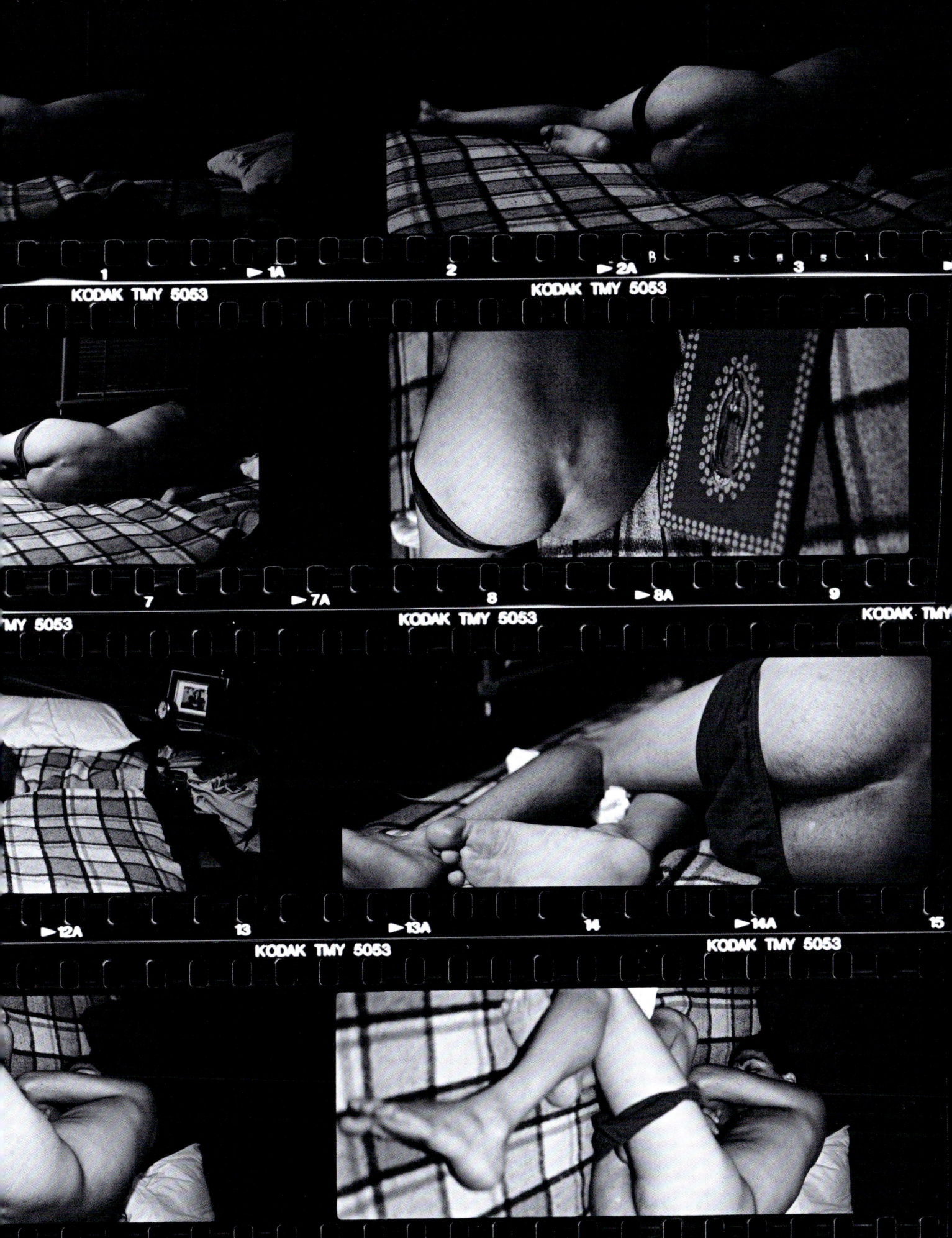

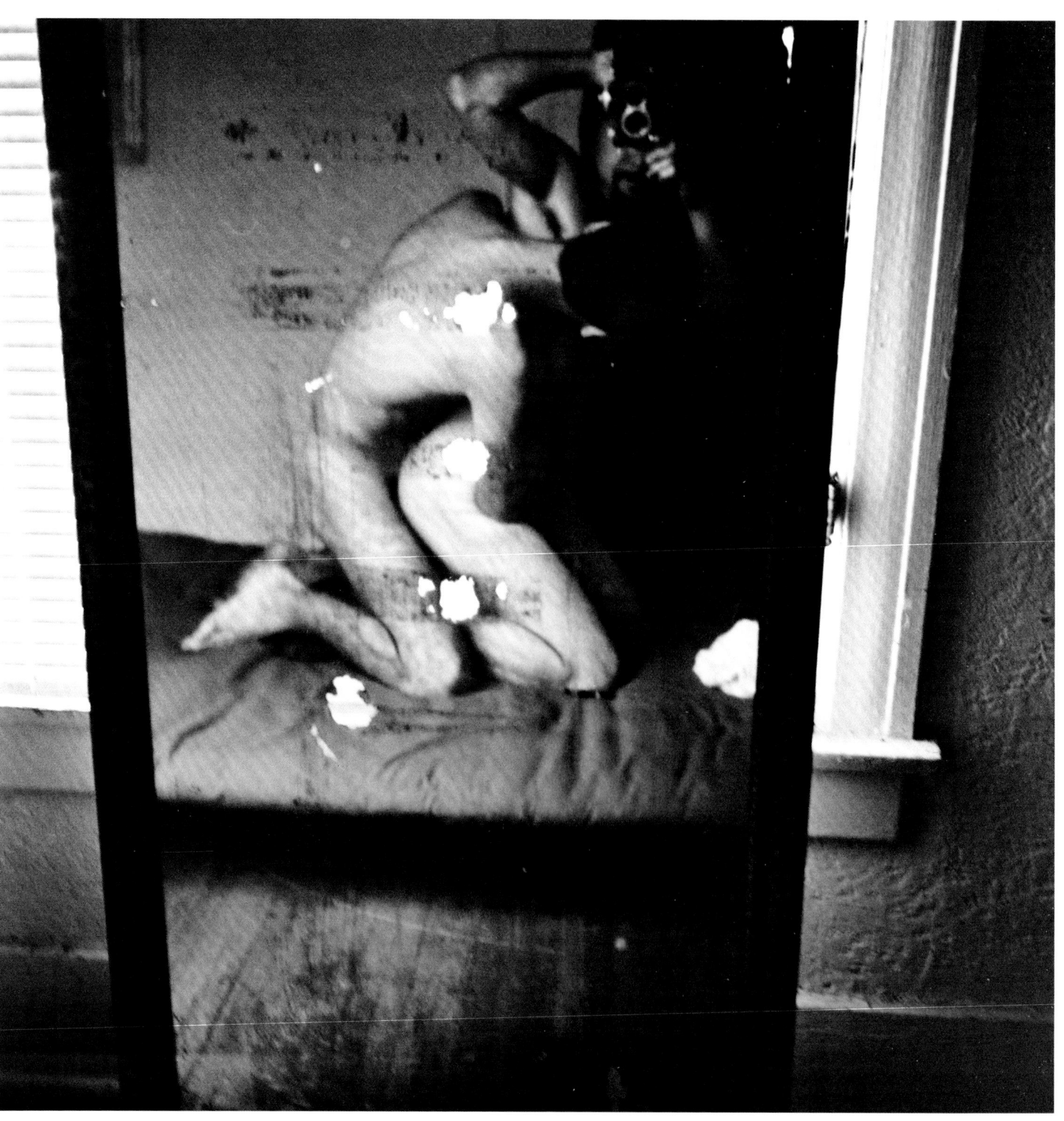

Bianco, Reynaldo, Echo Park, ca. 1992

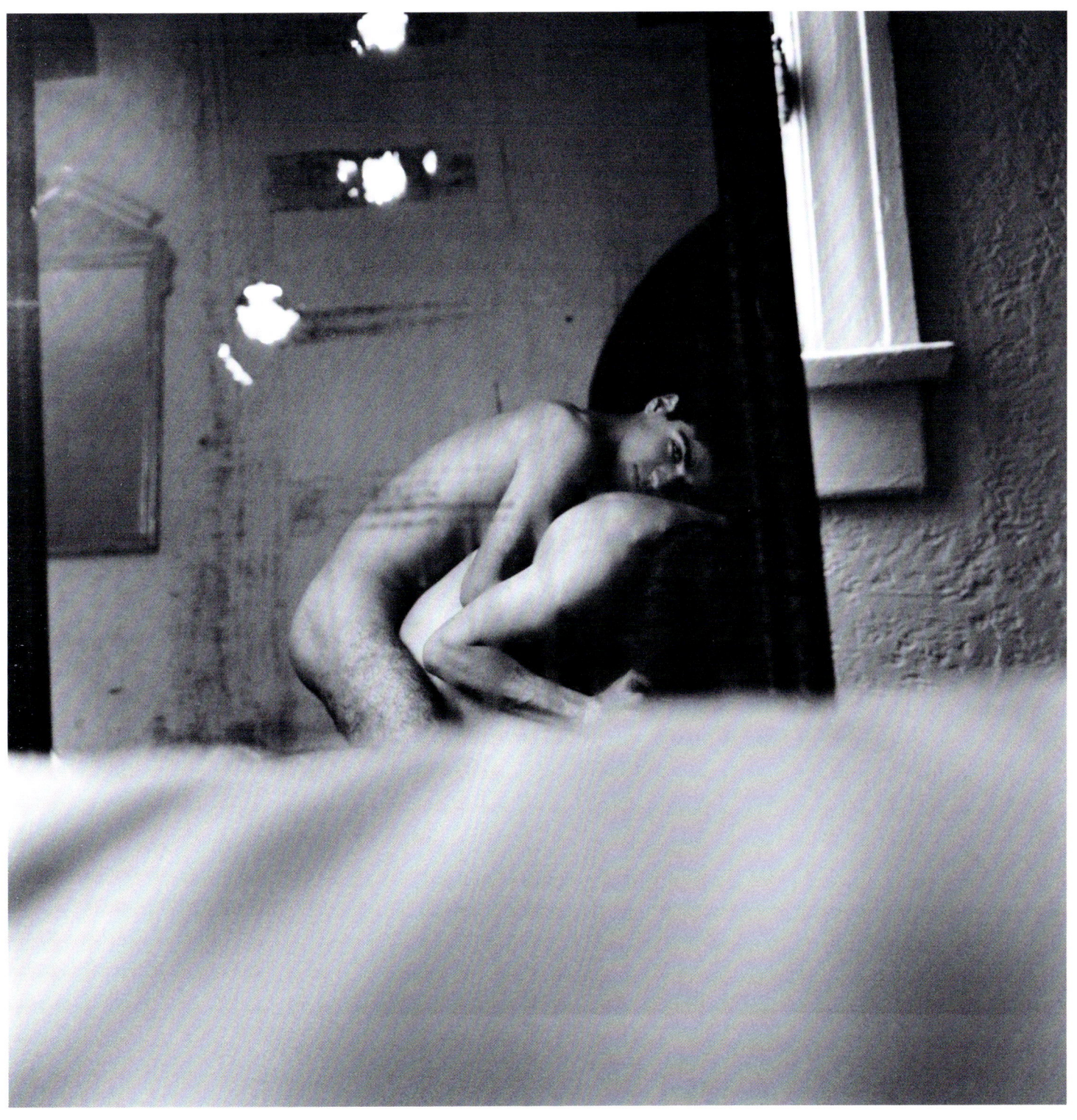

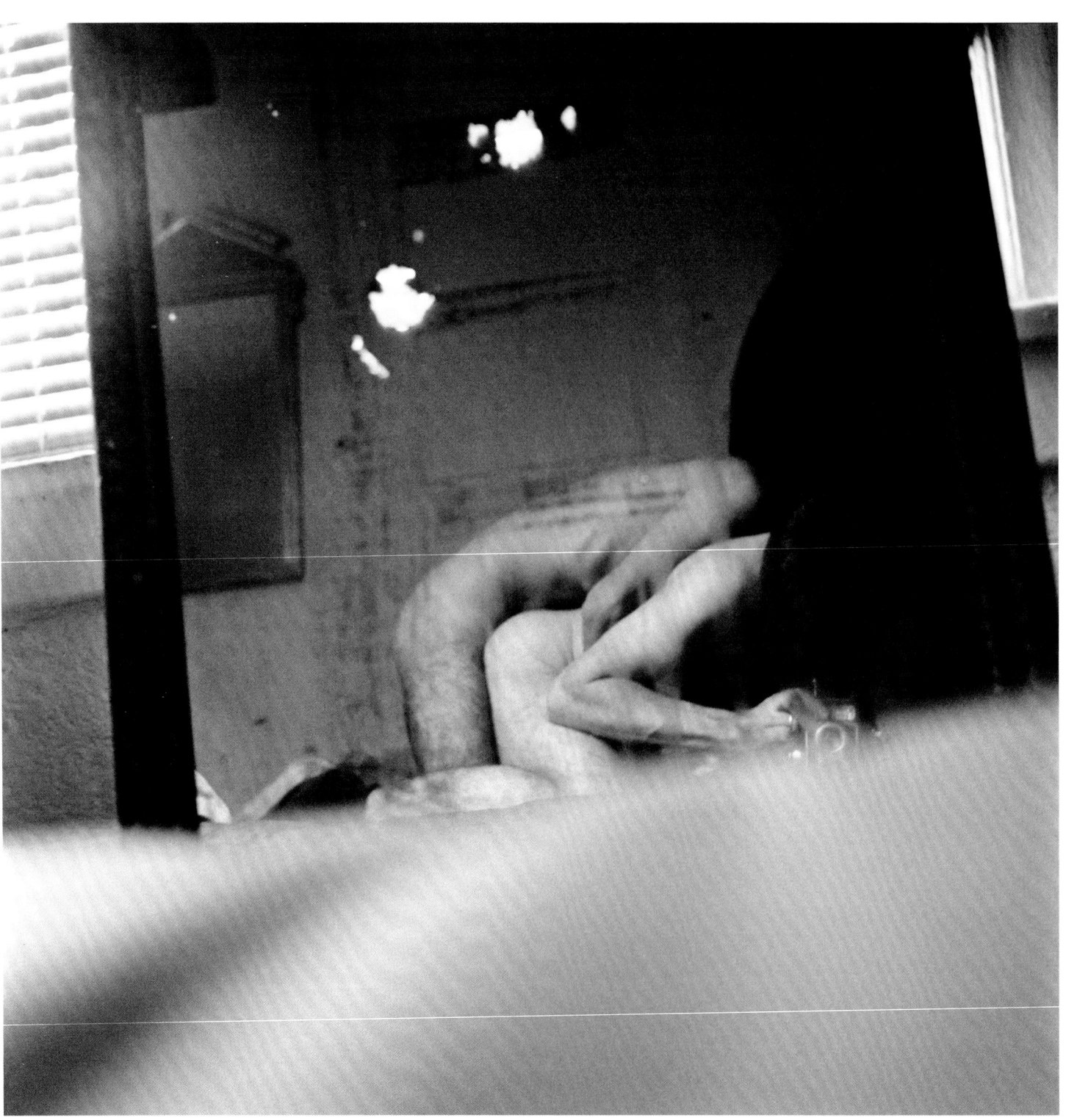

Bianco, Reynaldo, Echo Park, ca. 1992

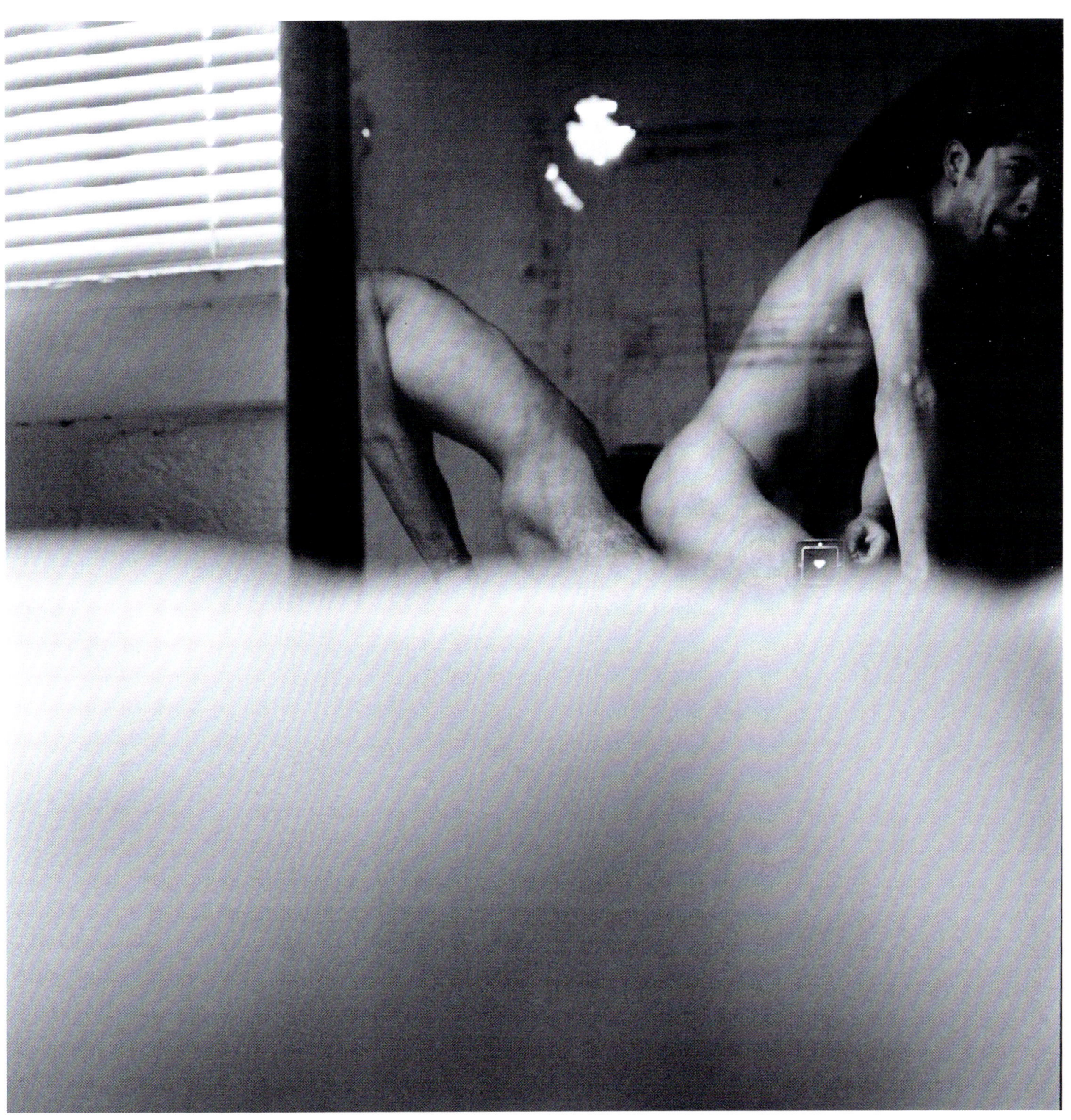

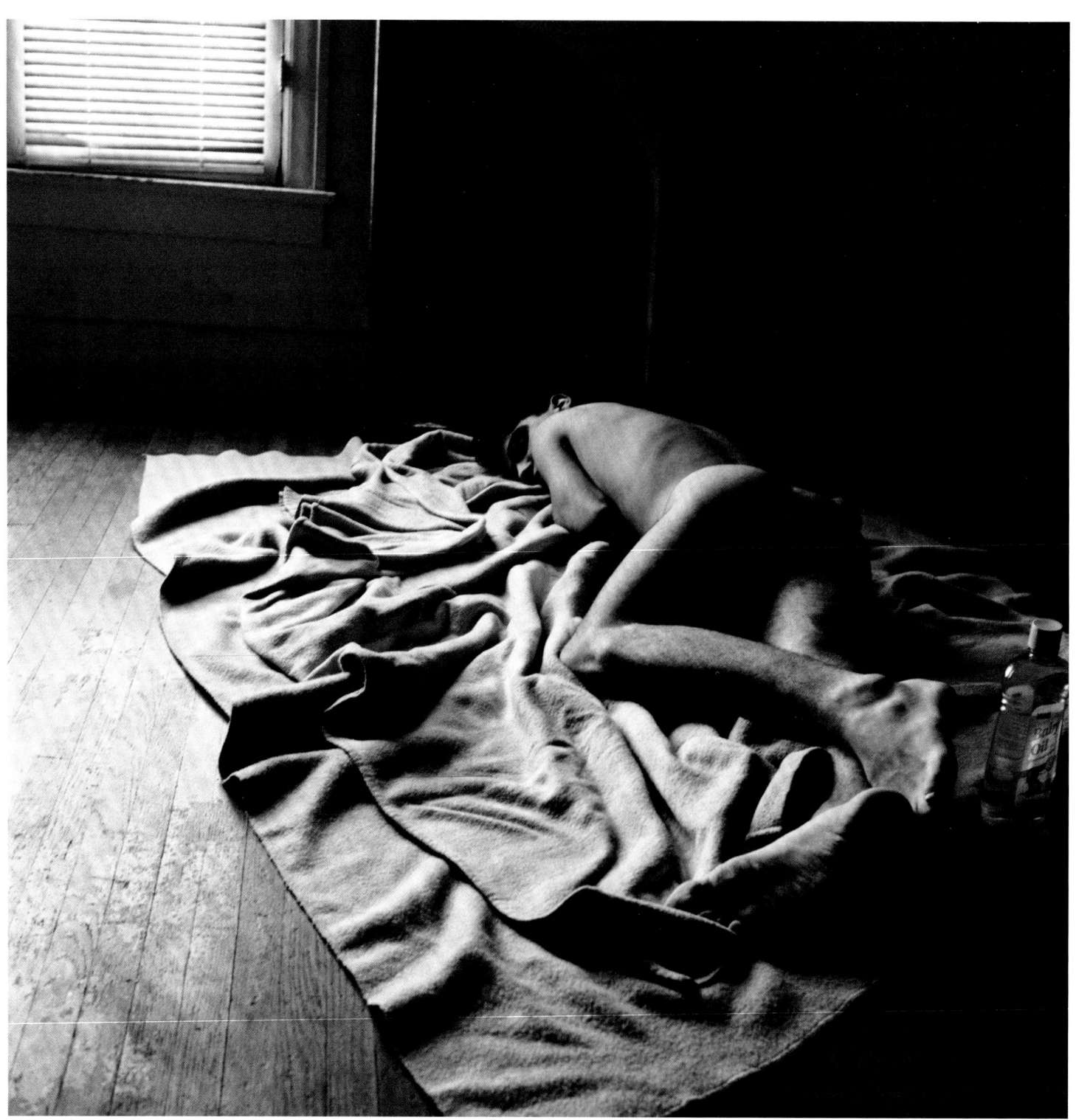

Bianco, Echo Park, ca. 1993

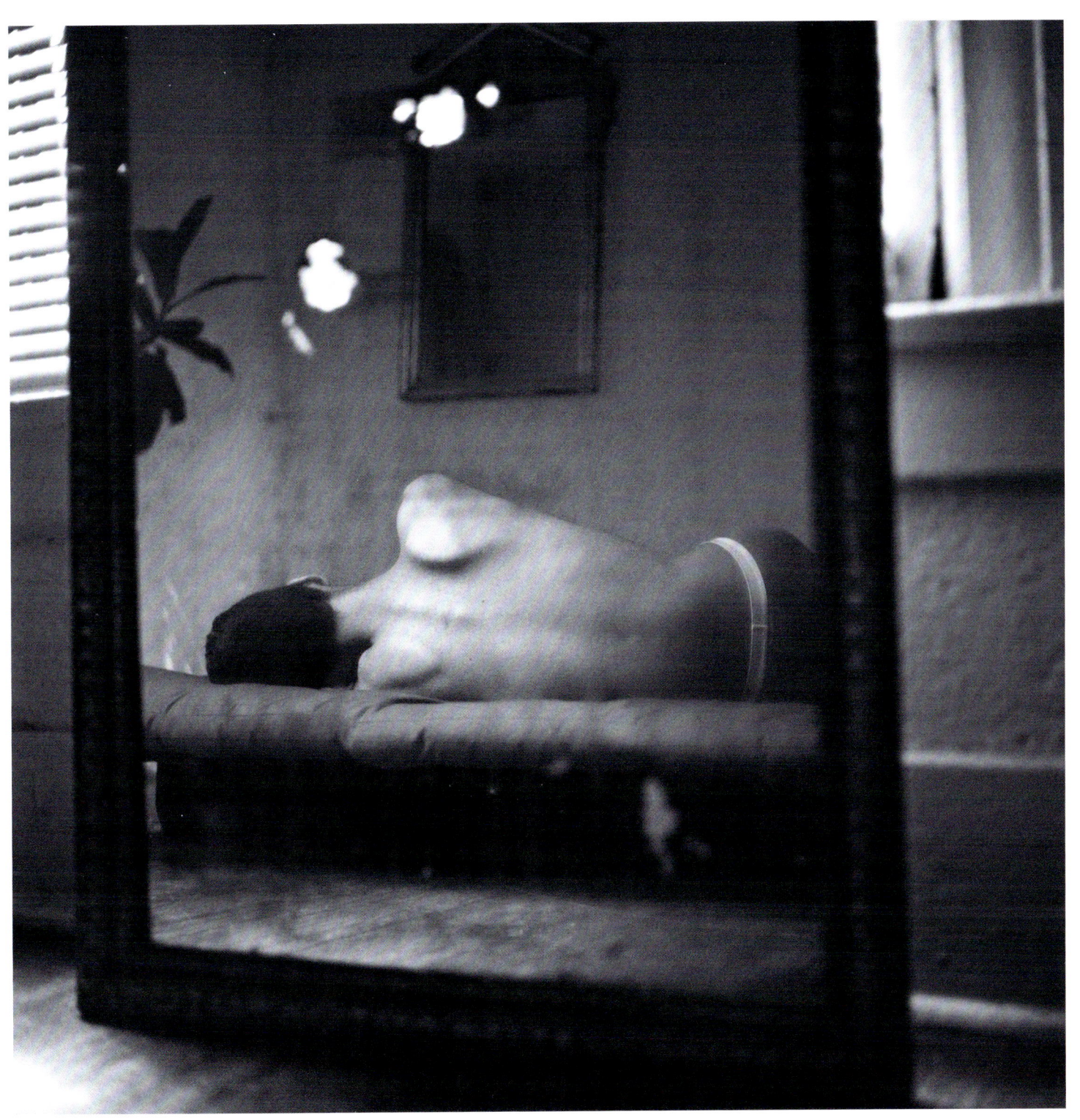

Bianco, Echo Park, ca. 1992

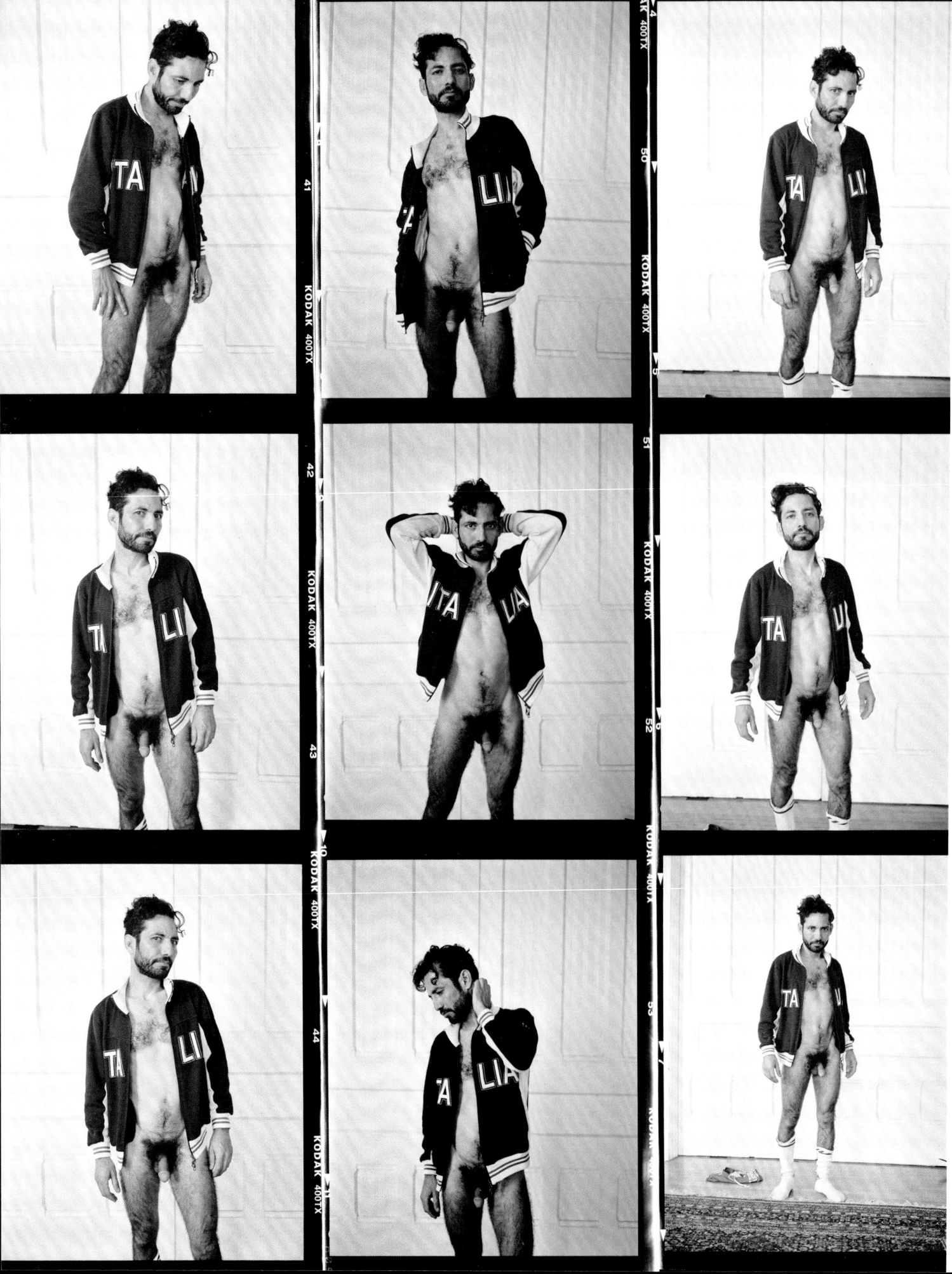

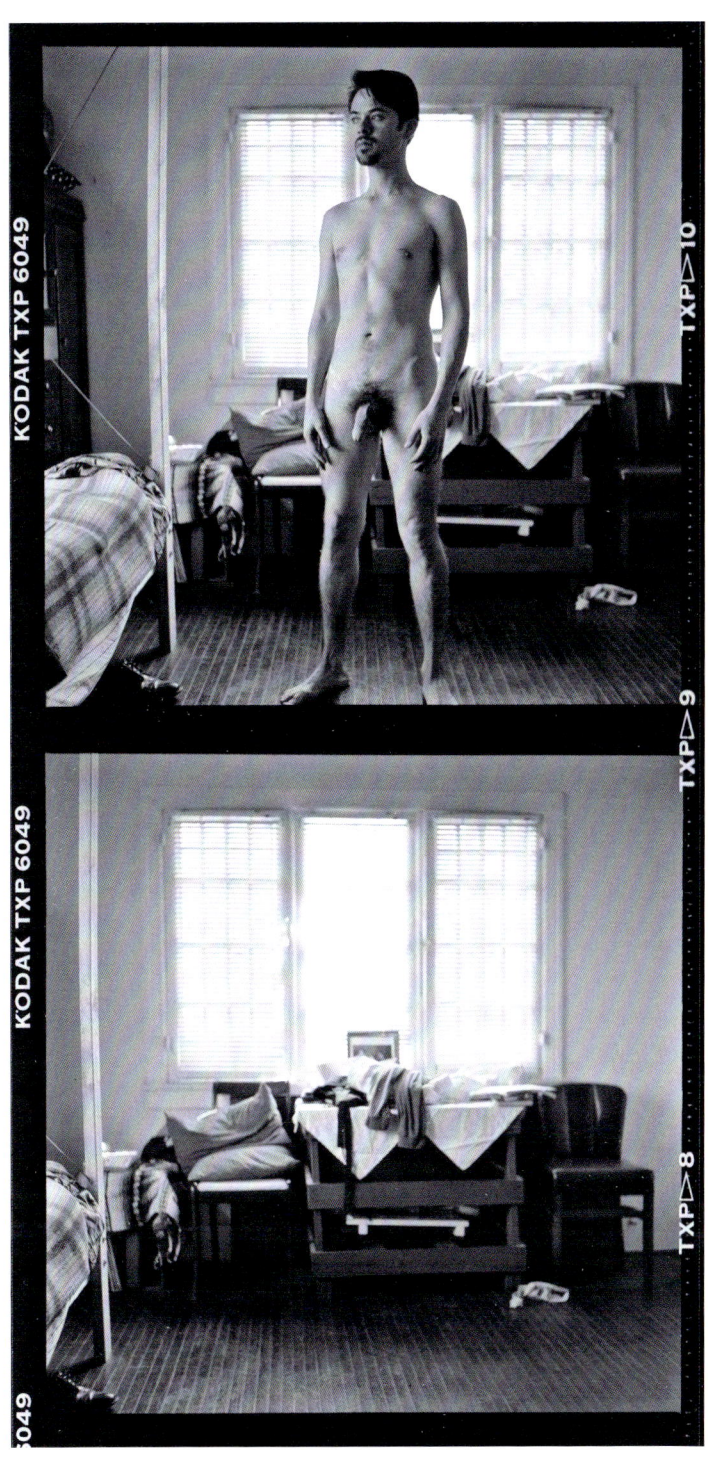

LEFT: *Justo, Lincoln Heights*, ca. 2015
Self-Portrait, Echo Park, ca. 1994

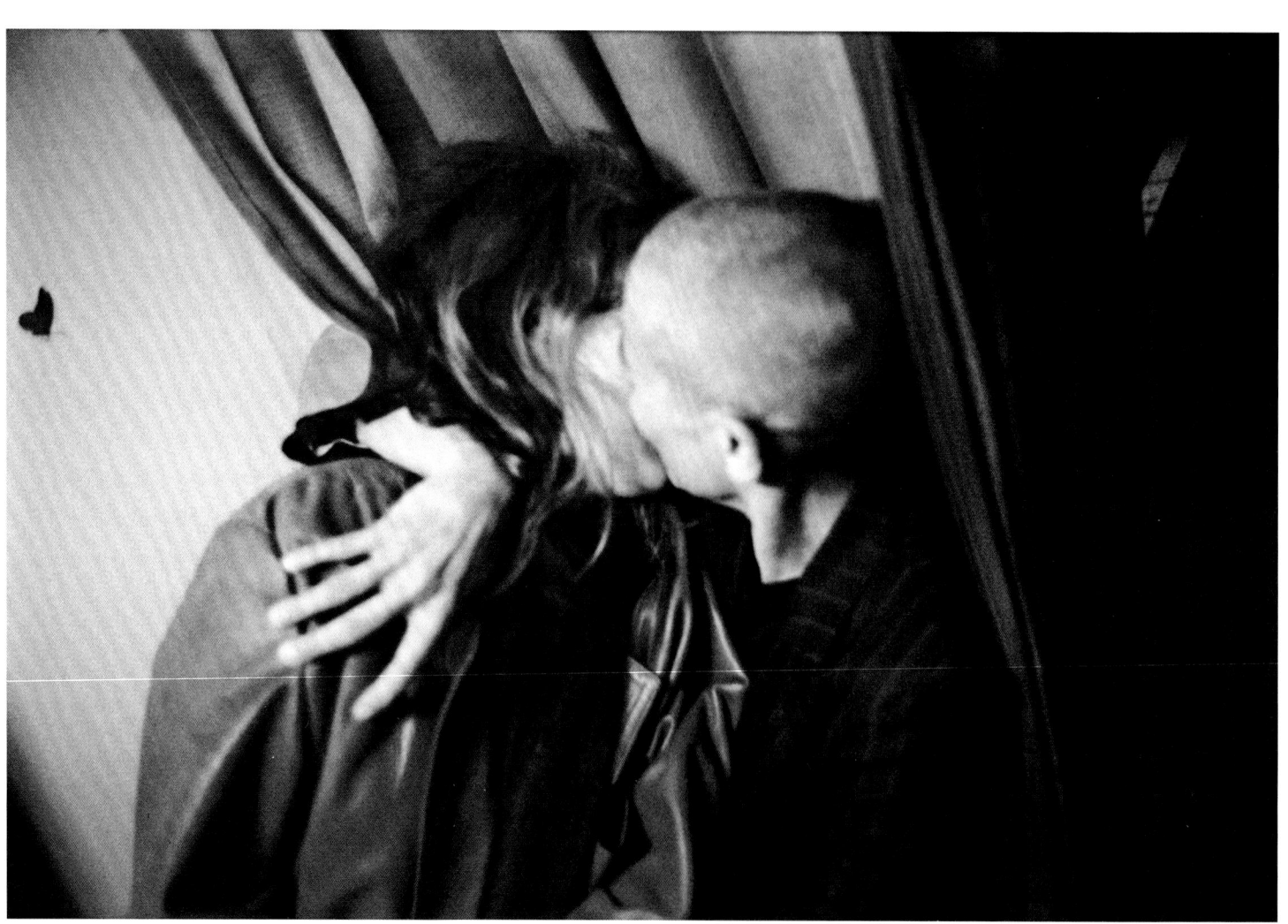

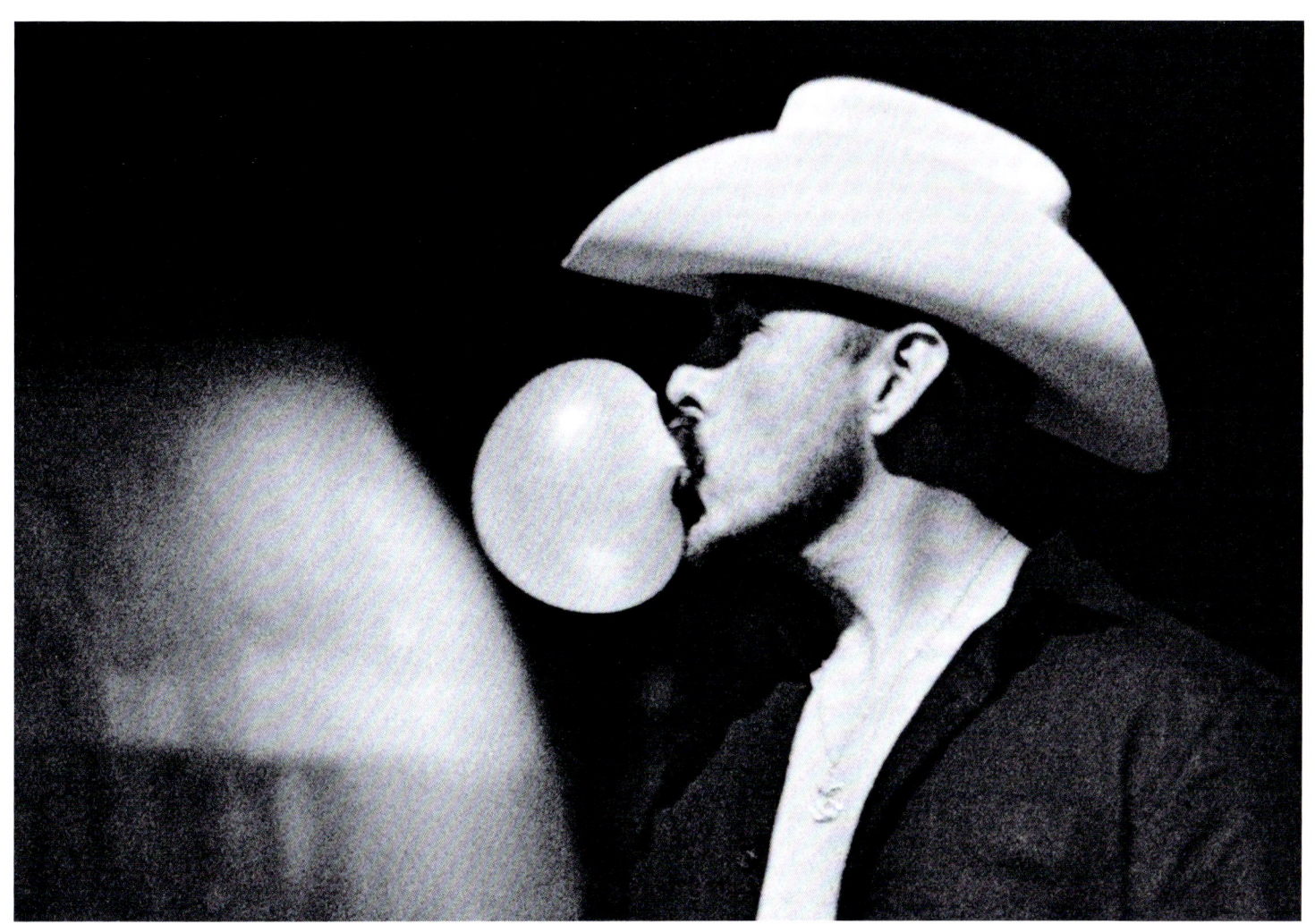

Richard, Downtown Los Angeles, 2023

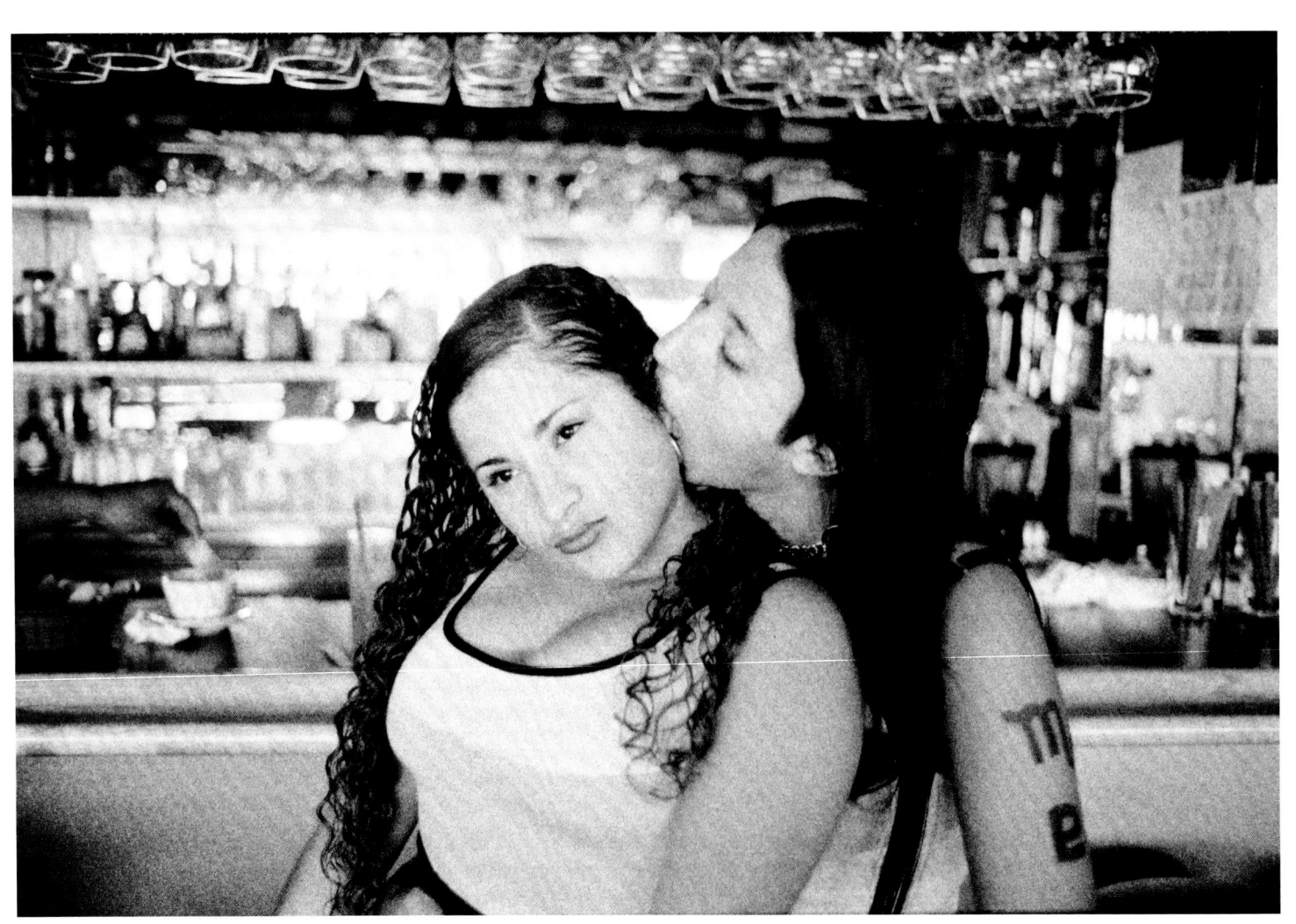

Girls, El Conquistador, 1997

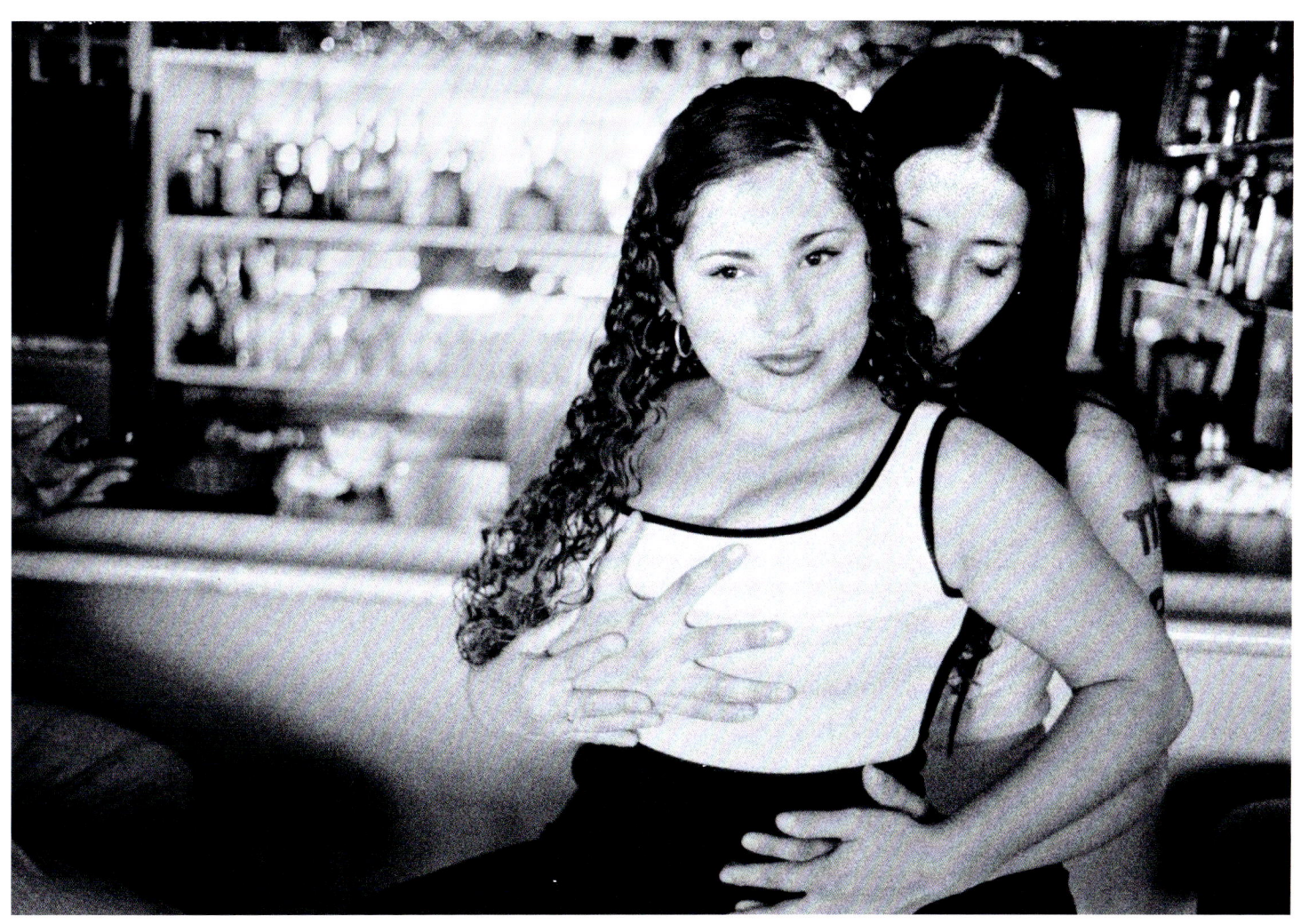

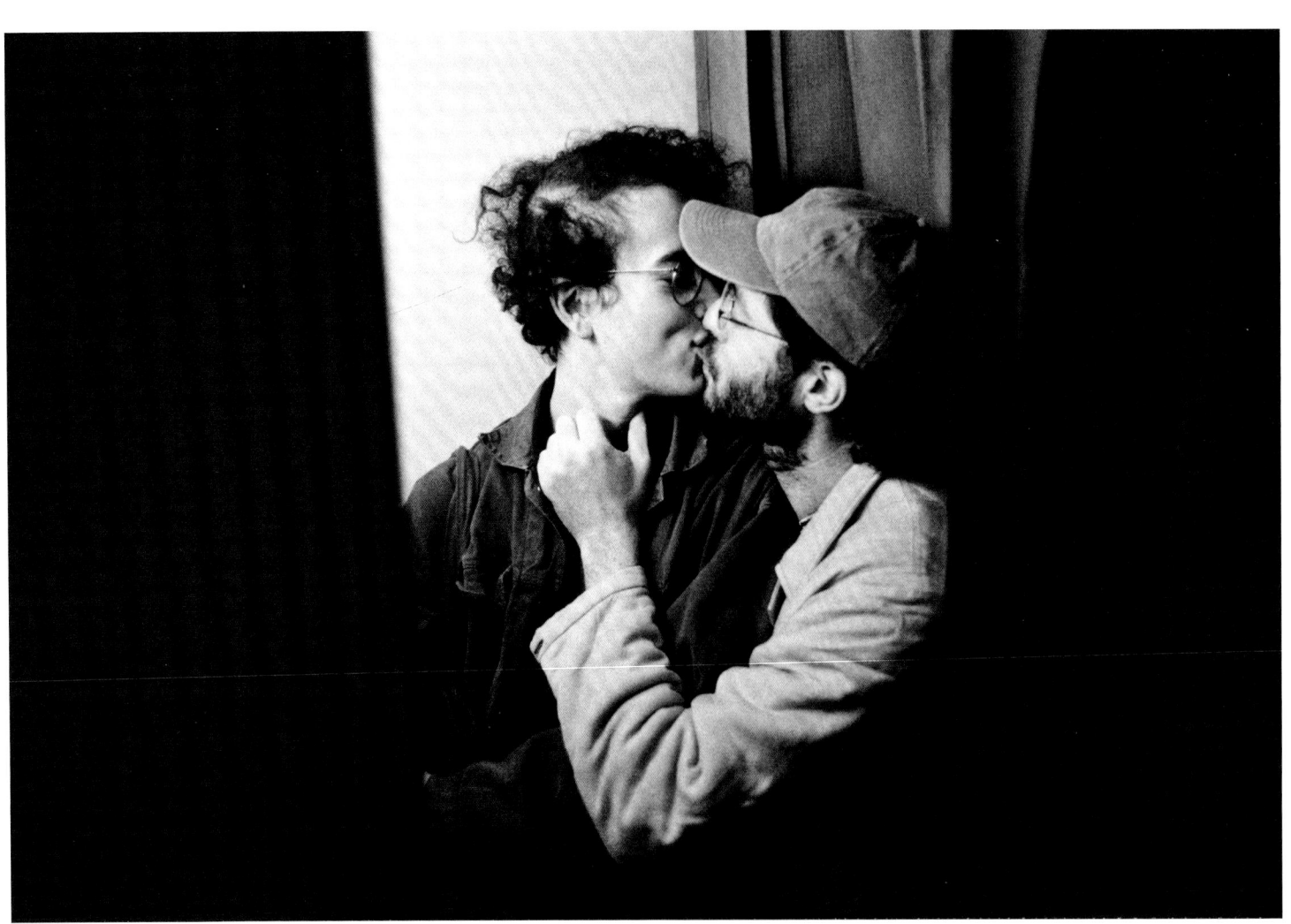

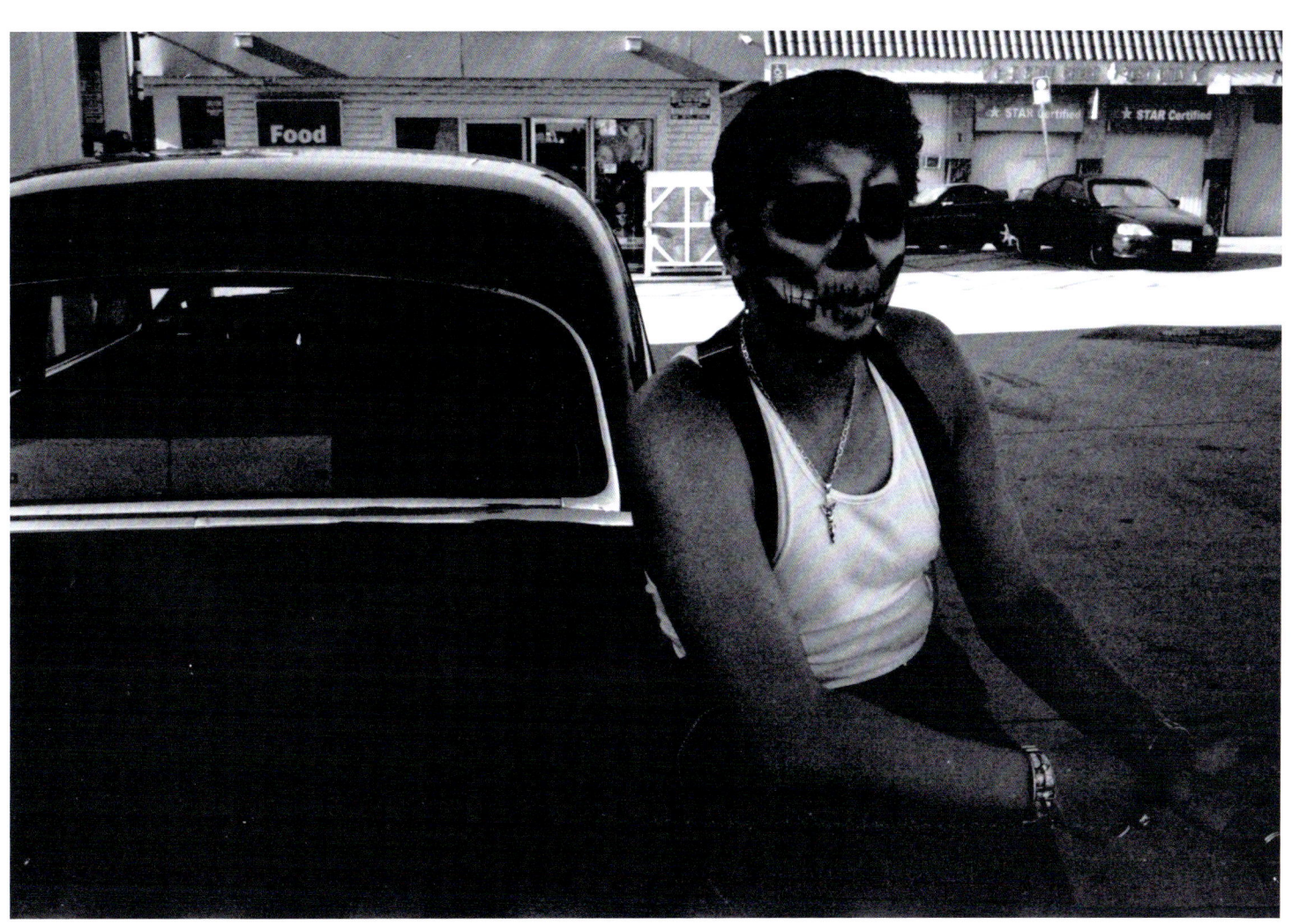

OG Kid, Lincoln Heights, 2021

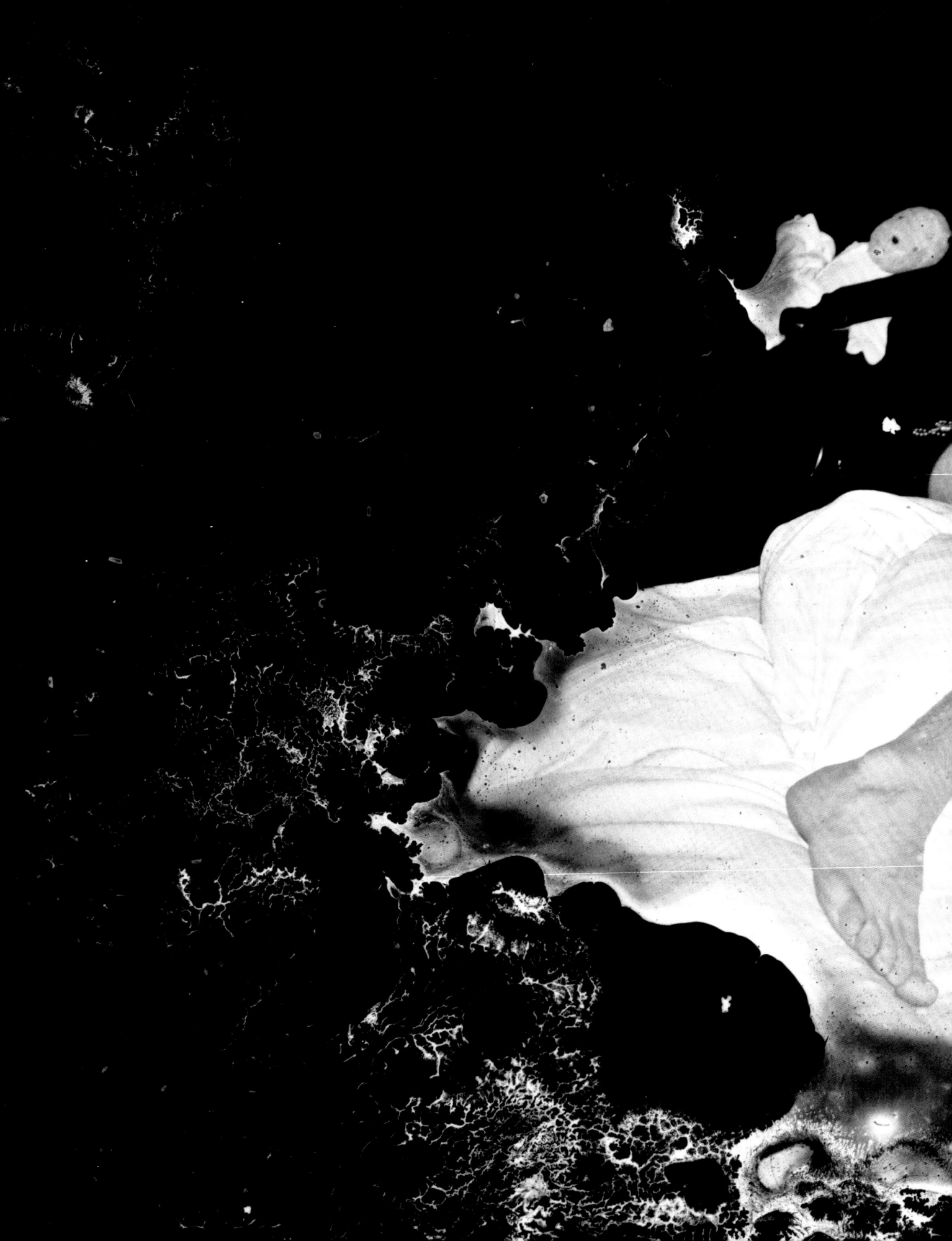

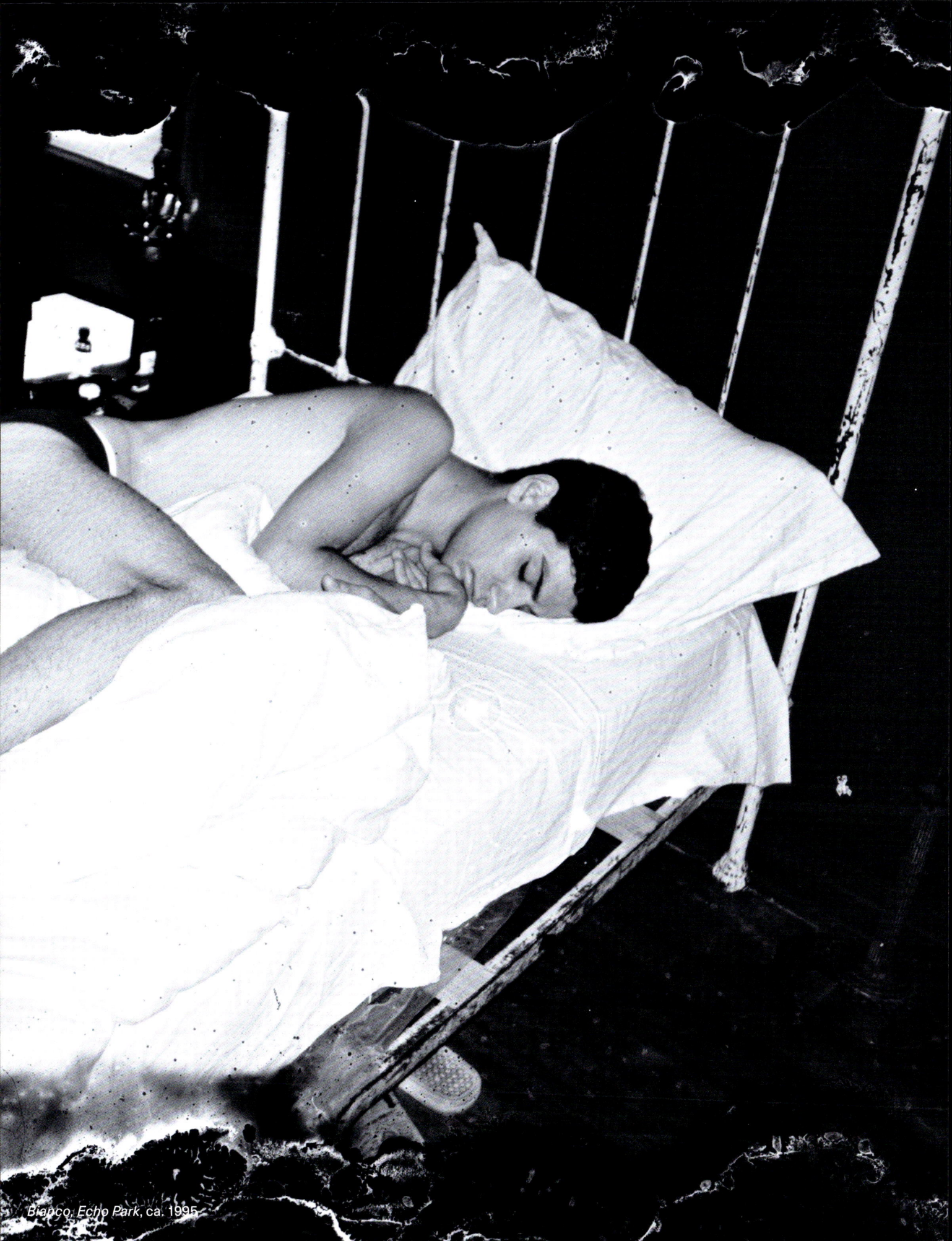

Bianco, Echo Park, ca. 1995

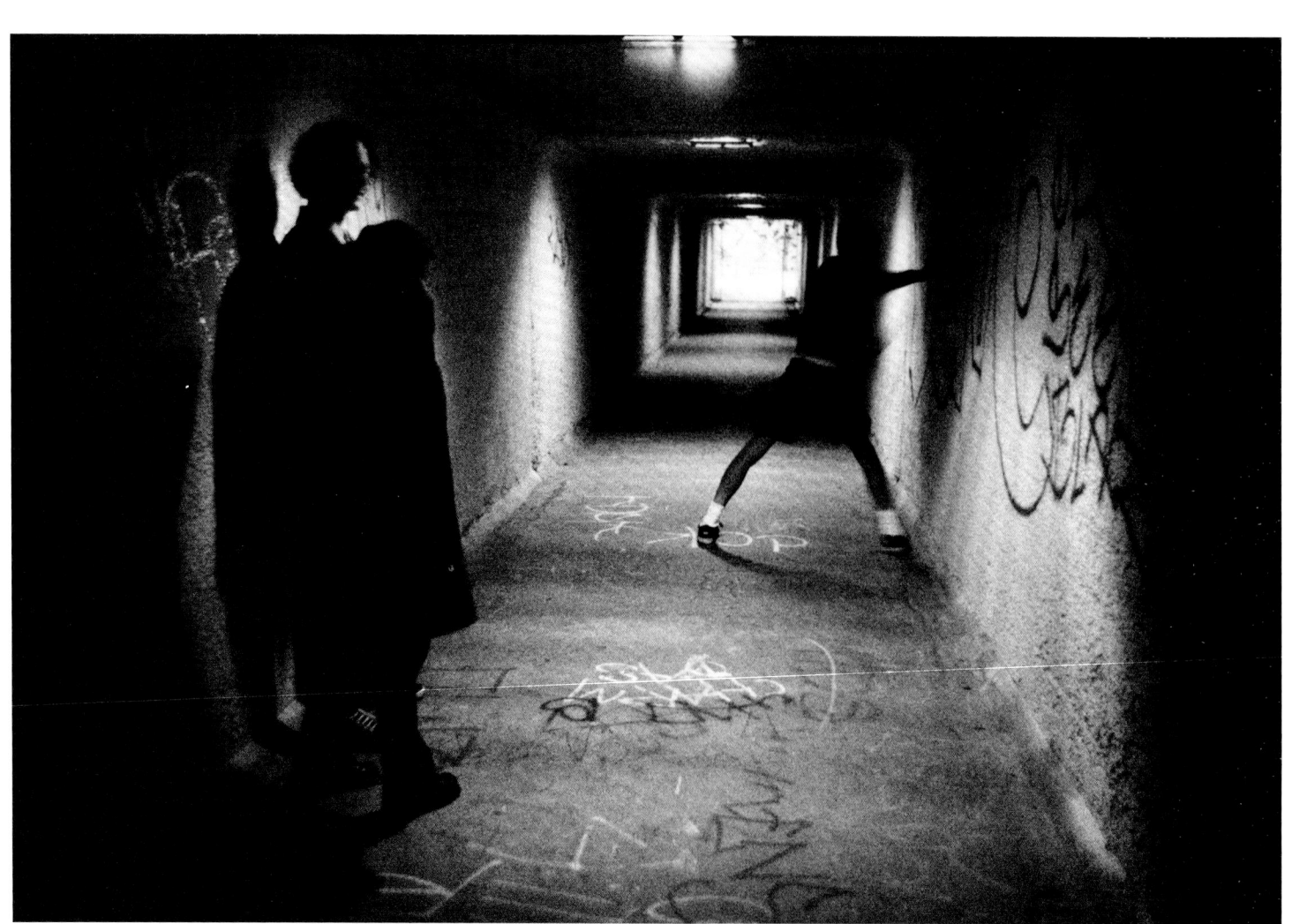

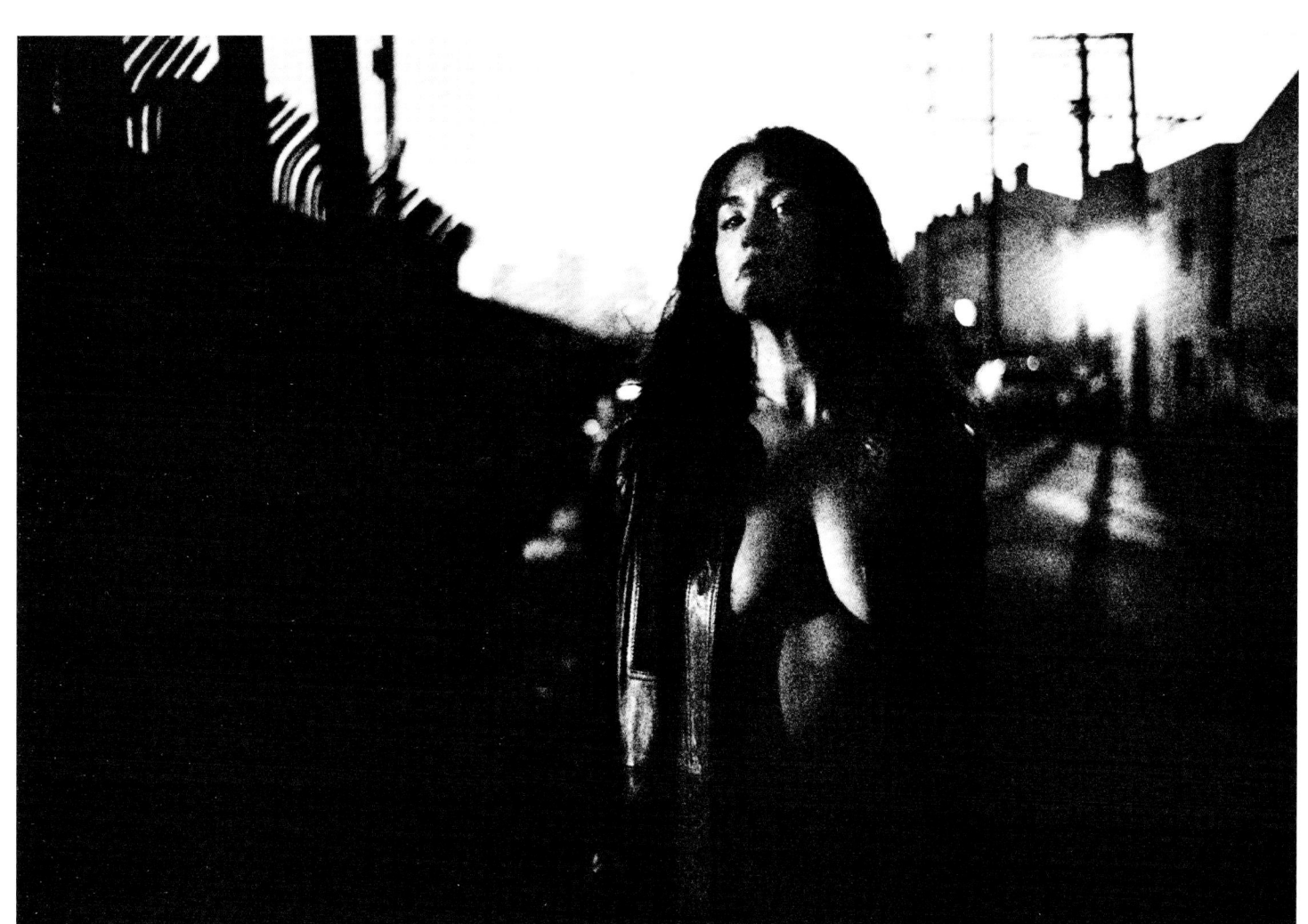

Gabriella, Lincoln Heights, ca. 2015

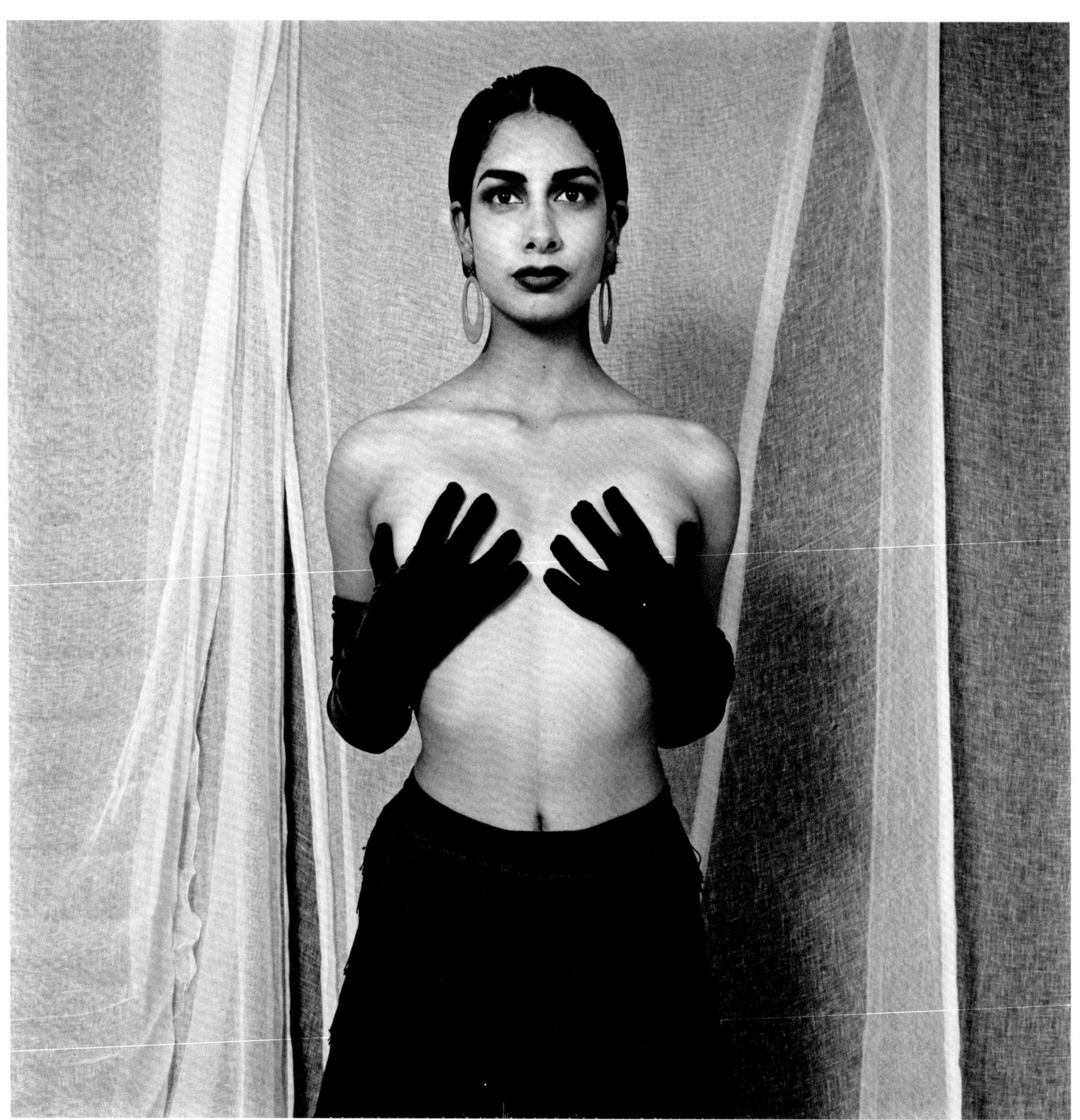

Cynthia, Hollywood, 1989

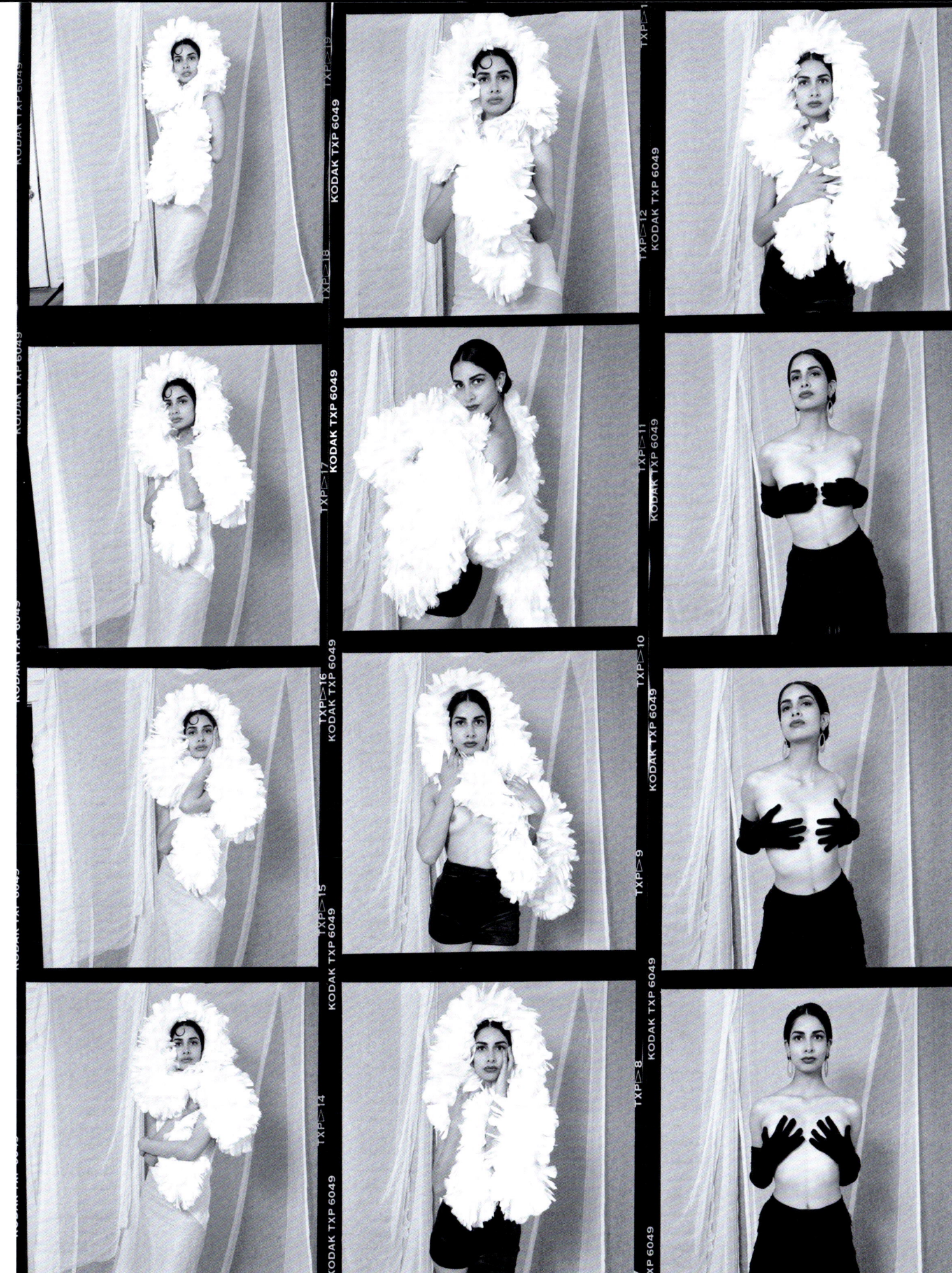

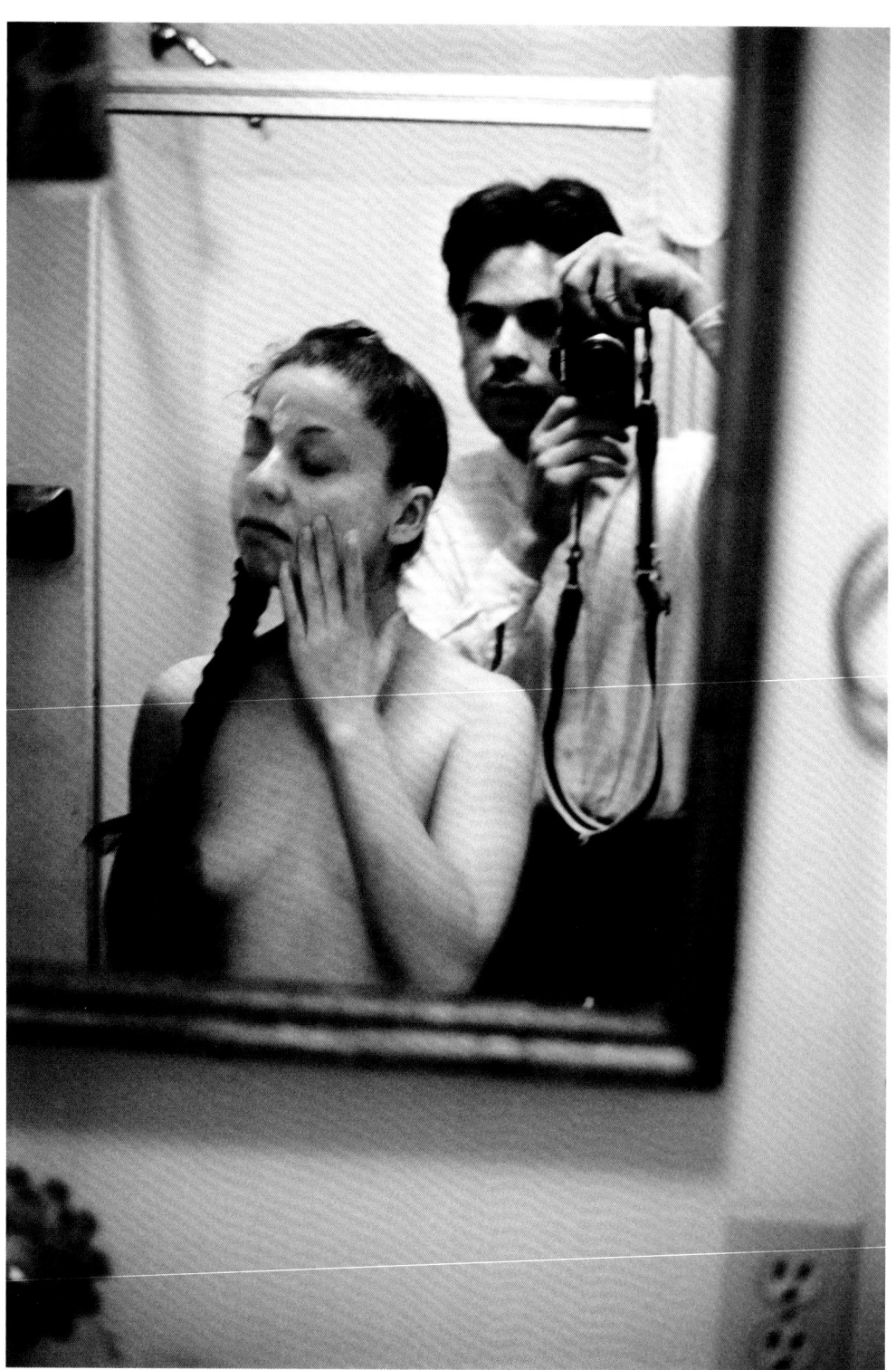

Martine, Reynaldo, Echo Park, ca. 1990

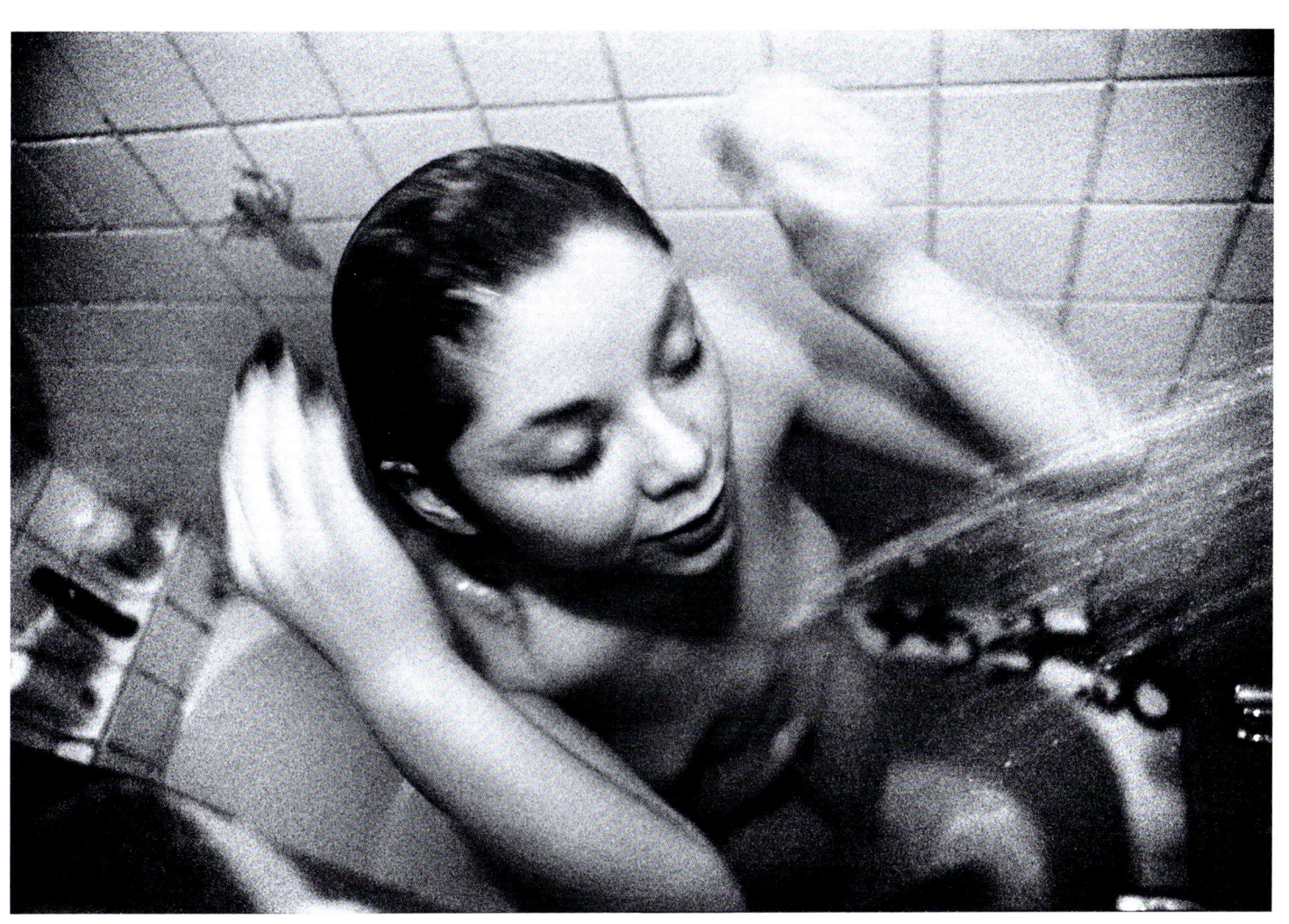

Connie, Echo Park, ca. 1990

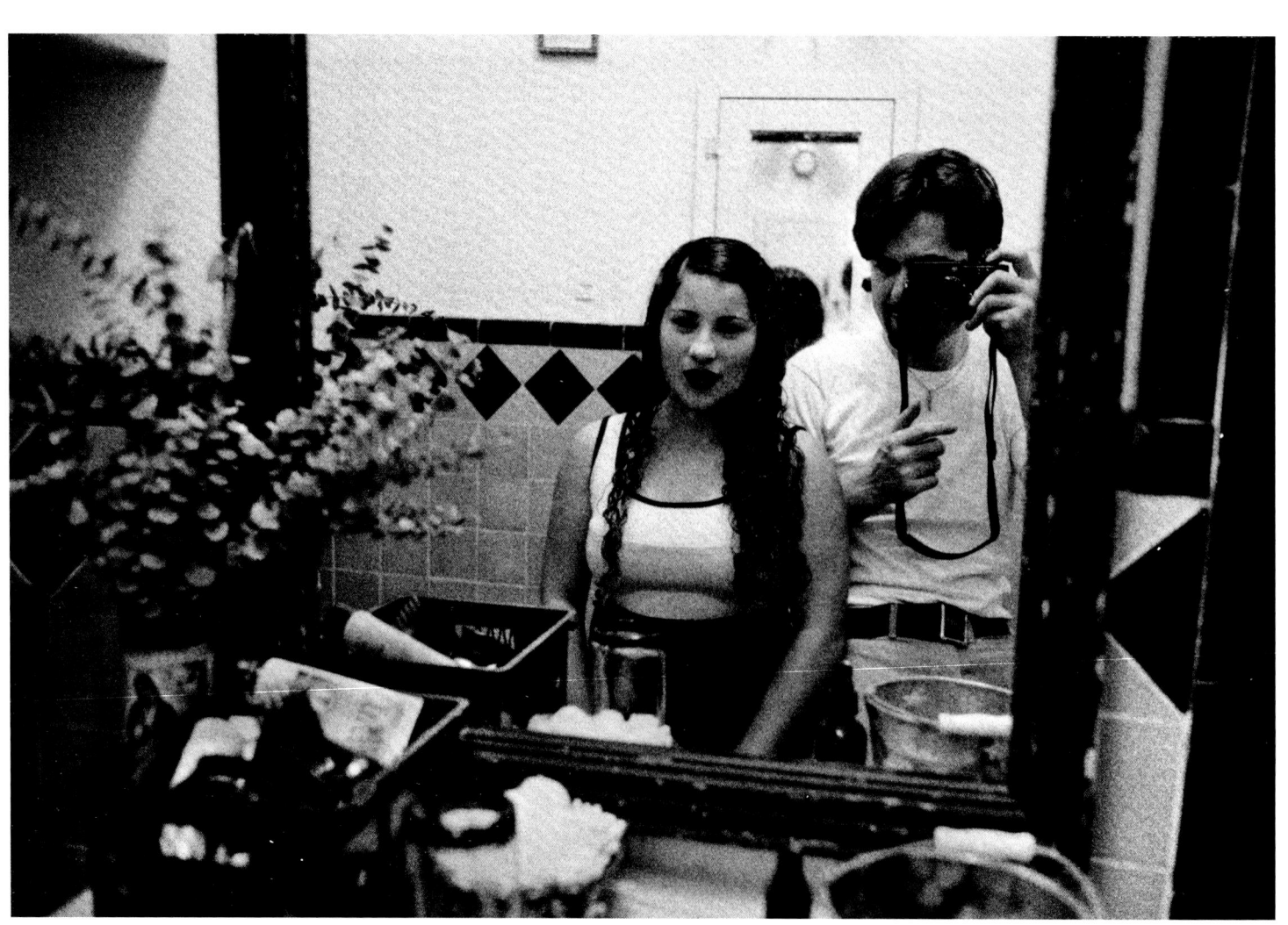

Reynaldo, Irene, Echo Park, 1997

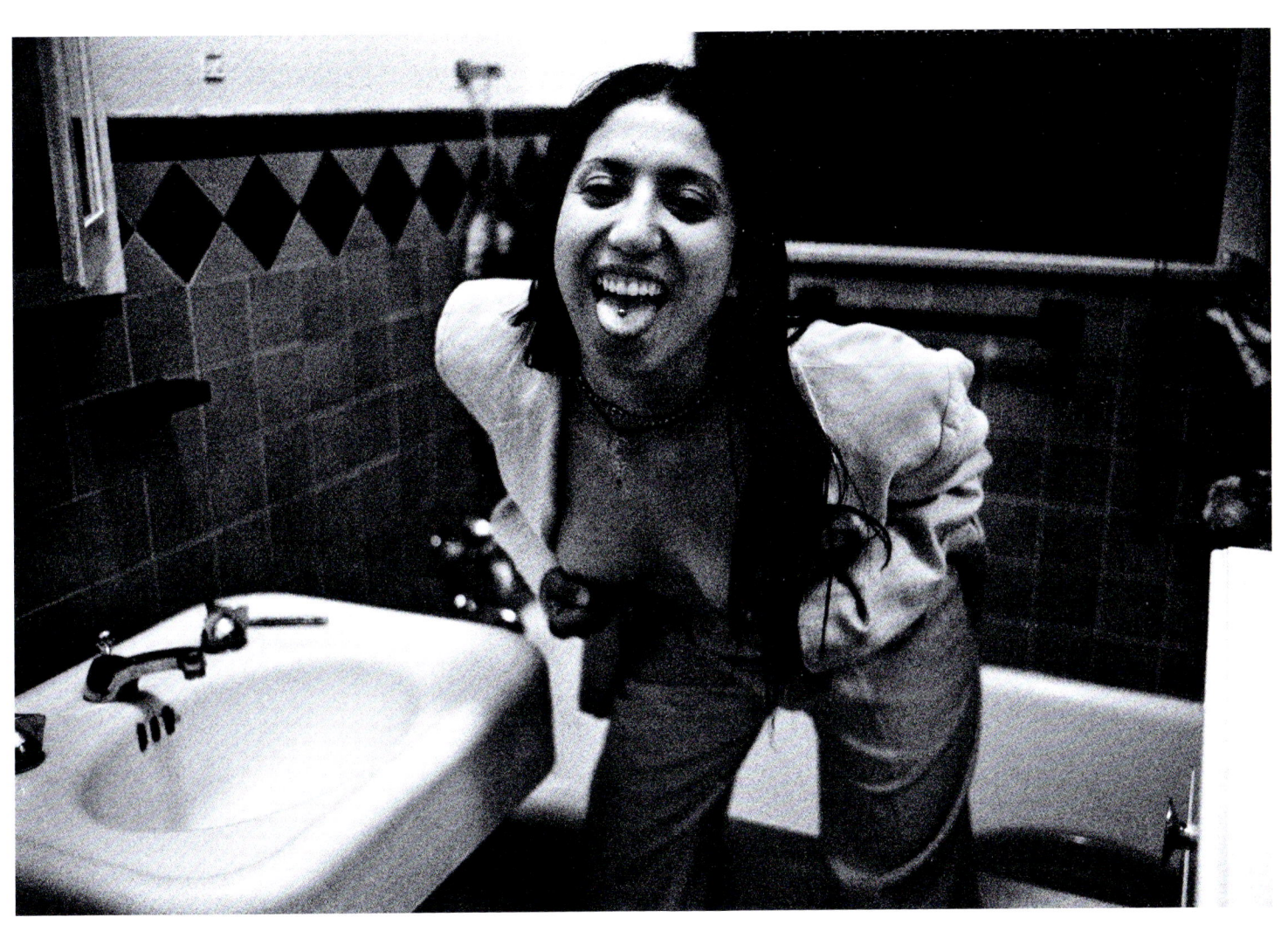

Laura, Echo Park, 1997

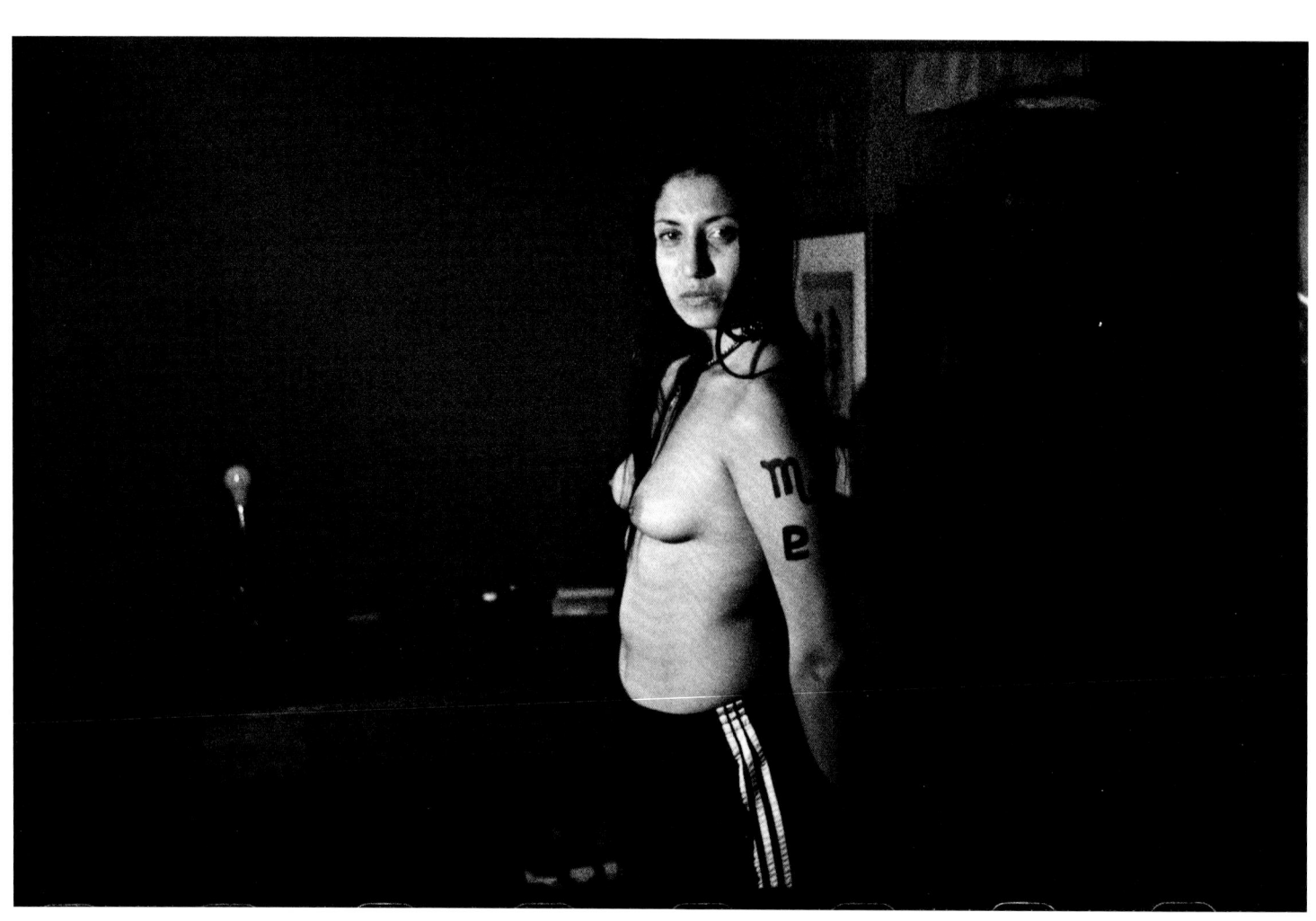

Laura, Echo Park, 1997
RIGHT: *Bianco, Echo Park*, contact sheet, ca. 1992

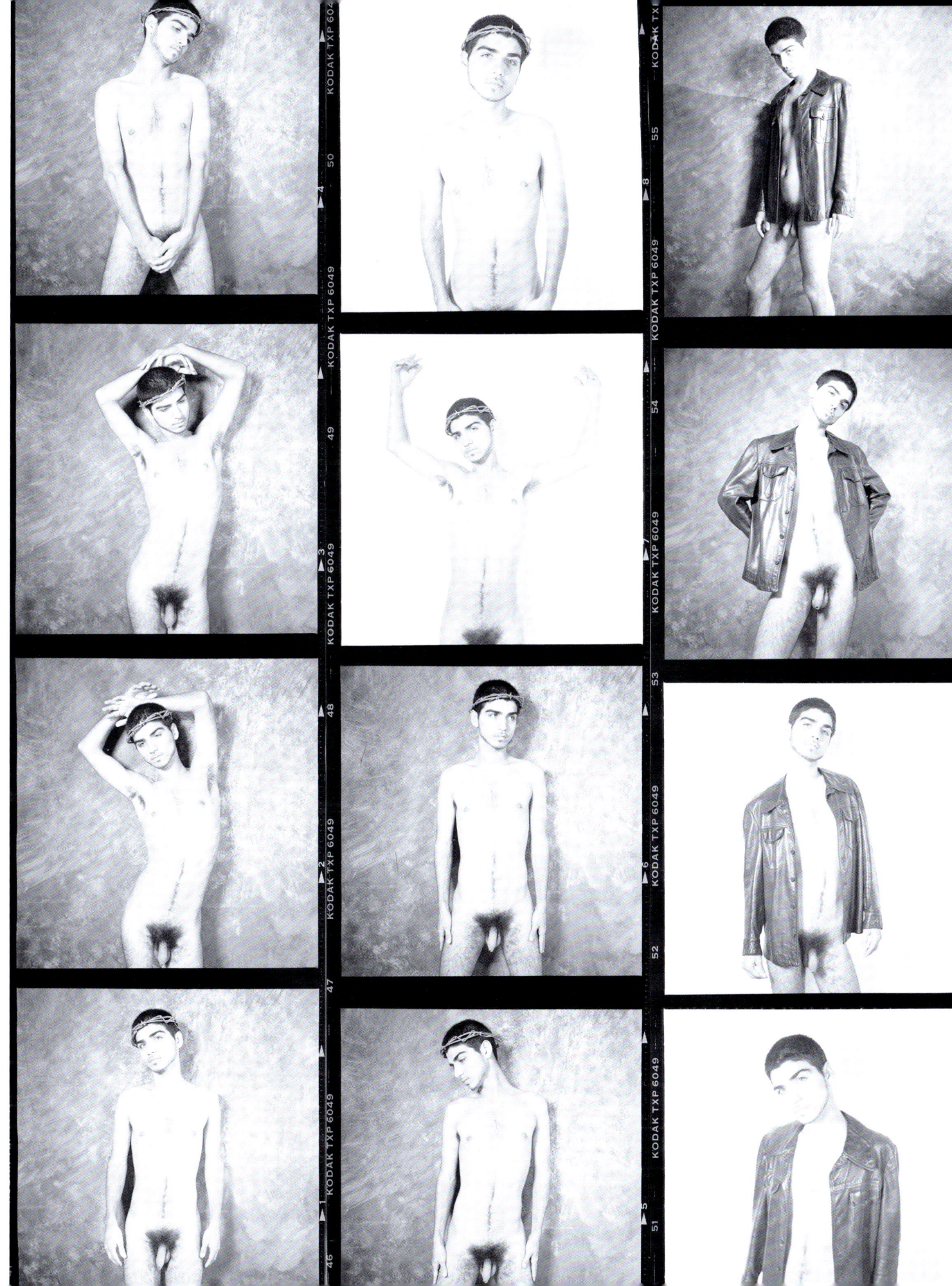

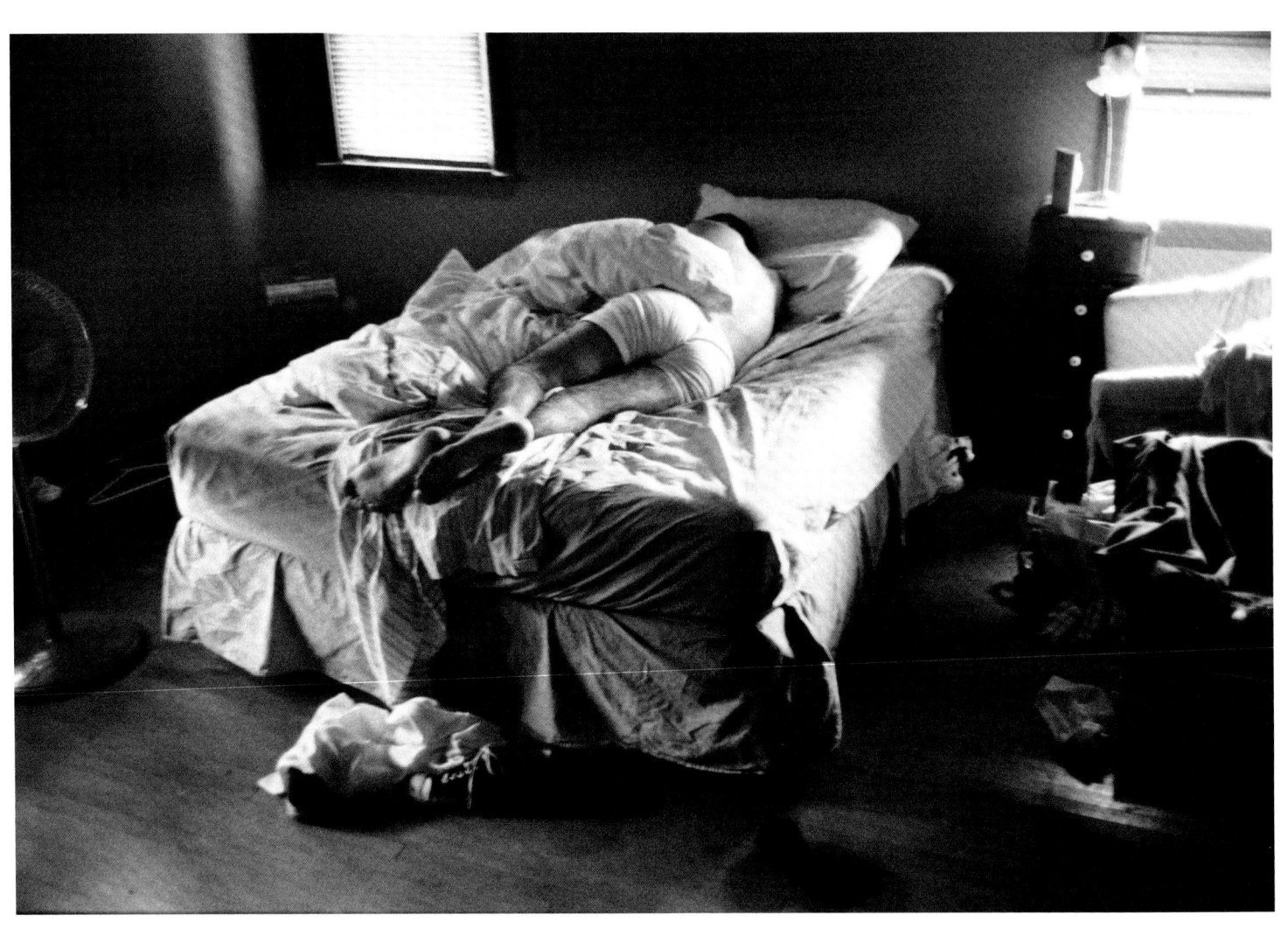

Bianco, Echo Park, ca. 1993

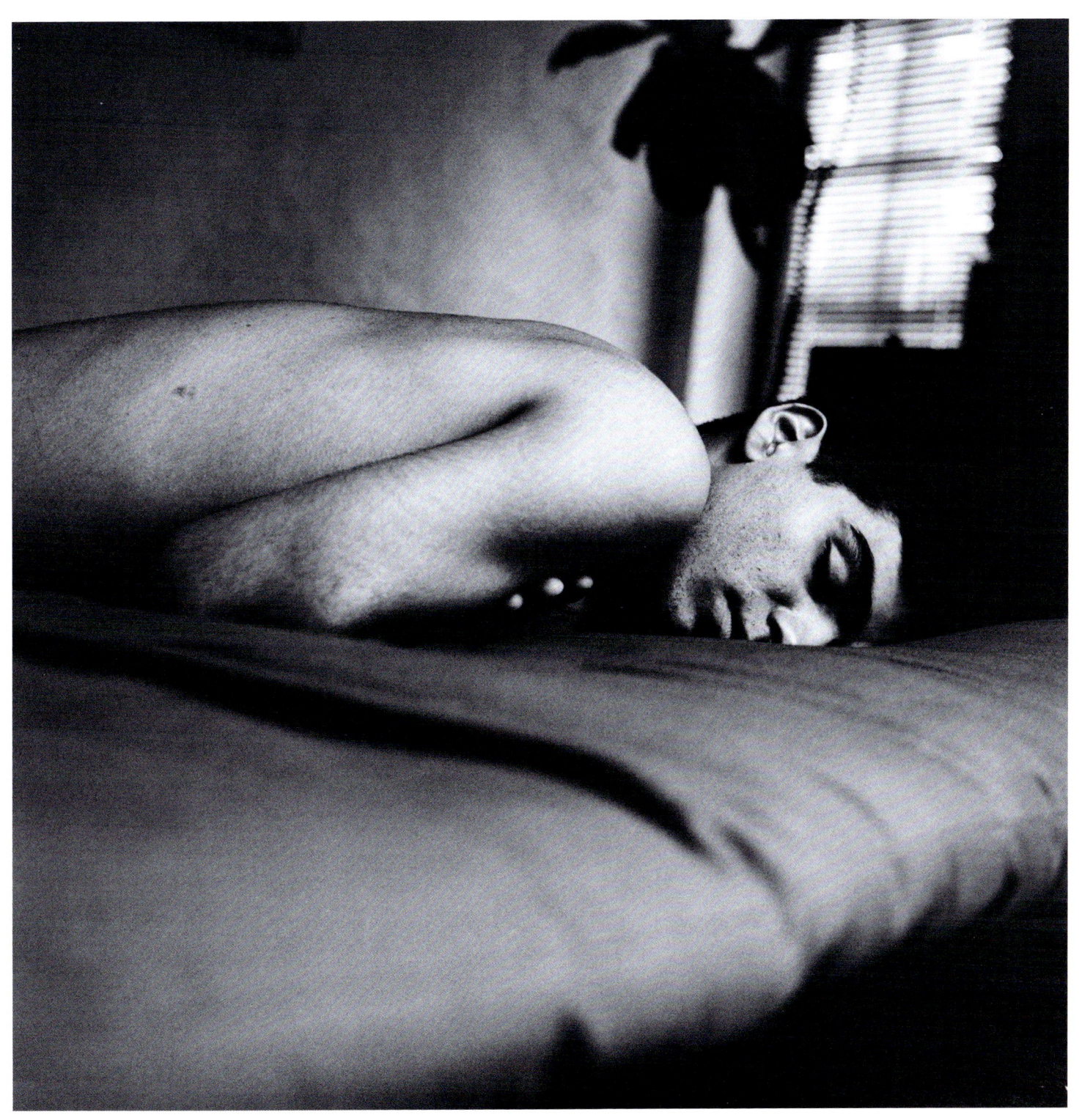

Bianco, Echo Park, ca. 1992

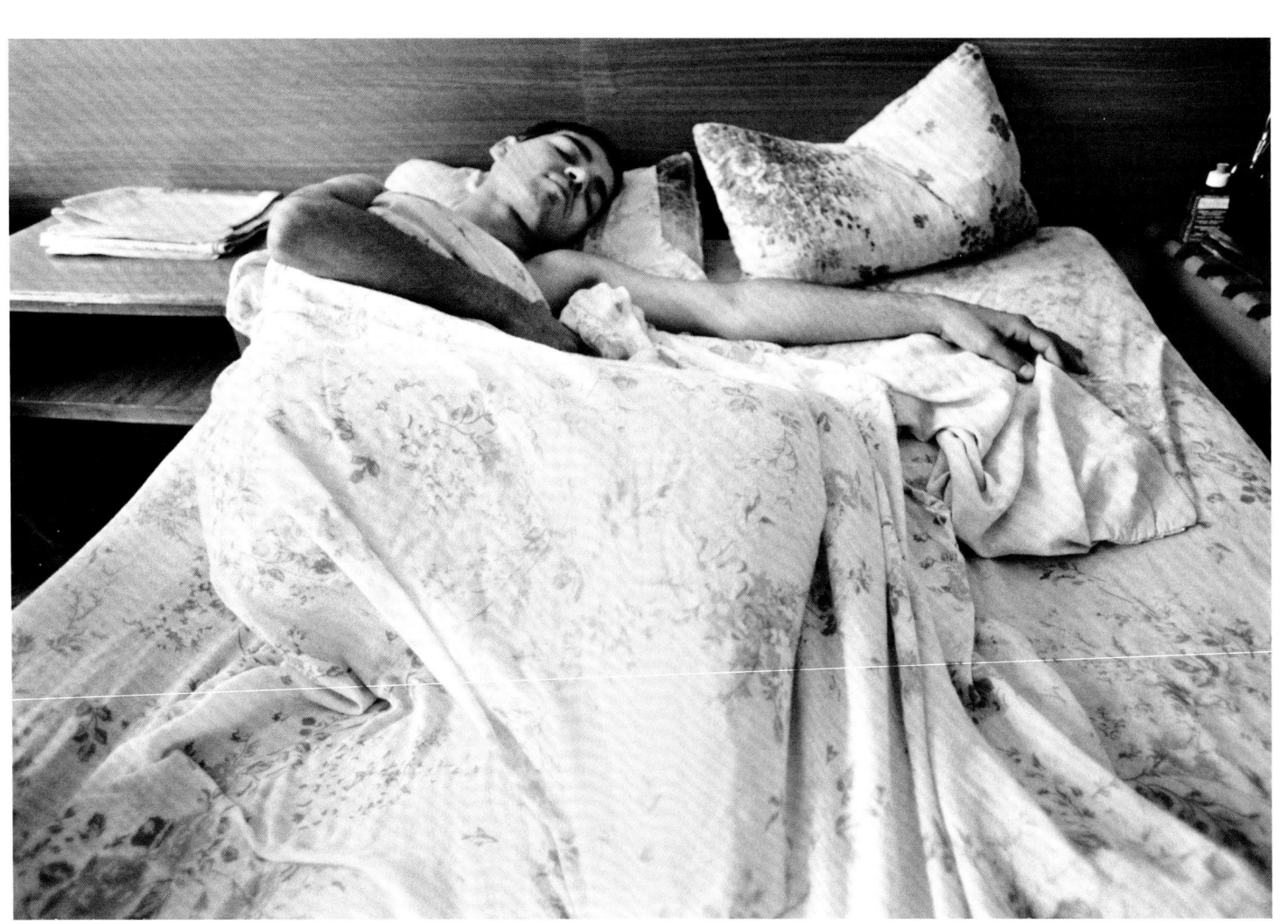

Bianco, Echo Park, ca. 1994

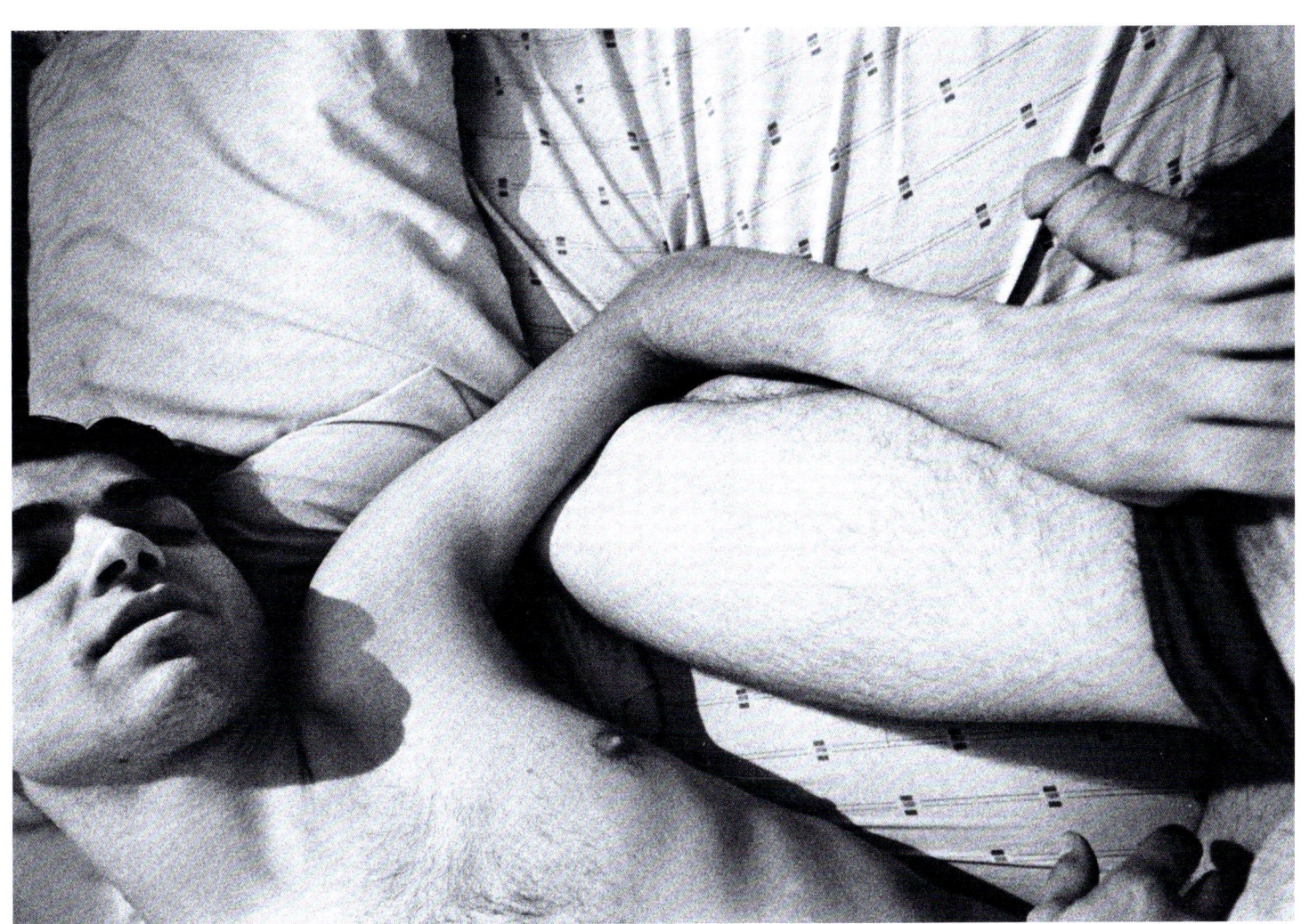

Bianco, Reynaldo, Echo Park, ca. 1994

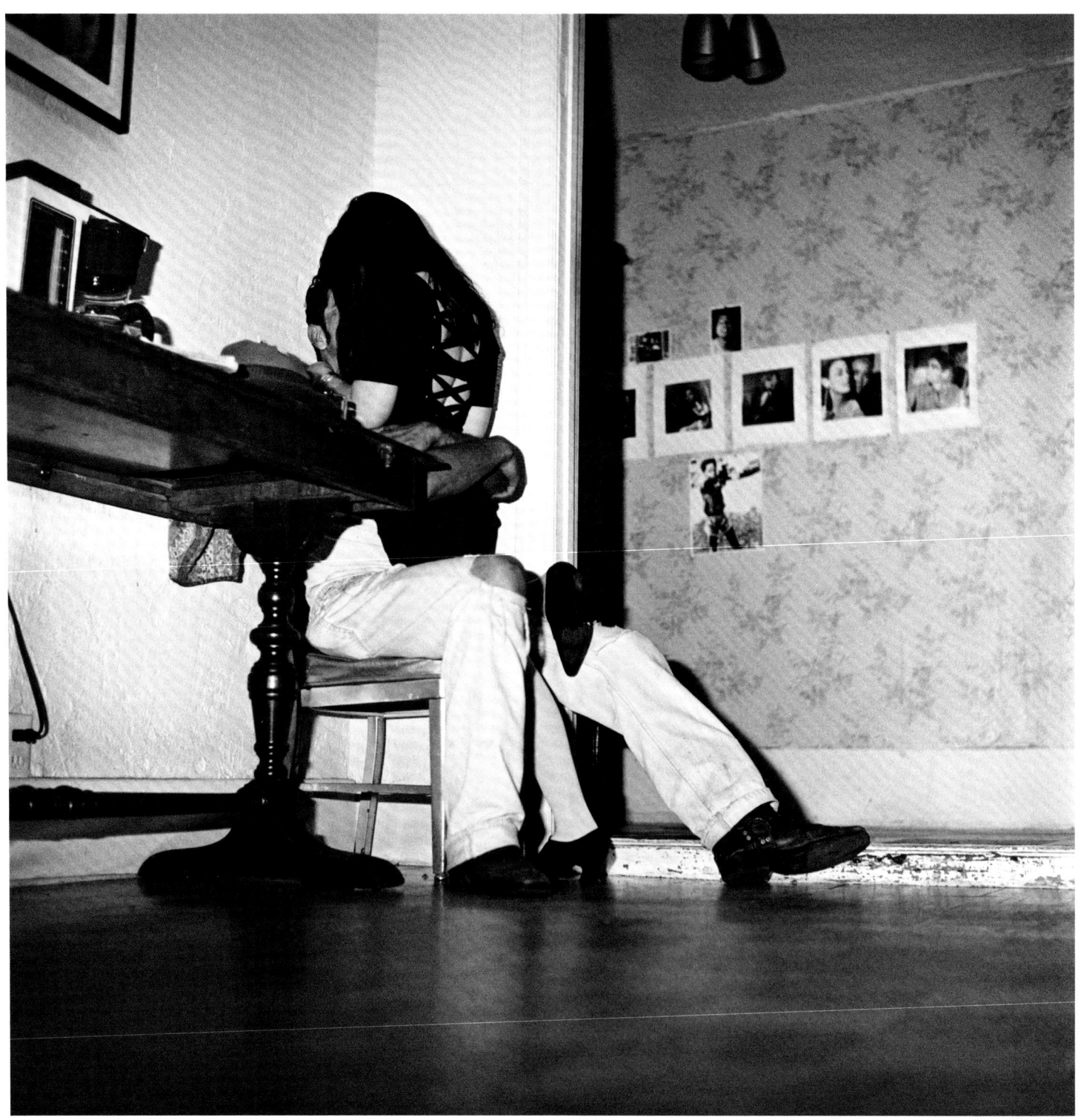

Rosie, Unknown, Echo Park, ca. 1993

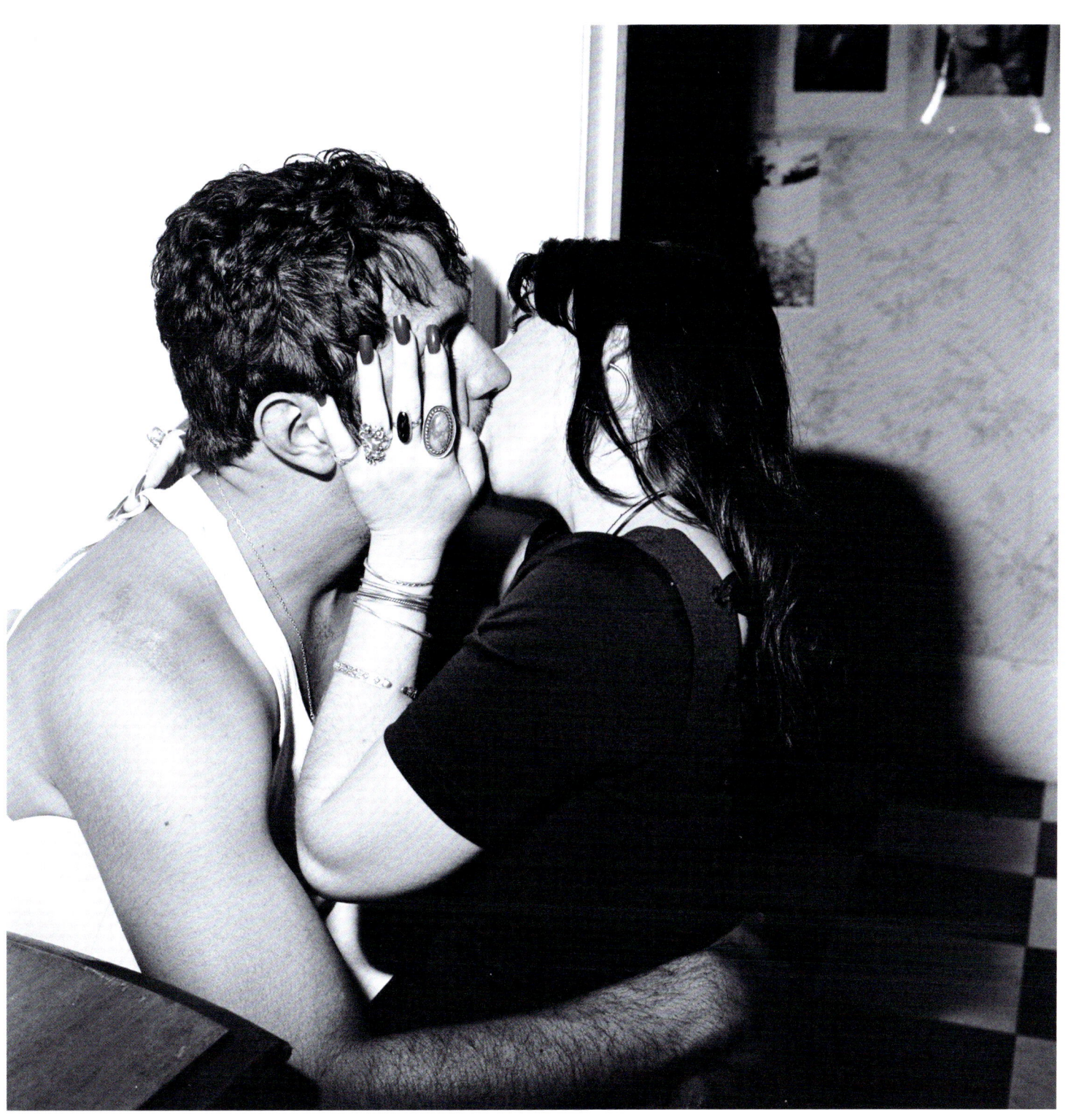

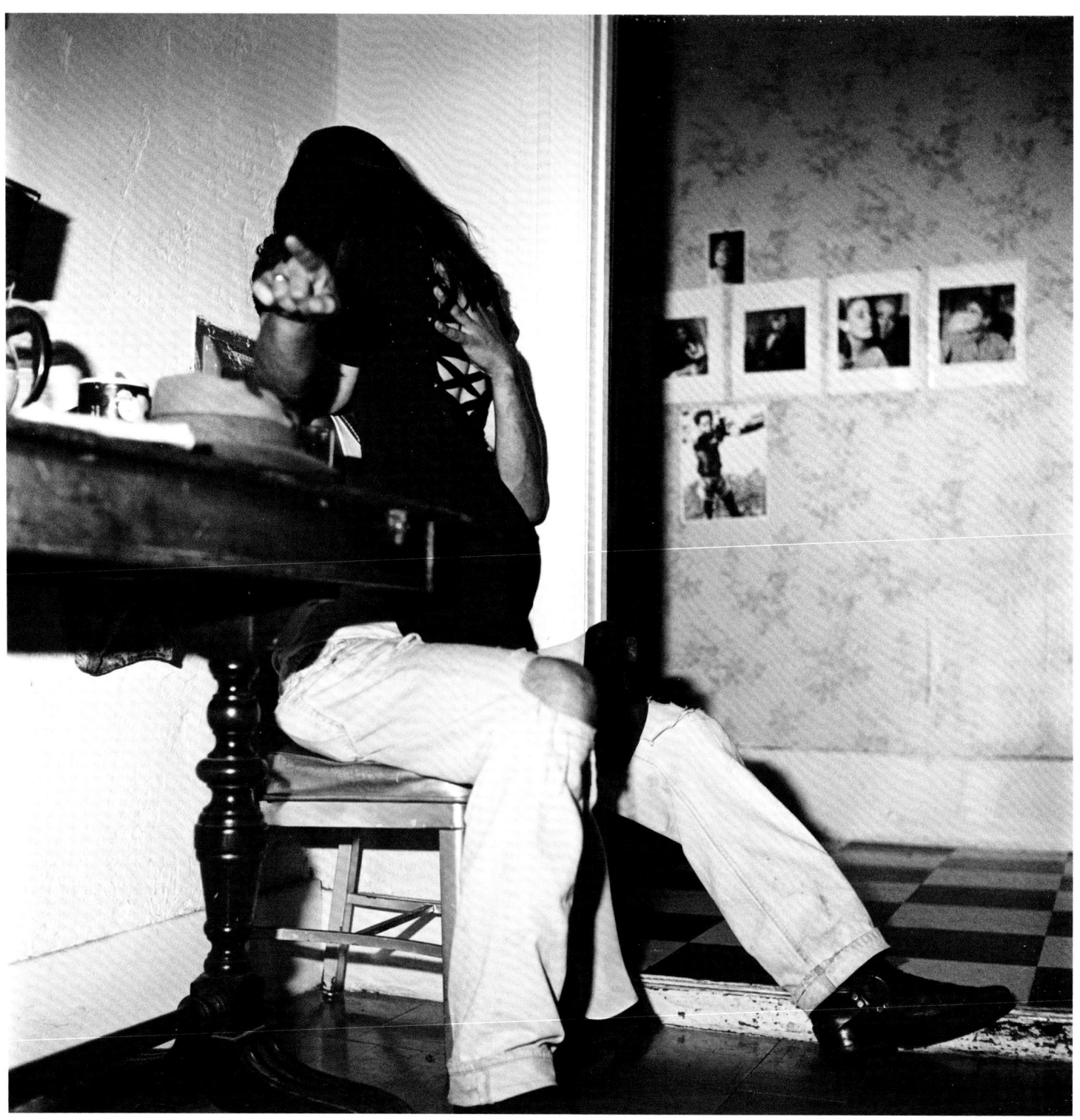

Rosie, Unknown, Echo Park, ca. 1993

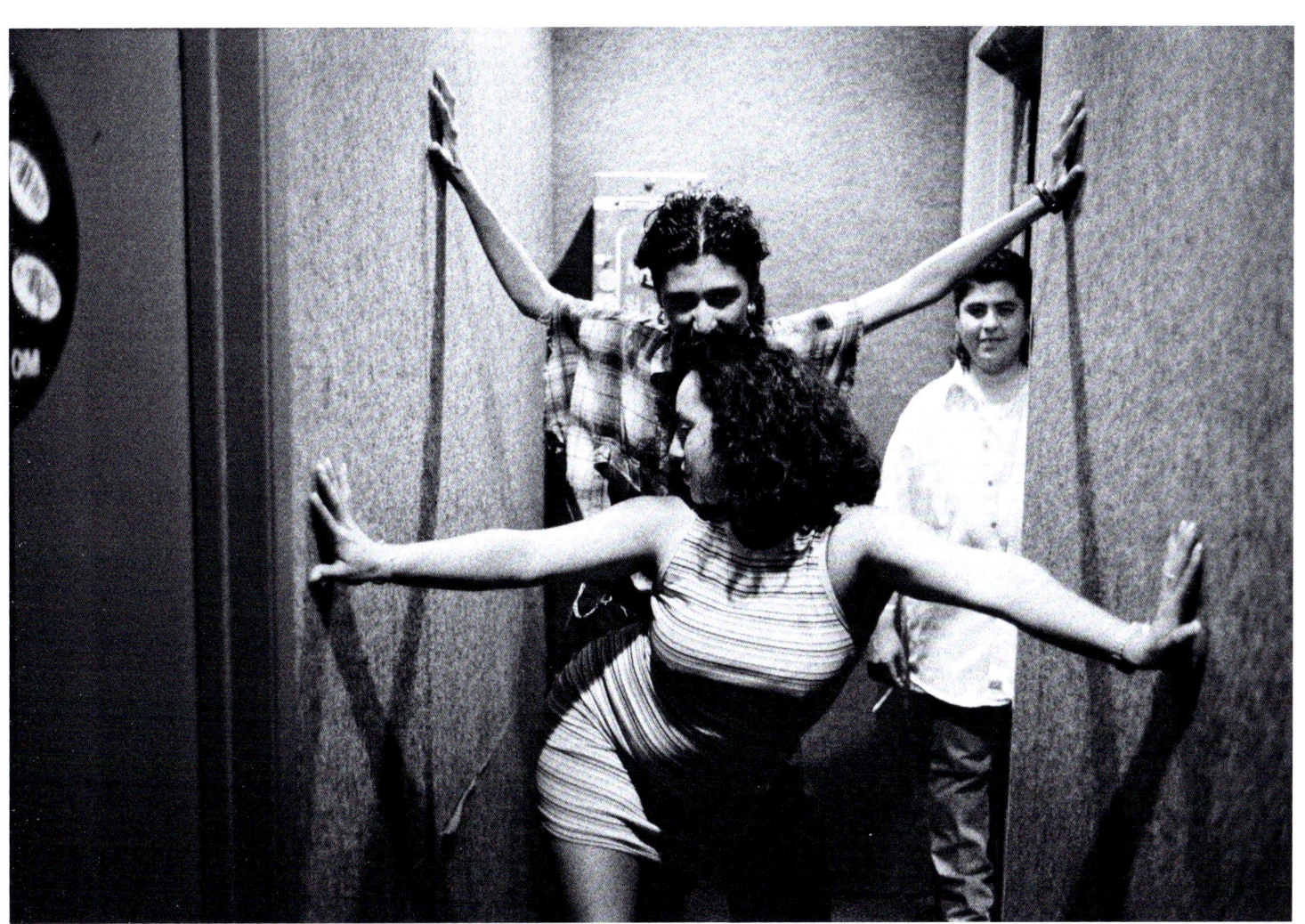

Ramona, Gia, Friend, Dreams, ca. 1995

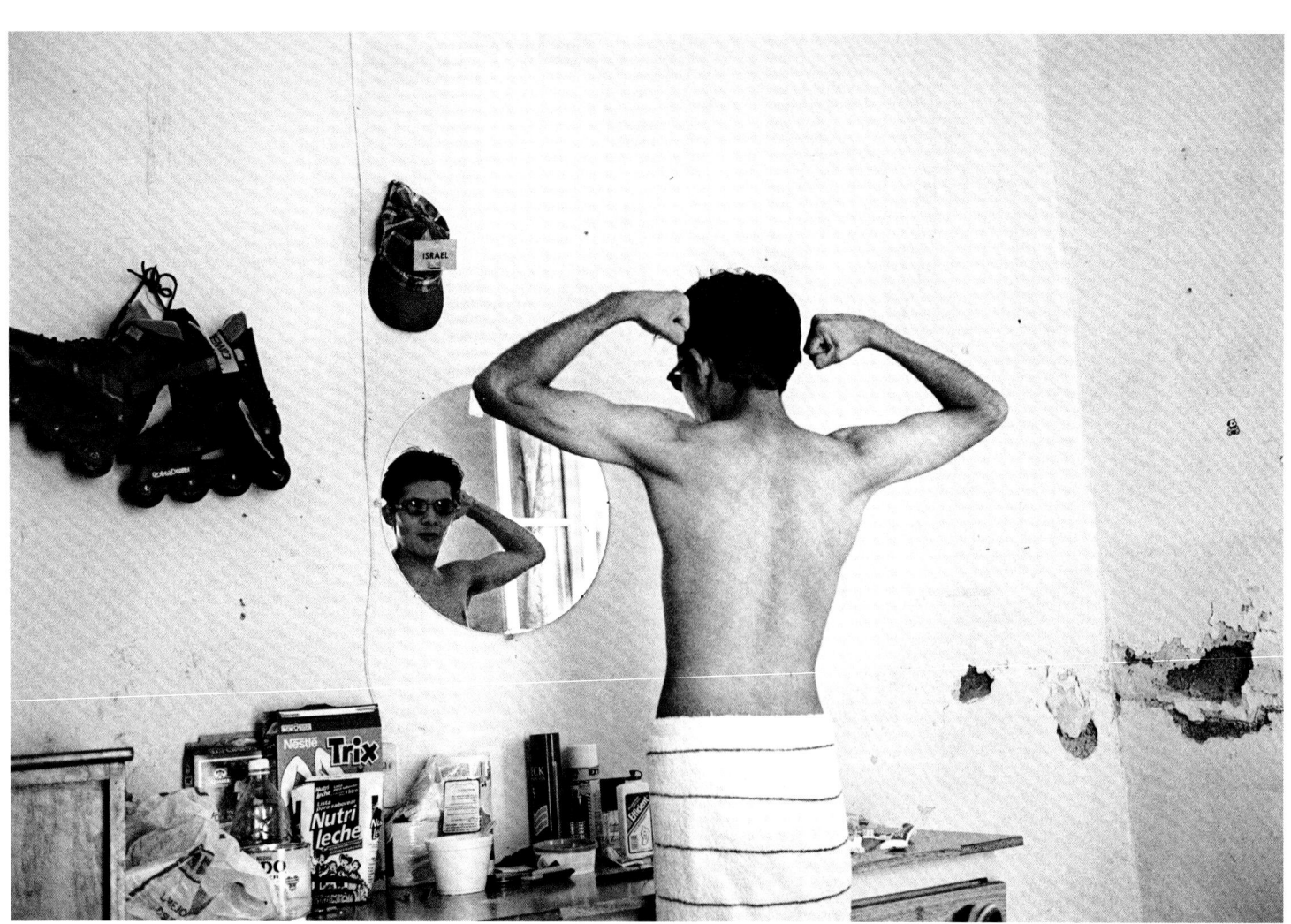

Guanajuato, ca. 1997

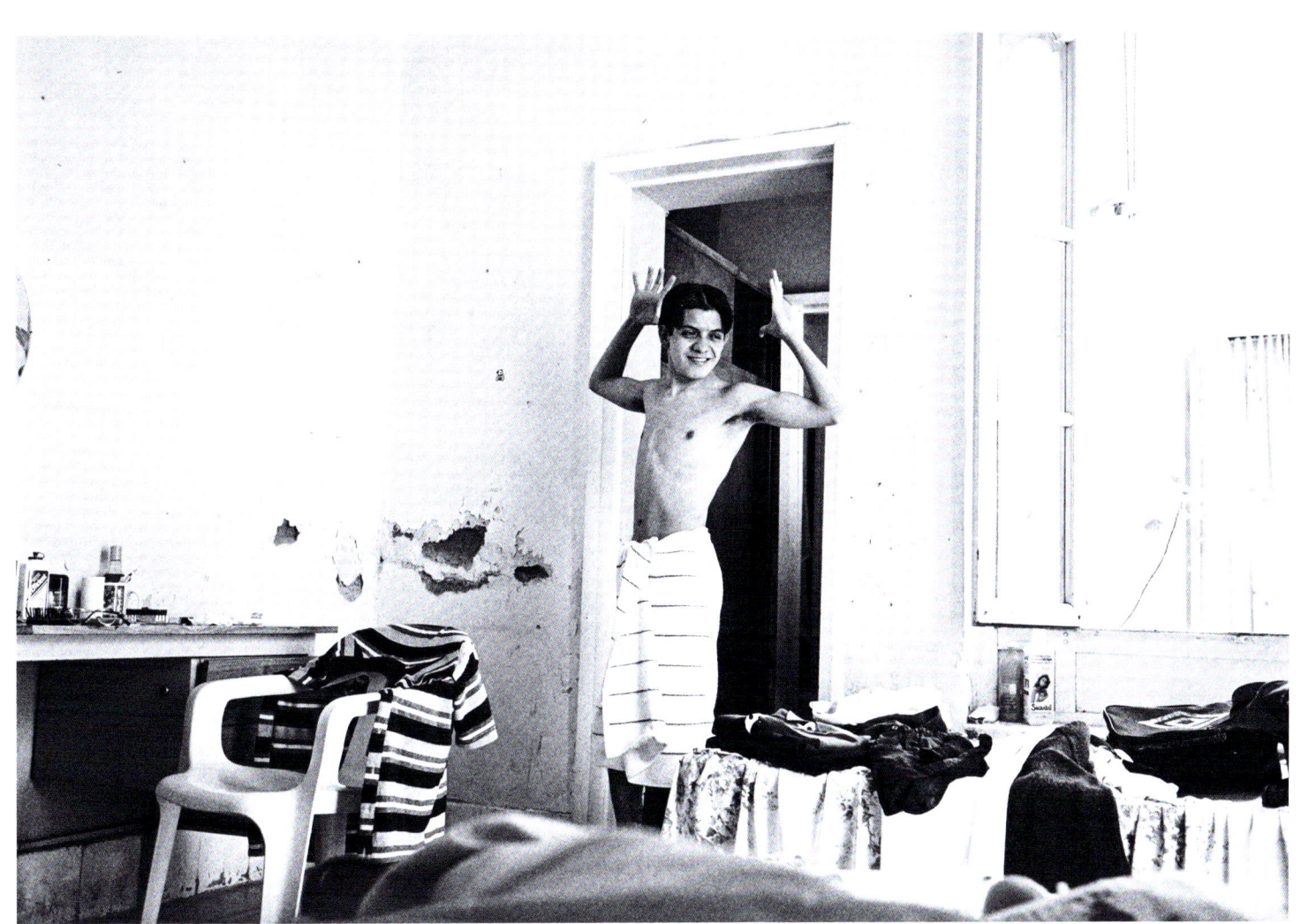

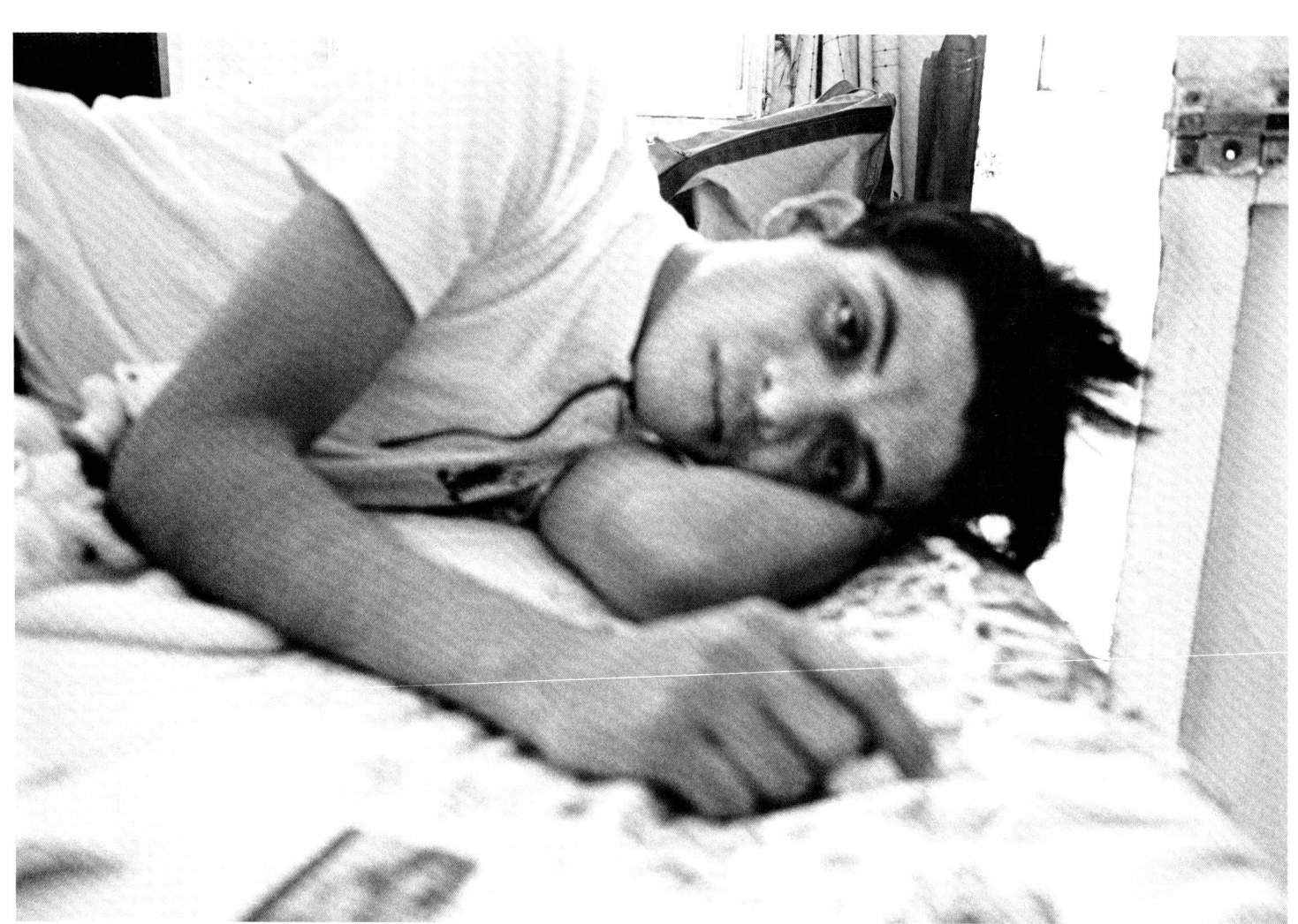

Guanajuato, ca. 1997

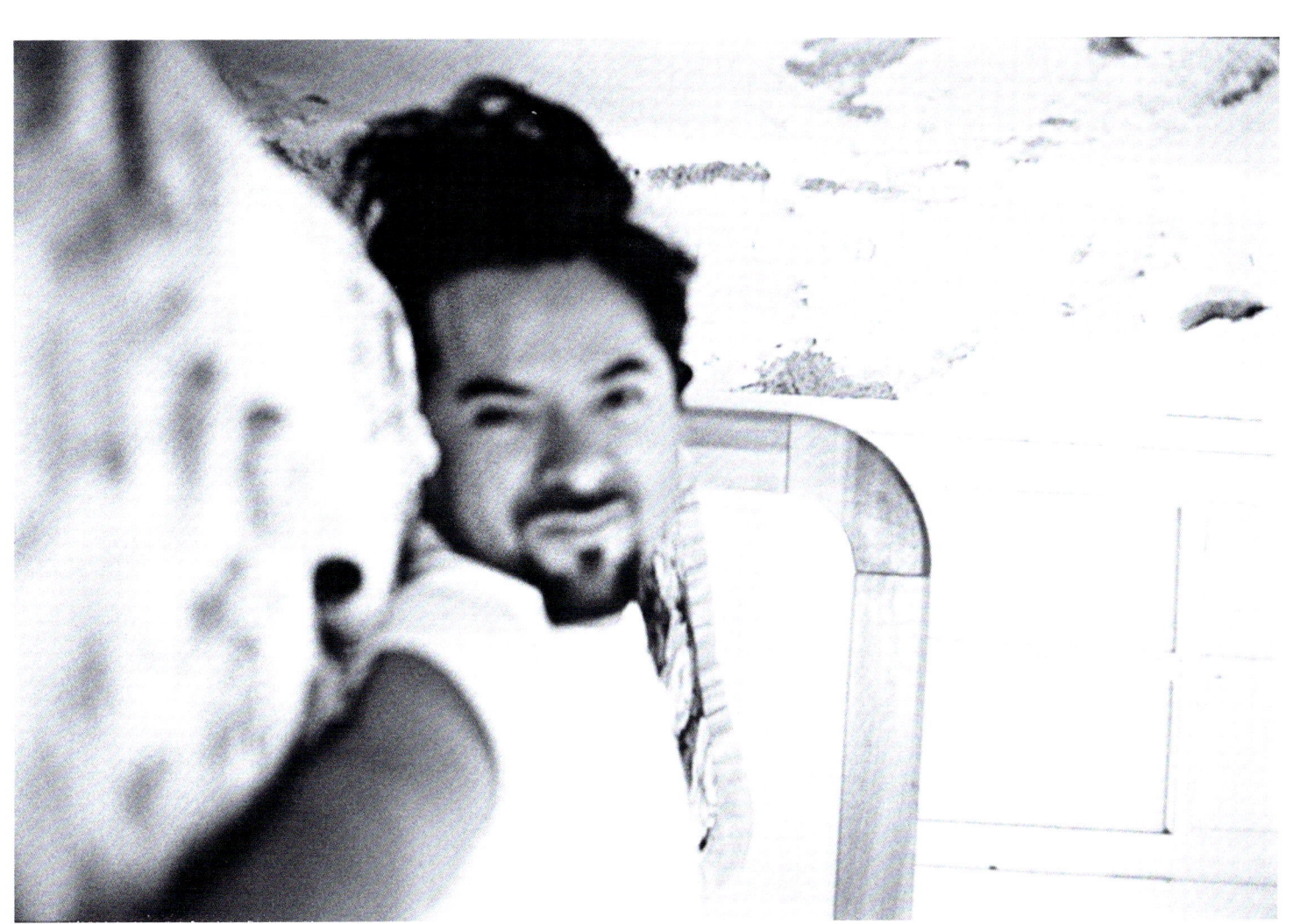

Reynaldo, Guanajuato, ca. 1997

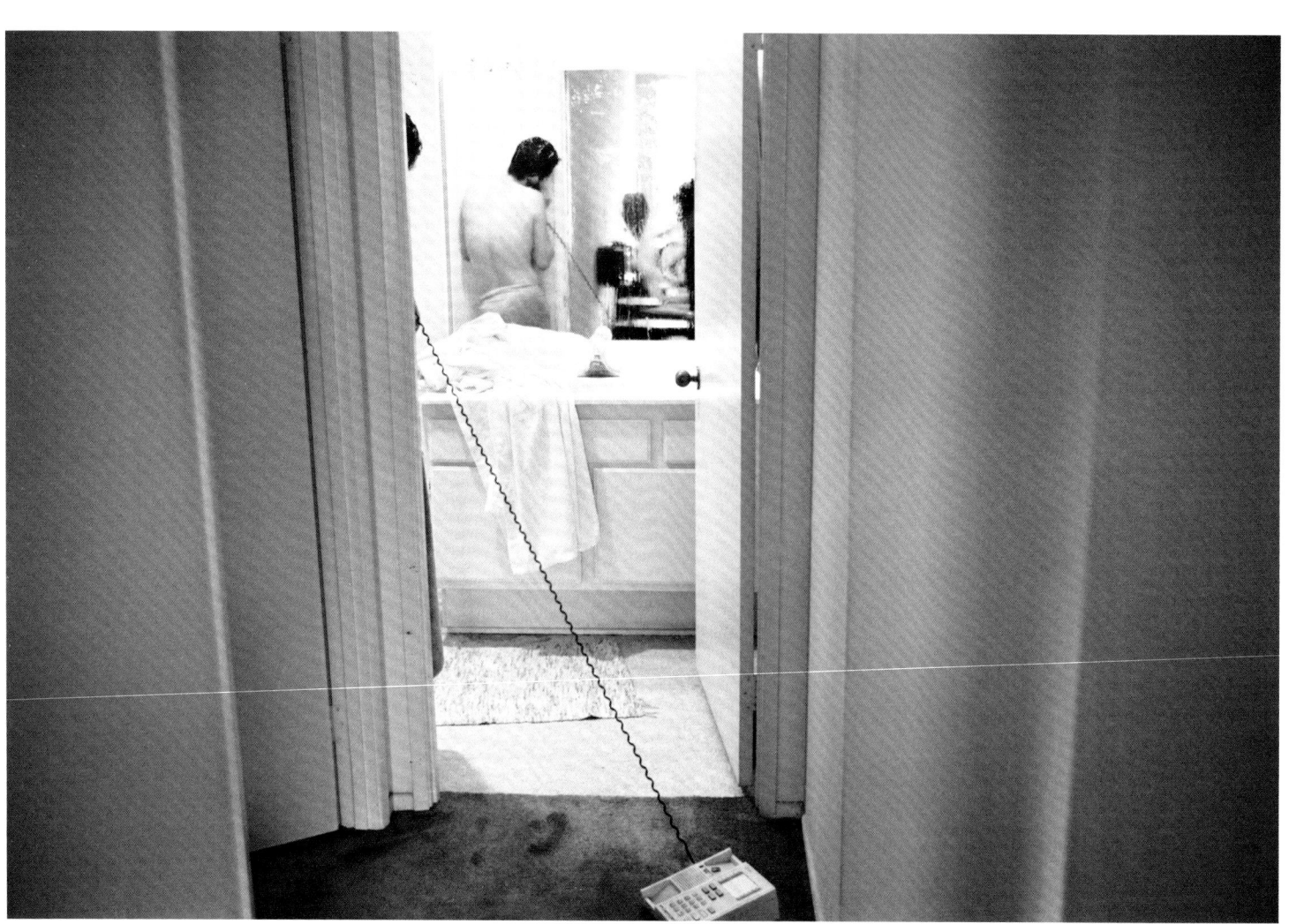

Steven, Echo Park, ca. 1991

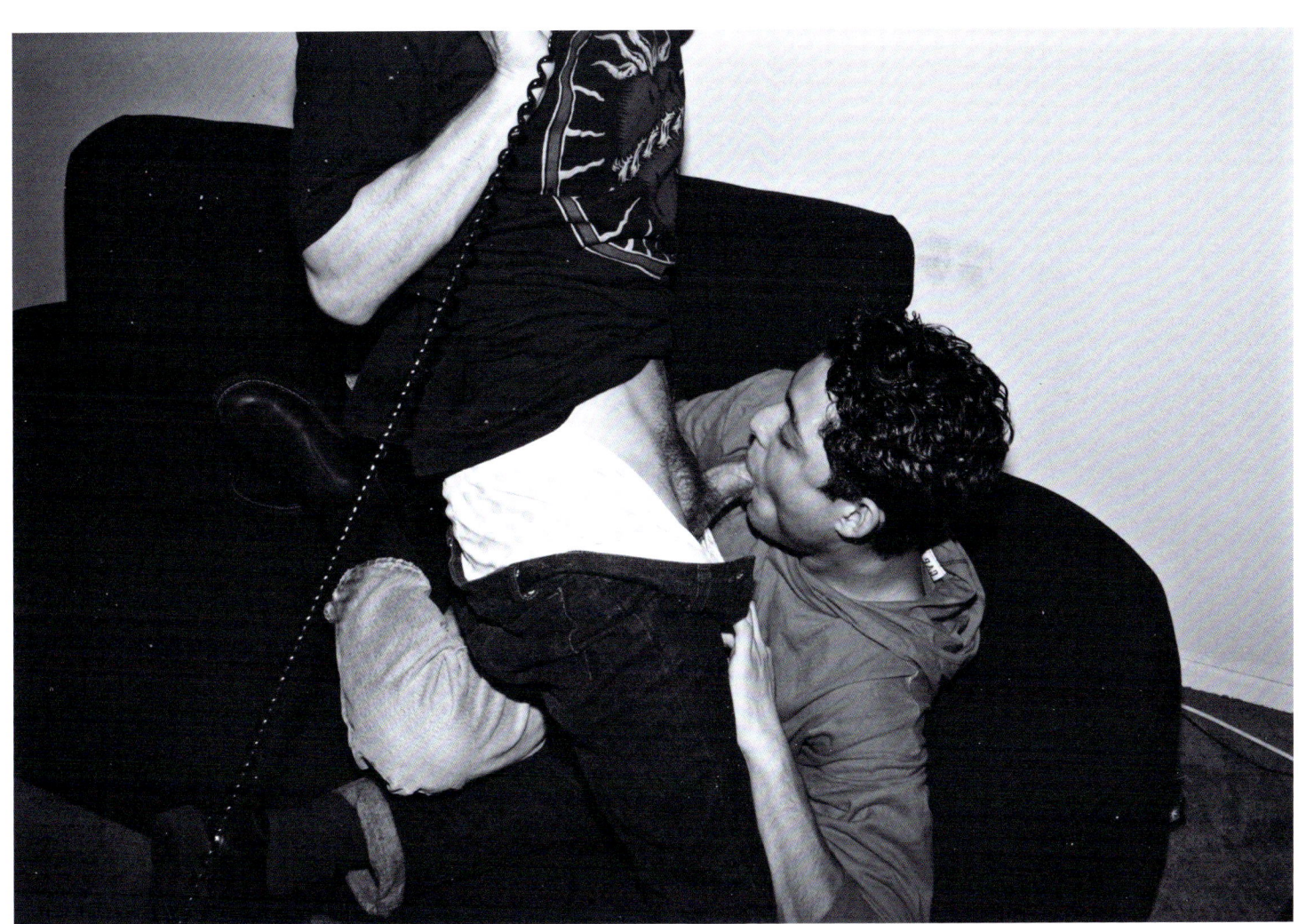

Reynaldo, Steven, Echo Park, ca. 1991

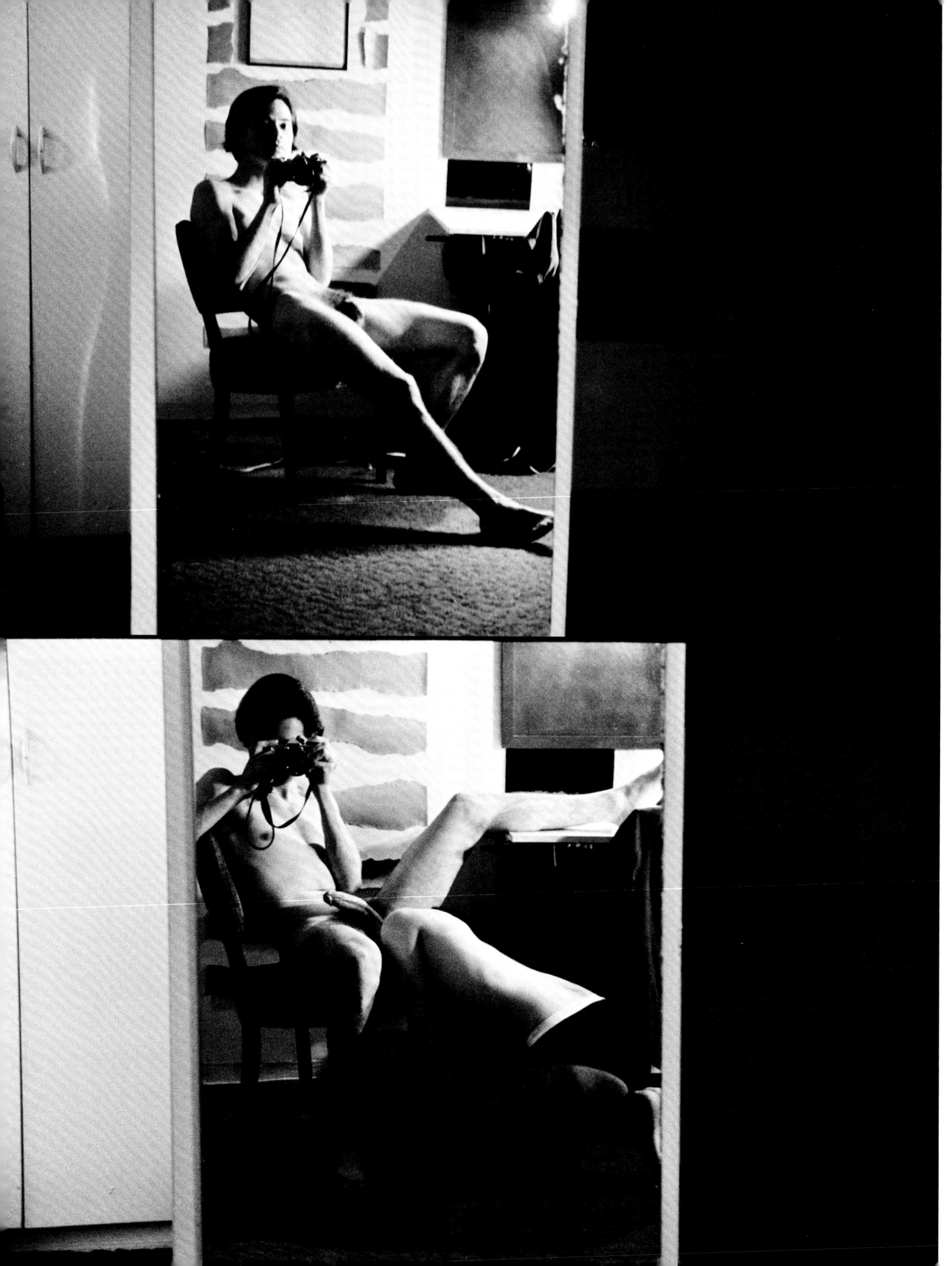

A SENSUAL CURRENT
—Chris Kraus

Who loves you? I'm madly in love with you. I love you so much! He said these things to me so many times I started to believe them and expect that we'd begin to do the things that people who love each other do ... watch TV, hang shelves, cook meals, consult each other about long-term travel plans. But that wasn't what he meant at all. He had to dignify his lust with the illusion of romantic love. He meant: I want to have continuous sex with you.

But what is the heart ... ? It's worth less than people think. It's quite accommodating, it accepts anything. You give it whatever you have, it's not very particular. But the body ... Ha! That's something else again. It has a cultivated taste, as they say, it knows what it wants. (Colette, *The Pure and the Impure*)

But then again, there is the moment—more powerful than any sex—when the potential lover abandons their well-rationalized defense and restraint and despite their better judgment just reaches for you. The electric jolt when the mind leaves the body and it acts involuntarily—the moment of the reach, the first touch.

Mike Farrell's room was next to mine upstairs in the 80 Webb Street share house. Our lives were separated by a thick twelve-foot-long plaster wall. Mike was a graduate student in comp lit and English and I'd just started university that fall. He was Irish, tall, with a broad chest and narrow hips. A short dark beard, blue eyes, straight longish hair. Mike was moderately friendly to the other people in the house (a mix of students, former students, stoners who worked as few odd jobs as possible, and a pregnant

eighteen-year-old girl named Prue), but all in all he remained somewhat aloof, which I understood to be a sign of his superior intelligence. He was writing his dissertation about the French writer Paul Nizan.

Prue lived in the big room across the hall on the other side of the stairs. Prue had the nicest room in the old Victorian house, the conjugal room, at least twice as big as ours. She'd asked to have that room when the previous occupant moved out. We split the rent evenly no matter which room we lived in, but considering Prue's pregnant and solitary state, we all agreed that it should go to her.

Except for occasional food-shopping trips, Prue spent all her time communing with her unborn child while she rocked in an old wooden chair. On rare sunny days, Prue's chair—positioned several feet away from her quilted bed, a bed that was never unmade—would catch a honey-colored slab of light through the double bay windows that faced south onto the street. Sometimes she knit. Glowing and soft and alone, Prue had achieved an almost vegetal existence that we all witnessed daily through her open door. As time and Prue's pregnancy advanced, her slow, gentle presence in the room just a few feet away from ours became the node through which Mike's and my attraction to each other passed. This attraction was based on the digust-we both felt but didn't dare express. *I was twenty. I will let no one say it is the best time of life*, Nizan's most famous novel, *Aden, Arabie*, began. Nizan arrived in Aden, a small city in Yemen, in 1931 and was appalled by French colonial rule:

TOP: *Self-Portrait, Pasadena*, 1987
BOTTOM: *Reynaldo, Ricardo, Pasadena*, 1987

Aden, he wrote, *was Europe compressed, and at white heat. ... There are only two human species left, and the only bond between them is hatred: the one that crushes and the one that does not consent to being crushed.*

Although Mike's voice was soft and his demeanor was very subdued, he'd formed some hard judgments about the writers he'd read. He knew who was real, who was fake, who'd sold out, whose heroic stance was just a pose. *You know*, he said once, *I don't think you're really as superficial and dumb as you seem*—a high compliment coming from him. Mike's position on the US was that, as a race overall, Americans were much stupider than average New Zealanders but there were exceptions like William S. Burroughs, Delmore Schwartz, and Richard Fariña who were much greater than any great New Zealander could hope to be.

Although I have never lacked close friends, Colette writes, *rarer in my life have been the friends who were not close, between whom and me passed a sensual current, a mysterious force that made them, to begin with, rather cantankerous and sparkling, then dull, snuffed out like a candle.*

That summer I'd lost my virginity at a demonstration, organized by the Progressive Youth Movement, against the US military installation outside the small South Island town of Blenheim. About forty of us traveled down on the overnight ferry and pitched tents outside the base. We made bonfires on Friday night and all day on Saturday we waved signs and chanted *Burn Woodbourne* and *Yankee Go Home*. There was something thrilling about this, being a Yankee myself. By late afternoon, news of our camp had spread to other "progressive youth" in nearby towns. We were joined by a gang of gearheads from Nelson who worked as mechanics and welders and had never read Marx but were drawn to our camp as a good source of student-activist ass. I hadn't yet turned seventeen but the clock was ticking fast toward the birthday deadline that I'd set for losing my virginity. So

when Murray Parker ducked into my tent, I didn't say no. It was purely technical sex and I never saw or even thought about him again. Whatever was happening in the house with Mike was so much more erotic. Exchanging glances, brushing past each other on the narrow stairs, we circled each other like two timid beasts.

Except for weed there weren't regular drugs at the house but one weekend Richard, the geology student who lived in the front room downstairs, got hold of some acid and everyone but Prue bought a tab. Webb Street was in the central city and it barely had a yard so Richard agreed to drive us all to Mākara Beach on Sunday afternoon. Piling out of Richard's car, everyone took their blotter with some Thermos water and then wandered off alone or in pairs to explore. Some people walked along the beach on the volcanic rock but a few of us walked up the sheep tracks into the steep green hills.

Nick and Jan walked fast ahead and I was straggling somewhere behind Mike when the acid hit, and hard. There was a tree with smooth bark and towering branches and on the ground, there were hundreds of black-and-white pebbles, quartz and granite. Picking up the bits of stone, turning them to examine them from every side, I was completely mesmerized and when I saw Mike pause ahead I called out *Look!* Mike walked back toward me down the hill and I held out my hand. He was standing very close. His index finger touched my palm as he turned over one of my gathered stones and then everything peaked and I was overwhelmed by an oceanic, electric charge.

After that I became obsessed with arranging a full consummation.

My friend Penny helped. The plan was that, the next Friday night after everyone came back from the pub, she and her boyfriend Steve would stage a small late-night party in my room. They'd get completely drunk, pass out on my bed, and refuse to leave. Then, I'd knock on Mike's door and tell him I was tired and had to sleep and could I lie down in his room?

74

Self-Portrait, Echo Park, contact sheet, ca. 1998

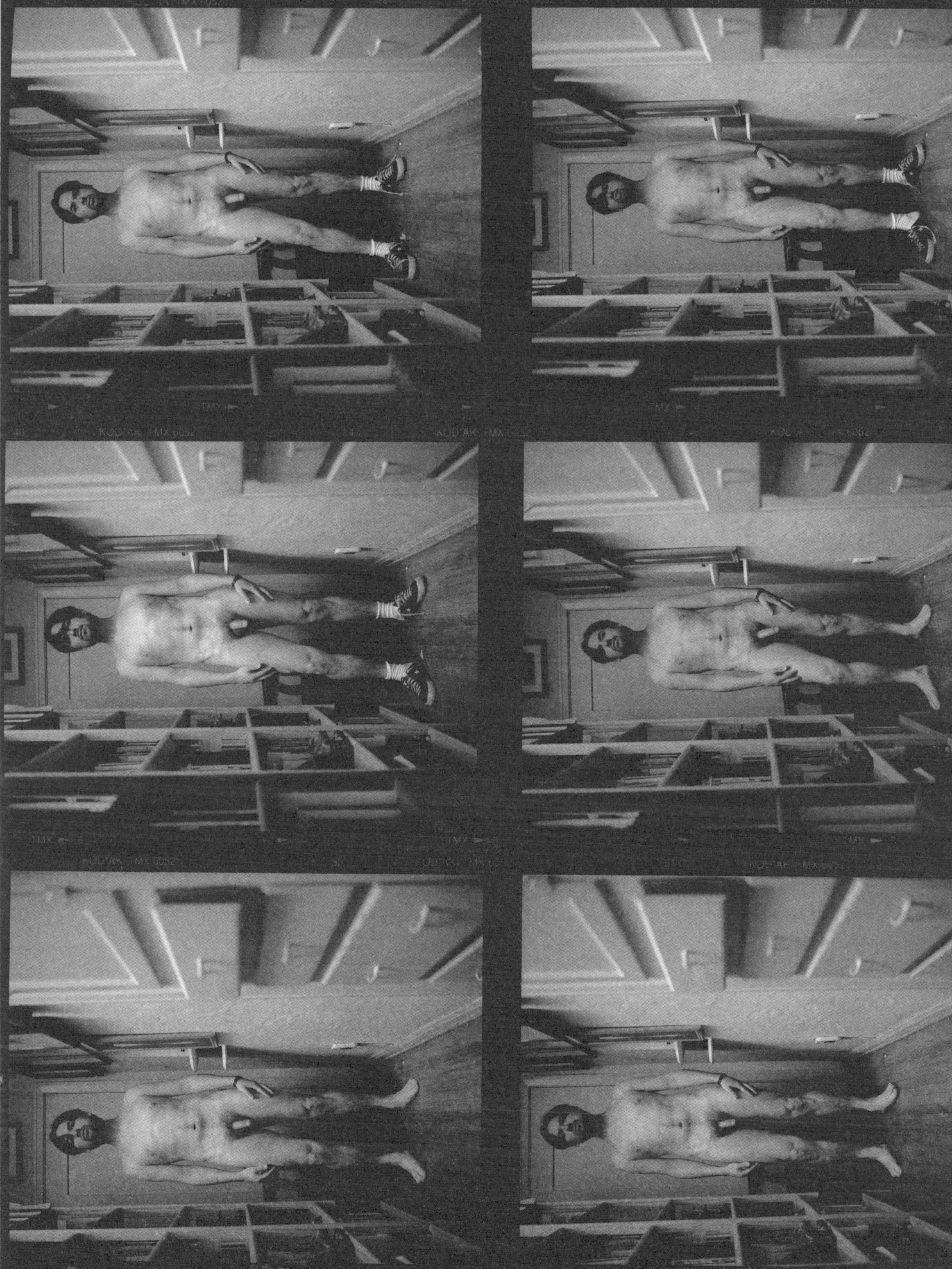

Everything happened just as Penny and I planned. Mike answered the door and allowed me to sleep like a dog at the foot of his bed under a blue-wool plaid blanket he'd got from his mom. Curled up like a shrimp, I folded my arms two inches away from my calves. And then I heard him breathe. The room was pitch dark and I knew this was my chance. Accidentally-on-purpose, I let one hand drift across the hairs on his leg. Mike's arm shot down and grabbed my wrist, pulling me up alongside him on the bed.

I don't remember what happened next in Mike's room on that night but for the next two and a half years we spent together, it was all downhill from there.

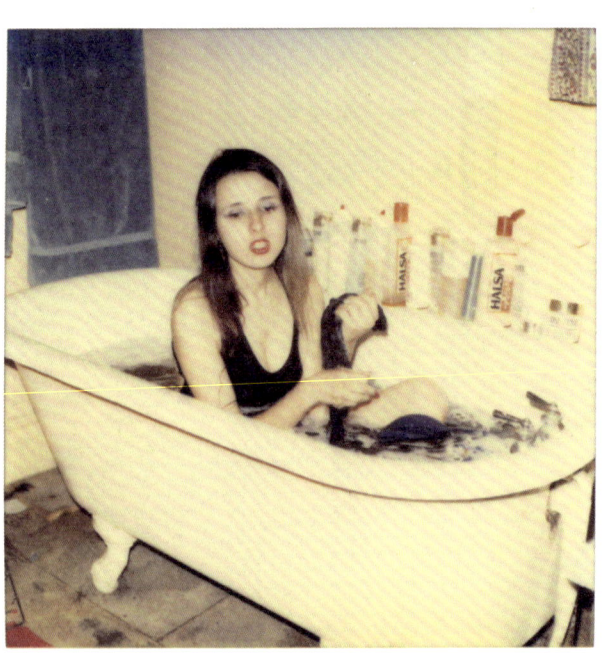

Tatiana, Polaroid, ca. 1985

RAIN
—**Abdellah Taïa**

Translated by **Noura Wedell**

Hell, literally.

Summer had lasted too long that year. It was February, and all over Morocco the sun continued to triumph daily, burning lands, souls, bodies, and skin.

It was a real economic catastrophe for the country. For everyone. Our future. Our projects. The radios and TVs kept repeating it.

Everyone was tired of that unbearable, intolerable heat. Except him and me. We liked that the sky stayed completely blue day after day. And we adored the sun. Our god.

We had our ritual. To walk for hours and hours after school. To walk with and under the rays of the sun, crushing and voluptuous. To walk so as to melt into the heat. The eternally peaking heat. Merging him and me. A boy and another boy. Two brothers. More than that. To walk without ever tiring, to reach night, blackness, a bit of calm, secret intimacy. Our corner behind his house. To dream in silence side by side.

He was older than I. He was fifteen. I was thirteen.

His family, who lived across the street, didn't like my family. Our mothers especially. They'd hated each other for years, and fought regularly in the street.

I sided with my parents, of course. But deep down I didn't care. Ever since my life had begun, just across the small street of our poor Salé neighborhood was my double, simply taller, gentler, more beautiful. Me: him. Him: me. He, always further along than I. He, timid. I, cheeky

by necessity. Close and far away, a double fiction between us. At the beginning, without words.

It took years and years for what I was preparing for us, alone, to finally come about.

His hand that reaches toward mine. I take it. I keep it in my hand. I force him to come closer to me. I feel his body. His heart. I see his sweat. I breathe the warm air coming out of his nose. There is no doubt, it's really him, it's really me.

He says, "My name is Abdellah."

I say, "My name is Abdellah."

He doesn't believe me. He smiles. He's beautiful, more beautiful, with that smile, that wide-open mouth.

I repeat, "I'm like you. My name really is Abdellah."

He inches closer to me and whispers, "You're like me? You'll have to prove it!"

I didn't know what to say. Not realizing the meaning of the words that were coming out of my mouth, I ended up saying this: "Let's have a contest, a competition, if you want ... Man to man?"

He liked that offer, that challenge, that audacity. I could see it in his eyes and on his skin. He was excited. Without even lowering my eyes, I knew he was hard. He was breaking free of his borders, all of a sudden. Abdellah then made that inconceivable gesture that will stay with me my entire life: he put his left hand on his sex and as he would for a crying baby, he caressed it soft to calm it and lull it back to sleep. This lasted a very long time. A full minute. To me, an eternity. Then he offered, "You give me your milk. I'll give you my milk."

In a flash I cried out, joyfully, "Sperm! Your sperm!"

He put his hand on my mouth, the hand that had touched his sex for so long, and revealed the program. "I'll teach you everything, Abdellah."

Abdellah was suddenly no longer just my name. It had become an immense sky, a large notebook where I could write everything about myself through the other, him. My life before me. My future in the present, thanks to him. Thanks to what bound us, those secret, mysterious, and very concrete ties. A volcano. Milk. Overflowing milk. Exploding milk. On the verge of flooding the entire world through me.

Abdellah expected me to think of all the details. To find a good place, the right hideout to realize our challenge, our promise.

I told him to meet me after school.

"Wait for me next to the small door to your middle school, not the big one. No one uses it. I'll meet you after class. Around 4:20 p.m., when all the students have left."

"OK ..."

"I know where to go."

"Where will we go, little Abdellah?"

"To hell, big Abdellah."

"Suits me."

As we waited for nightfall, I didn't know where to bring him, to say the truth. So I suggested that we walk, and walk some more.

Our steps guided us far, beyond the big forest, all the way to the river, the Bou Regreg. Across from us was Rabat, the capital, and its Hassan Tower. Another world that had nothing to do with us and with our project. We lay on the ground and tried to find inspiration. It didn't come. But that didn't stop us. Someone had to make the first move. I thought this would be Abdellah's role, not mine. He didn't do anything. He was probably overthinking all he had to do. His responsibility toward me. I wanted to reassure him, to tell him not to be scared. I watched the sun as it moved away. I turned my head toward him. I opened my mouth just as the muez-

zin started to call the fourth prayer of sunset. I didn't say a thing.

We listened very carefully to the masculine voice, explosive and strangely very spiritual, filling the air and the world with Arab words celebrating God. Then, we rose to go home.

It was a failure. Nothing would happen. God was against us. We had to forget our scandalous project quickly, and quickly repent.

When we arrived in our neighborhood an hour later, it was completely dark. The street was empty. God had disappeared. And desire had returned. Strong. Urgent. Dictatorial.

I understood that I'd have to force big Abdellah to go all the way. I had to be both actor and director with him. Take his hand. Open his fly. Take out his sex. And demand the miracle.

Behind the house was a tiny garden that belonged to no one. And in the middle of that garden, if I can call it that, was a small tree with large leaves, still green despite the drought. That's where we should hide. And act.

Without asking, I pulled big Abdellah under that tree. We sat down at its foot. I stuck my body against my friend and brother. And still without concern for his opinion, I moved in close to

his face and kissed him on the cheek. A hot kiss. Very hot. Very humid. In a fever. And in love.

Happily, he reacted quickly. He lifted his head toward the leaves. Breathed deeply for five seconds. Put his right hand on his fly. And as if illumined from inside, his whole body began to vibrate, to tremble, to shake.

I could see it. I adored it already. Still hidden in his pants and underwear, the other Abdellah's large sex couldn't take it any longer. I drew in again toward my friend's face, and set another hot kiss on his cheek. He turned toward me, and opening his fly he kissed me too. On the mouth. For a long time. He hurt me. I didn't object.

His sex was there, exposed, erect, large, proud, as high as the Hassan Tower. Beside itself. Crazy. Tender. Volcanic. And so red.

The big Abdellah put his arm around my

neck and invited me to follow closely everything he did.

"Watch this. Remember everything. Rejoice. The rain is coming soon."

He was right. He spoke truth. The miracle that everyone in Morrocco was waiting for was going to occur at last. Any second. Water. Water everywhere, for everyone and all at once.

A flood.

Now, big Abdellah's sex was more than red. It had grown black. It screamed. It rumbled. It was about to die from being so alive. I inched my hand toward it. I touched it softly.

Big Abdellah took my hand and put it in his mouth to bite it hard. I let him.

That's when the milk appeared. It shot out violently from Abdellah's sex. In abundance. The jets reached far. Up to the leaves of the tree. Up to the sky.

It was beauty itself!

Abdellah let my hand go. He looked at me. Smiled sweetly. And after a short minute of rest, started masturbating again.

To encourage him, I whispered in his ear: "Go for it, go for it. This time, I want to drink your milk, swim in it. Go for it! Go for it!"

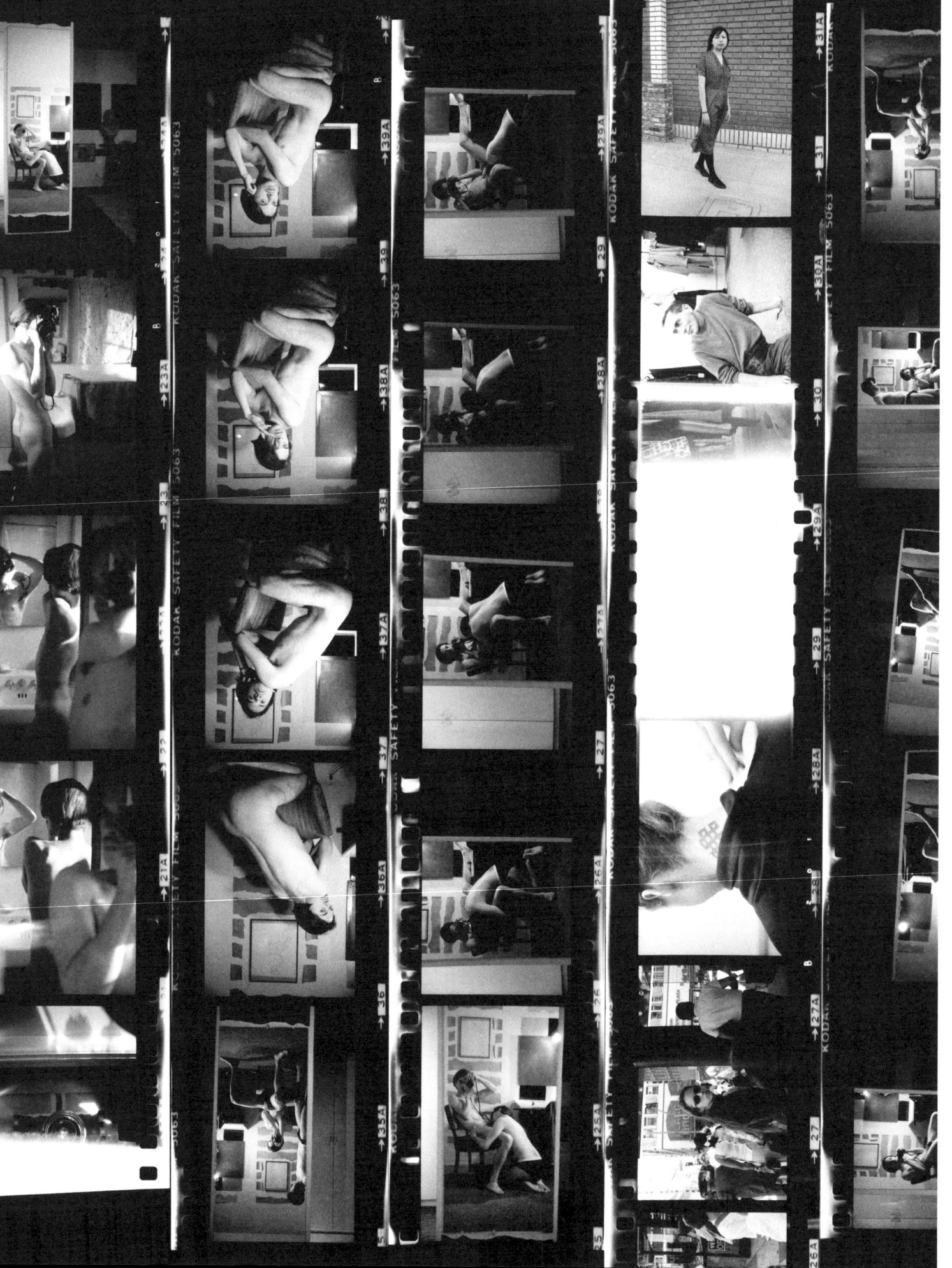

MOMMIES & DADDIES
—Devan Diaz

The apartment wasn't in my name, so I left without a thought for how my ex would pay my half of the rent. A broken emotional lease. For a long time I couldn't refer to her as anything other than "my ex," because when I tried to recall the experience, a large *X* obstructed my view. Resentment formed one slash, guilt made the other, and together they kept me outside of the truth. I left in August 2021, and in the year and a half since lockdown my ex had gotten what she'd wanted: permission to fuck other people.

I took her desire for others as a rejection, and instead of rejecting her back, I got vindictive. I wasn't enlightened enough to see nonmonogamy as anything but cheating. So I cheated. Worse than even cheating, at the end of it all, was that I left. Neither of us could fess up to what we had done, why we had done it, or how badly it all hurt. Only now can I admit it lasted three and a half years—when it ended, I said it had been four, because the half year spent fighting felt like it counted for double.

Hailey knew all of this and summoned me to the last month of her summer rental on Fire Island. I'd never been to Fire Island, never understood how this gay island for the wealthiest among us could exist, but her invitation came as a blessing. Hailey knew I needed out. I've followed Hailey many places, all glamorous, most fast. She's taught me how to say no, to think harder, to get more. We met at 61st Street–Woodside to take the Long Island Rail Road to Sayville. A short bus ride and a two-level ferry took us from Long Island to the Pines. As always, Hailey wanted to ride on top. The orange Hermès scarf tied around her head whipped behind her like the combustion of a rocket.

Every home is each gay's version of paradise, Hailey told me that first morning, waving a manicured hand over the beachfront homes. Butterflies, bamboo, muscles, wealth. The whole island felt like a drift, no roads, just an endless boardwalk. Everyone waved hello to each other, as if to say, *Yes, we're really here*. Herds of deer roamed the island, cute but untouchable due to ticks. "Don't pet them" Hailey told me as I stopped to take a picture of a white-tailed doe and her fawn. The doe's eyes were chewed up and drooping, heavy with its parasites. She sniffed her surroundings before sticking her head in a bush. In one photo I took, the fawn is looking up at me, neck bowed and spotted white. In the next, she's tucked behind her mother, hiding again.

I began to believe in Hailey's paradise. Gays who never bothered to learn my name in the city asked me how I'd been. The powerful producer or gallerist becomes the doting housewife, eager to display domesticity by nursing the nighttime girls to health. Hosting, for those with stamina, becomes sport. Those who have, give; those who need, take. I know a girl who chartered an entire bus of dolls to the island for her birthday, and she ended up housing and feeding them for the better part of a week. On the island, everyone's a mother and everyone needs a mother.

My guilt throbbed despite the fun I was having. *You do guilt so well*, Natasha recently told me over text, as I talked about this time in my life. The other day I got paid to pass out pamphlets at a church a few blocks from where my ex lives, who now goes by Maia. She's a transbian DJ who lives in Bushwick, just as I told her she would be. We caught up in Maria Hernandez Park on one of the first hot days of spring, burning the winter off our skin on the brightest bench. Her silver-and-gold curls spilled over the same glasses she'd worn when we were together. I told her this was still hard for me to write; she asked me to try and tell the truth.

I met Maia the day after her forty-first birthday and ten weeks and two days before my twenty-sixth. At first she asked me to call her Daddy as a sex thing, then she asked me to do it outside of sex, then she was paying for my life. By that point in my life I'd had many mothers, but never a daddy. Daddy helped me lose weight and heal my new boobs, and she cooked every meal. Daddy even delivered coffee by hand every "morning" at 1 p.m. Eventually my livelihood became dependent on her. I washed dishes and folded clothes—chores I couldn't ever do for myself, but for Daddy, they became easy.

Really, what we exchanged was shelter, and we were equally generous. She was newly divorced; I was recently unemployed. I was ready to quit writing but she, like many of my mothers, made that impossible. Together we got to know what the other truly wanted from life, and we knew how to bring it out in the other. It was the healthiest, nicest time of my life. It could've been her forever. When we meet now, she urges that we were really sisters, *That's all it really was*. Yes, we holed up together the way I've done with many girlfriends, but I desired her in every way. That desire wasn't reciprocated.

Or maybe it was, and I couldn't see it, because she wanted more than just me. Her marriage had been open, she'd always been nonmonogamous, it was all she could talk about. I live in a time of unpopular monogamy, and largely I find that fabulous, but it's still

something I prefer. I was so afraid of not being wanted that I became OK with being somewhat wanted. Nicki Minaj: "Is it wrong, wanting more for myself?" "More" by having less, focusing.

But I gave in, because happiness made me beautiful and I knew someone else would want me. I found temporary confidence in bigger, richer, stronger men to fuck. "Real" men, as opposed to the man I had at home, months before she would stop being one. When I arrived at Hailey's on Fire Island, I'd had enough of sex. Maia had had enough of supporting me, so for the year prior I'd performed live-cam shows, causing my imagination to grow to an uncomfortable size so it could fit everyone's fantasies.

Hailey hadn't had enough of anything. While I read by the pool, she was somewhere getting fucked by the brightest minds of our generation. I loved watching her freedom on the island, because I'd been there to help heal her pussy. Her mother and I slept by her side those first couple of nights in the hospital. I loved swimming in the ocean while she slept off the night before on the sand. I savored this existence because I knew my sugar daddy era had ended; I'd have to make my own money when I got back to the city.

One morning, my computer lagged—remote location, I thought—until the screen went black: *Starting internet recovery. This may take a while*. I'd cut off my cell service in 2020 to save money; the laptop was my only lifeline. I chose exercise over despair, joining a yoga session on the deck with a group of muscle gays. A butterfly landed on my finger in Warrior 1, and I felt the first glimmer of gratitude in a while.

But guilt lingered—my ex was still in our apartment, surrounded by our memories and her decision to transition. Our gendered relationship had shown her she no longer wanted to be a man, while I realized I no longer wanted to need one. I'd left her as a response to her asking me to stay and face her new life.

News of Hurricane Henri interrupted these

thought loops. The storm was set to hit land that evening, and the ferry would stop running that afternoon. I couldn't take not having a home, or watching this temporary home be washed away. I had to leave someone I loved, again. Hailey and her housemates didn't consider leaving; instead, they filled the bathtub with water and started crafting a play about Henri, eyes gleaming with excitement at the chance of witnessing something worth retelling.

A Latina contingent staying at a photographer's house were going to leave the island, and they had a car. I'd been to the house a couple of times and navigated back through muscle memory, as both my devices were now useless. The island's center was my compass as I retraced the long, familiar walk. That sweltering August day turned humid and cool; the gray swirls overhead made the island phosphorescent. Sirens echoed as gays in Speedos ran past, flying high on whatever they'd taken.

I was the only one moving deeper into the island. The bag with my belongings dug into my sunburned shoulder, and I couldn't turn back because I didn't remember how. It felt like a corny metaphor for my life, and I hated it. It wasn't just a cliché, it was a meme. I remembered the photographer's house as having a clear view of the ocean framed by greenery, right at the end of the boardwalk.

Every turn had a similar name: Bayview Walk, Beach Hill Walk, Beach Road. Every tree seemed to replicate itself the farther I got. Parties carried on in the houses I passed, the music at a volume I'd grown used to hearing at night. Their courting of Henri made me walk faster. I had no way of knowing if the last ferry had departed, or if my friends had left without me. I knew if I kept walking, I'd find it.

I arrived at a clearing I remembered from a few nights earlier. I wanted to be shown where to go, I wanted Daddy to handle it. In that moment of bratty longing, an adult deer stepped out from a bush to my left. Her fur was matted and uneven, but her eyes were clear.

She kept eye contact with me as I took her picture. Then she began nuzzling the ground, looking for something neither of us could find. I couldn't see any ticks on her and I wondered how she had escaped the fate of the doe I'd met before.

I wanted her appearance to be a sign, so I turned it into one, tossing her my half-eaten peach. I watched her begin to eat it before turning left. I knew I was there when I heard the photographer's voice on speakerphone, telling my friends how to hurricane-proof the place. I watched the waves grow even taller from his deck, nothing but sand separating them from the house. I felt that moving the outdoor furniture inside wouldn't save anything, but I helped my friends carry it in.

Don, our driver, insisted on a final lap in the pool before we left. His indifference toward the storm grated against my fear, but I was glad to be riding with him. Drivers should be indifferent. I took photos of Palma as we waited for him to finish, the dark gray sky like a light box, and through that we found a way to laugh. We were able to make the last ferry off of the island, hangers-on waving goodbye to us as we departed.

In the end, I learned that Henri never touched ground—I could have stayed in paradise, instead of returning to what used to be my home. I hadn't moved out actually, just spiritually: all of my stuff was still there. Maia wasn't happy to see me, but she didn't turn me away. We were relieved it was over, and grateful not to be fighting. She talked about her transition and I listened. Maia said she didn't want me as a mother—another transsexual showing her how to do drag, honey. I respected it. When I packed up my things to leave, I left behind a vintage lamb-fur coat. It was my insufficient apology. Things would take a while to get good again, but every time she posted a photo of herself in the coat, it renewed my hope that they would.

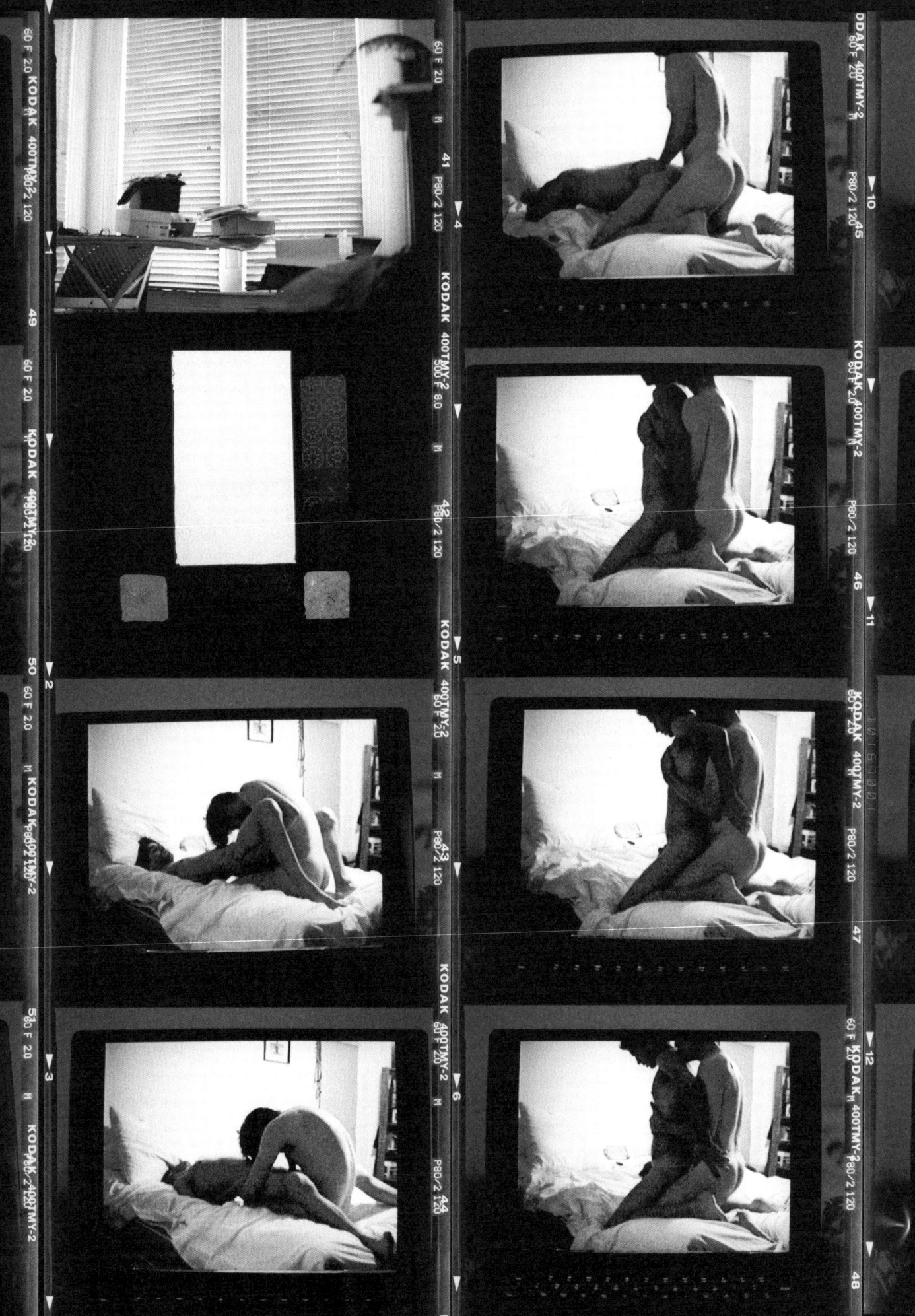

A HAPPY CHRISTMAS
—Colm Tóibín

It was Ireland in the late 1980s and many had left the country.

Not just the unemployed but others who couldn't bear the boredom, not to speak of the rain, the rules, the long winters, the short orgasms, the loving families.

In New York and Boston and San Francisco, Irish people became themselves. For example, the lesbians slept with girls and the gay boys with other gay boys. People were free and happy.

Until Christmas began to approach.

Then they got homesick and they booked transatlantic flights at exorbitant prices. In the week before Christmas close to one million Irish people came home to a country with a population of four million. They were filmed on arrival at Dublin airport by TV news. They were welcomed everywhere they went. Their families wept with joy. Drinking and elation followed even though the days were dark.

In 1989, on New Year's Eve, I was having an early dinner in the house of a friend, a psychiatrist. There were four of us at the table. As soon as we sat down, the phone began to ring and it seemed to ring throughout the dinner, the psychiatrist leaving the room to answer it, coming back each time looking preoccupied.

It seemed that many of the recently returned Irish people had so enjoyed their homecoming and the subsequent festivities that they had gone starkly out of their minds in the sunless days after Christmas. Their relatives were frantically searching for a facility that would take them in. They had found, by fair means and foul, the psychiatrist's phone number.

Gay people in the same season had basked in the warmth of their old bedrooms and their extended families. But by the morning after Christmas Day, the wine had grown sour and the excitement had dimmed. It was time for the coiled mass of gay men returned from abroad to descend on the few sad gay bars in the city and the cavernous gay saunas in search of something that they had not had since the night before they left in the first place—some gay raw Irish sex.

Somehow, fucking a white-assed American or sucking the long, lean cock of an Italian meant nothing. It happened elsewhere; it was something you did on your holidays. In those dark, depressed days between Christmas and the new year, old, decayed cruising places in Dublin, long abandoned, were freshened by returned emigrants who wanted something that was real and true and homegrown.

The saunas could have charged double. Within an hour of opening, they were full. And they remained full all evening and into the night until they closed. Men who had frequented the best clubs in the known world now desperately wanted to have sex in a Dublin cubicle with some freckled Irish country fellow who had, ostensibly, come up to Dublin for the after Christmas sales. He was looking for bargains. I can recall the look of surprise and glee on his face as, having come off big-time, he made for the shower as though butter would not melt in his mouth.

*

Where was I? I was with my family in the days before Christmas, sleeping in my old bedroom in the town in the southeast of Ireland where we are from. Even as Christmas dinner was served—and the same jokes, all of which I loved and relished, had been told by the same people—I longed for the lure of a wet night in a strange Dublin park, with no one stirring until someone did, someone slinking in by a side gate, someone in the bushes.

The saunas, unlike the bushes, had rules. You could greet someone only if you had met them in the sauna, not if you knew them from outside. In fact, there was no outside. Thus, a well-known judge, happily married with five children as far as the world knew, could wander freely in the sauna. The only thing that distinguished him was his total nudity. The rest of us wore towels; he had thrown all caution to the wind.

Sometimes, it was like going for a haircut. It was quick and functional; it worked. You arrived, you made your presence known, you had sex with someone, you showered (you could also shower as soon as you arrived), you left. But it was also like nothing else. During your time in the sauna, you were almost a ghost, almost invisible. Or the world outside was a ghost and its inhabitants unimaginable.

In one of those Christmas-to-New Year's seasons I met someone in one of the Dublin saunas who seemed not to know the rules. He wanted to make out as though it mattered, in ways that were supremely tender. I must have wanted that too. And after an hour or more—maybe much more—it seemed hard to know what to do. We could just come off and shower and leave and pretend we didn't know each other if we ever met in the future.

But he didn't want to come off. And he didn't want to let me know much about himself. He smiled a lot. Soon, I realized that all this was no big deal for him; he was home from somewhere for Christmas. This was what he had needed. I didn't think I would see him again.

It couldn't have been the following year that I met him again. That would be too neat. But it isn't impossible. More likely, however, it was that same season two or three years later.

I met him in the same place. And the same things happened almost as though we had learned our moves by heart or were working at the behest of a choreographer of cheap and furtive thrills.

There was a third time. Could it have been by arrangement? I don't remember except that it was clear that what was going on between us was unusual, a kind of connection that went against the whole spirit of the Dublin saunas of that time. We didn't want to separate. But out in the world, the place where people wore clothes and huddled up against the December cold, what was palpable between us might dissolve, float away.

Should we go to a bar? Walk along the street together? Have dinner? Behave like two guys on a date? Go home together? It felt as though we had bypassed these phases. But we had ended nowhere, without a clue what to do.

On that third time, as I got ready to leave, I saw him talking familiarly to someone I knew who had just come into the sauna. This guy too was home for Christmas, one of four gay Irish blokes, the same age as I was, who had gone to live in Milan after college. They had a famous apartment there, and there was much talk in our circle about the fashion and style and freedom they had won for themselves in gallant Italy.

I knew three of them, and now, of course, it occurred to me that this—the one with whom I had been making out—was the fourth. He was back from Milan. I even knew his name.

And this meant that he must have known all along who I was. I had not published much at the time, but he was close friends with several of my close friends. It had just happened we had never met.

But, of course, we had met. And maybe all the closeness and warmth and ease we enjoyed had come from a connection that was not merely governed by sauna laws. We lay in a locked cubicle in a twilight set of rules that allowed for more.

At that time, I didn't think much of it, as I imagined that stuff like that would happen again. It was life. It was what the future would be like, I thought.

Except it wasn't.

Soon, two of those guys from Milan— including the one I had been with—came home to live in Ireland, and the other two appeared in Dublin more. I saw them. I saw my friend with all his clothes on. I saw him wearing shoes. I saw him talking to other people.

It was hard to know whether there was more of him in this social world, or much less. It was easier to believe that maybe I had seen one negative image of him in the sauna and now I saw not a fully developed photograph but a competing negative image, or its companion. Both negatives were waiting to be printed, needing tender touching before they would come into being, needing more than a mere Christmas visit, more than a pale homecoming, needing something more than I could easily name or give.

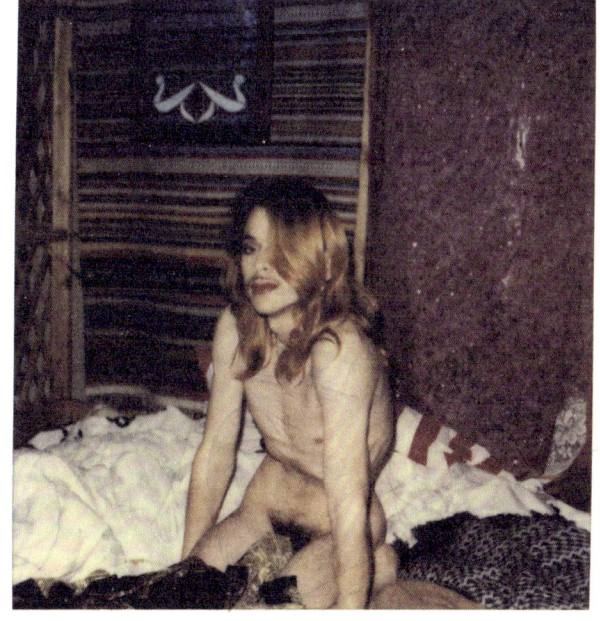

Reynaldo, Polaroid, ca. 1985

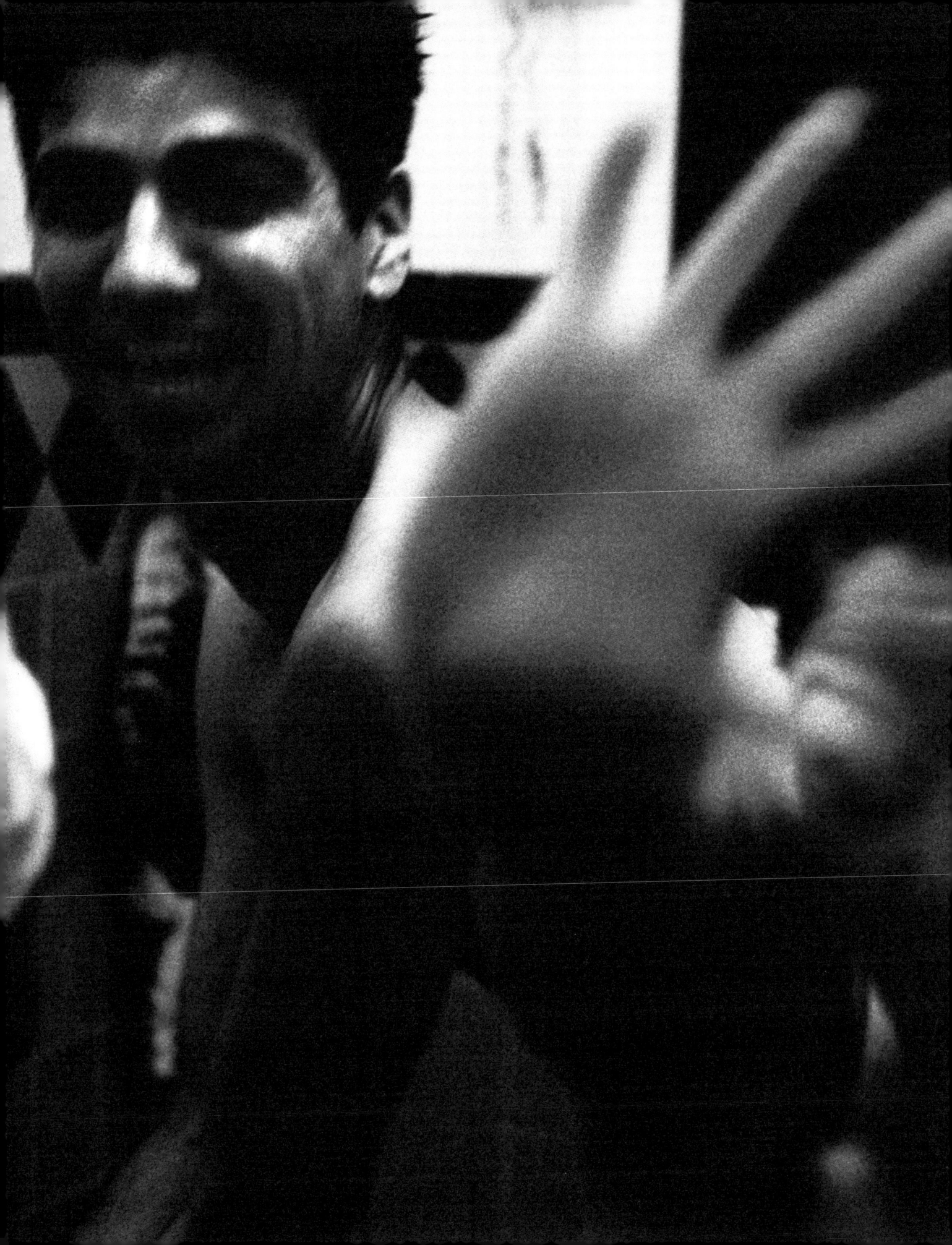

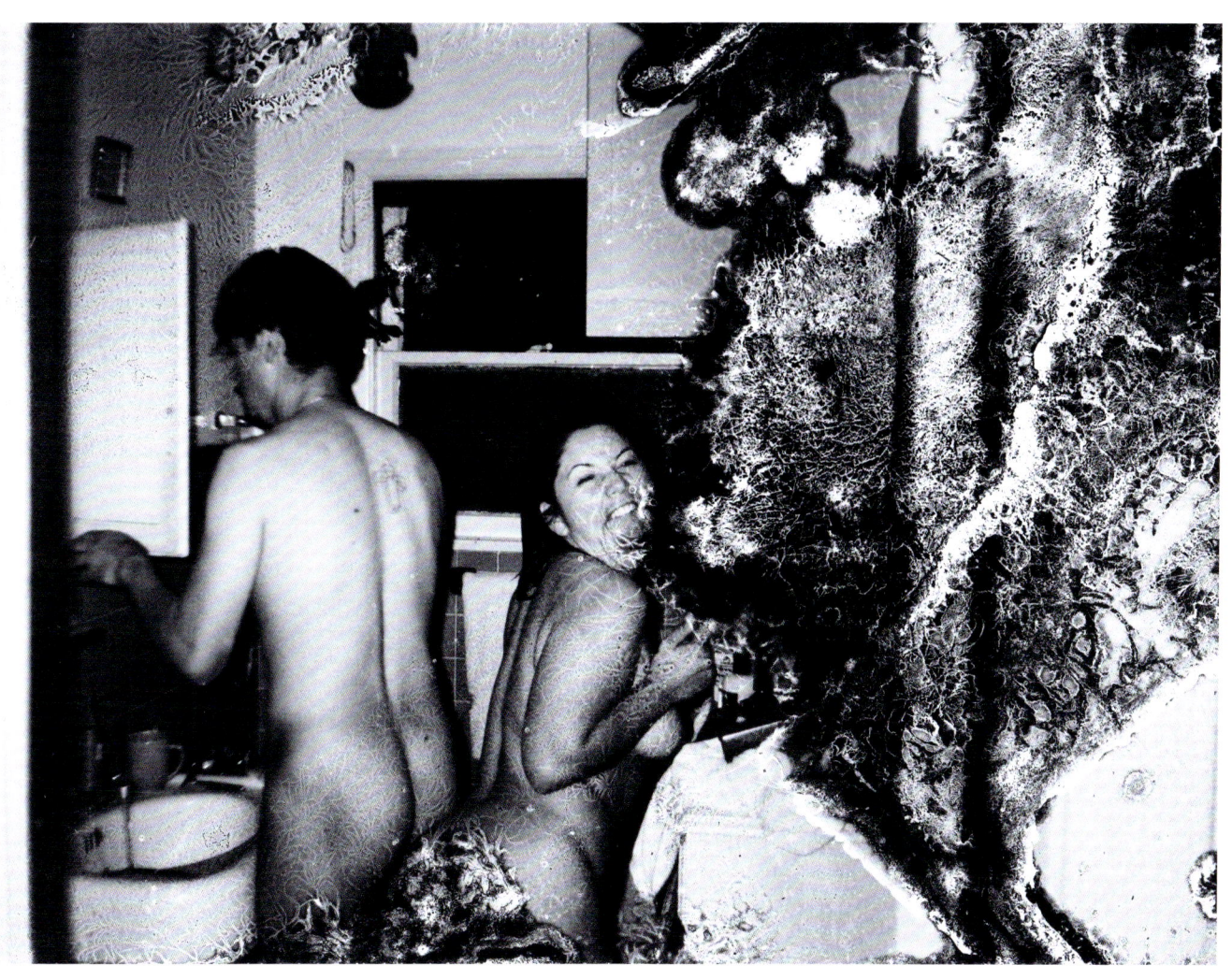

LEFT: *Bianco, Connie, Echo Park*, ca. 1997
Reynaldo, Connie, Echo Park, ca. 1997

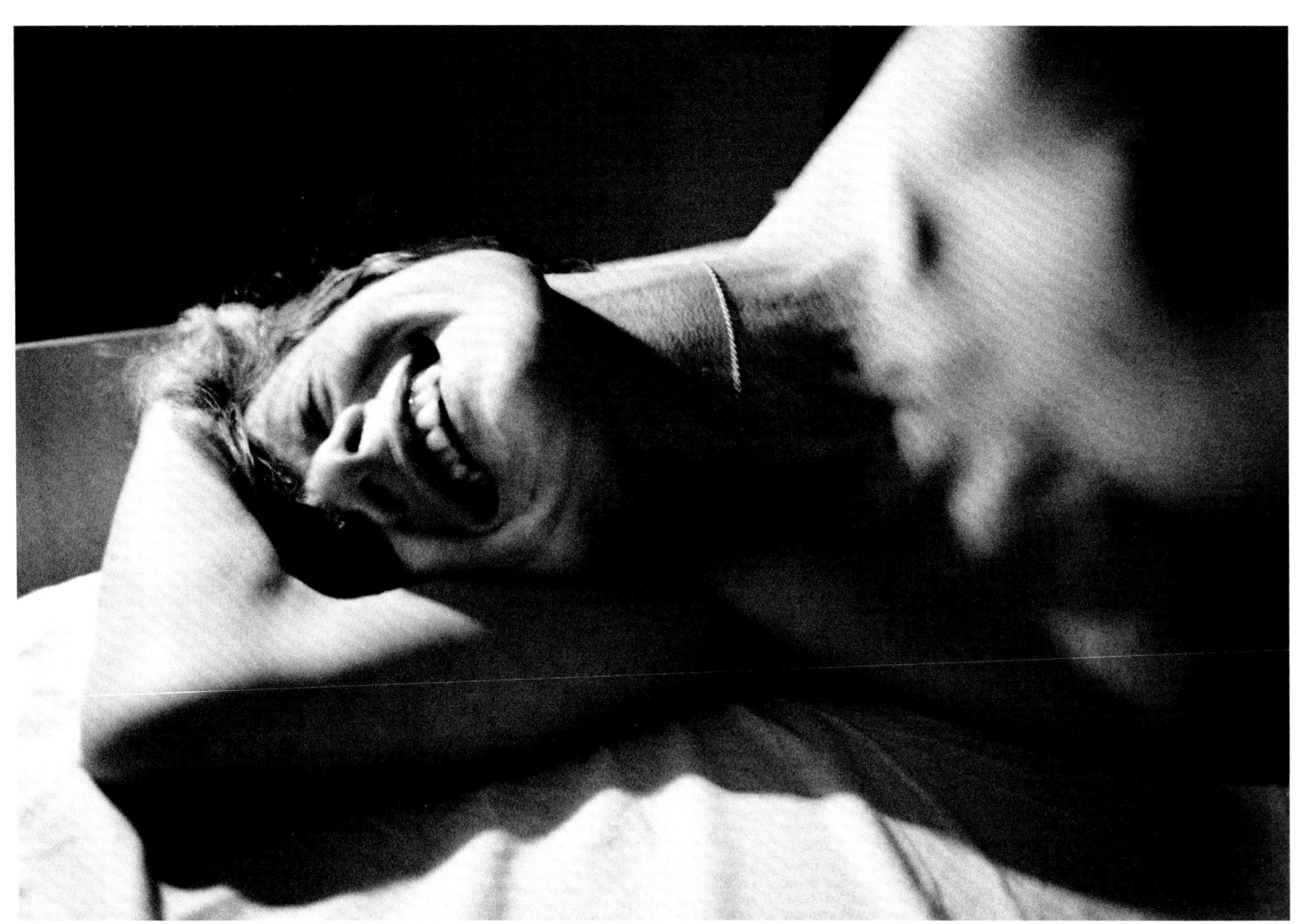

Monika, Berlin, 2000

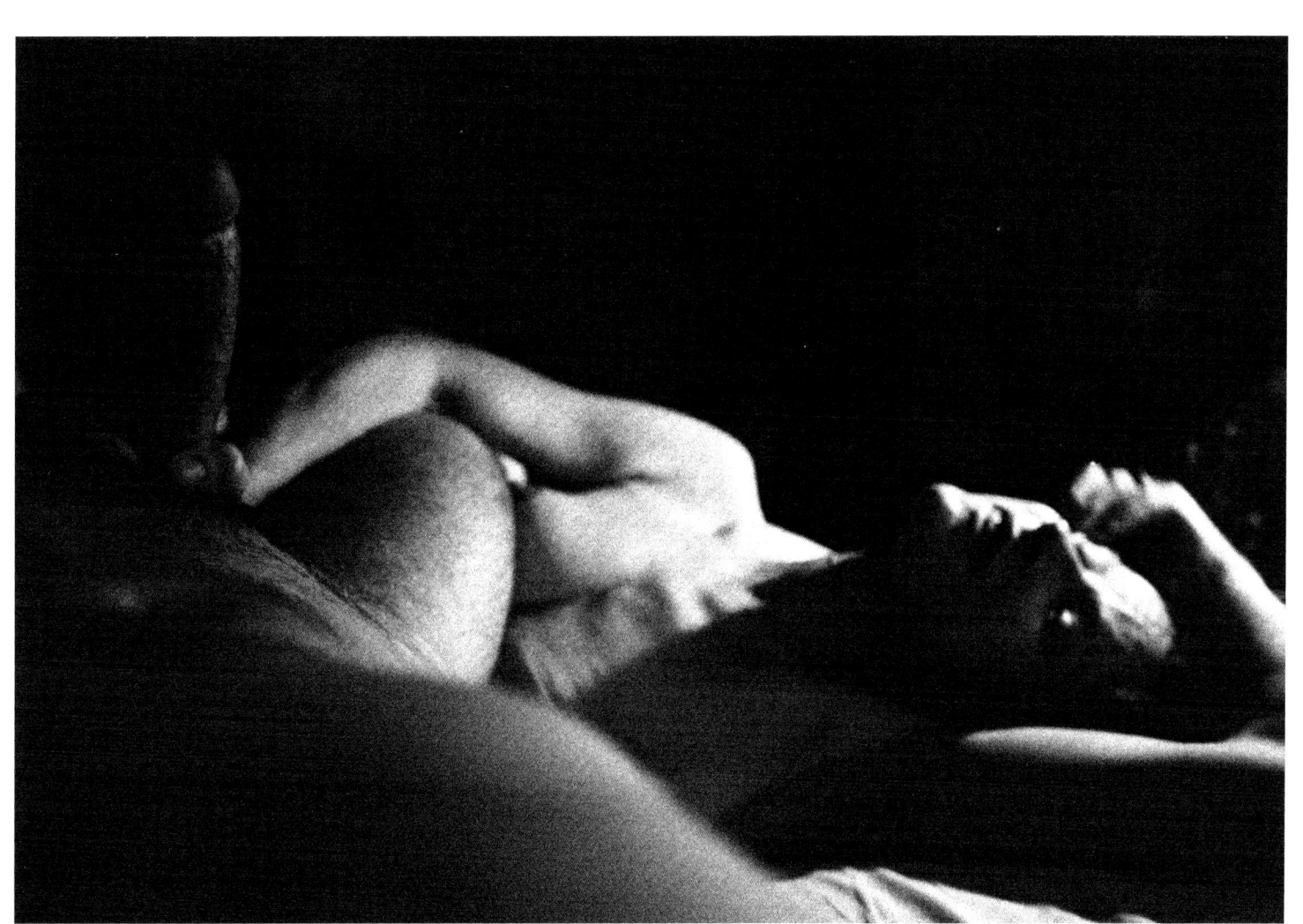

Reynaldo, Monika, Berlin, 2000

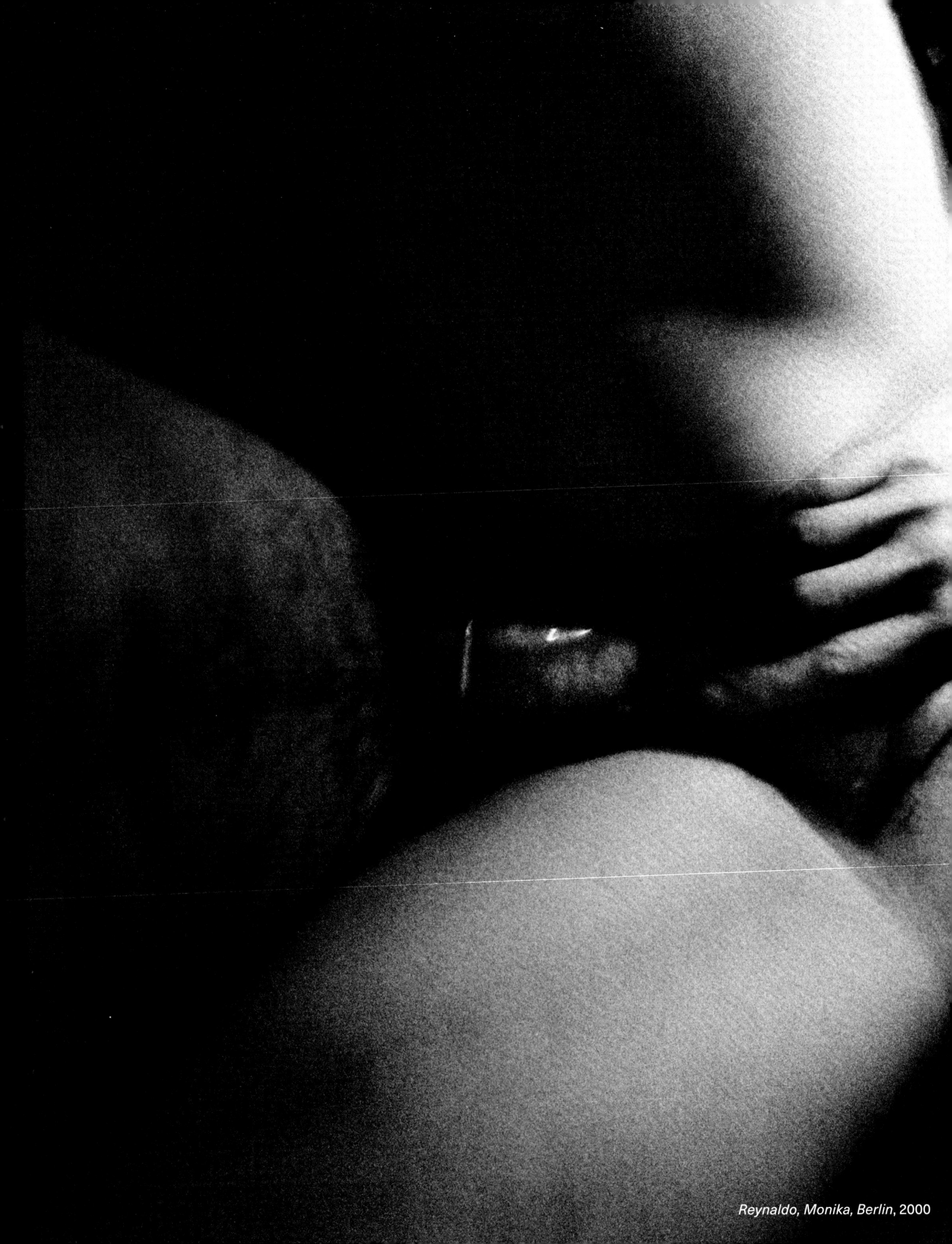

Reynaldo, Monika, Berlin, 2000

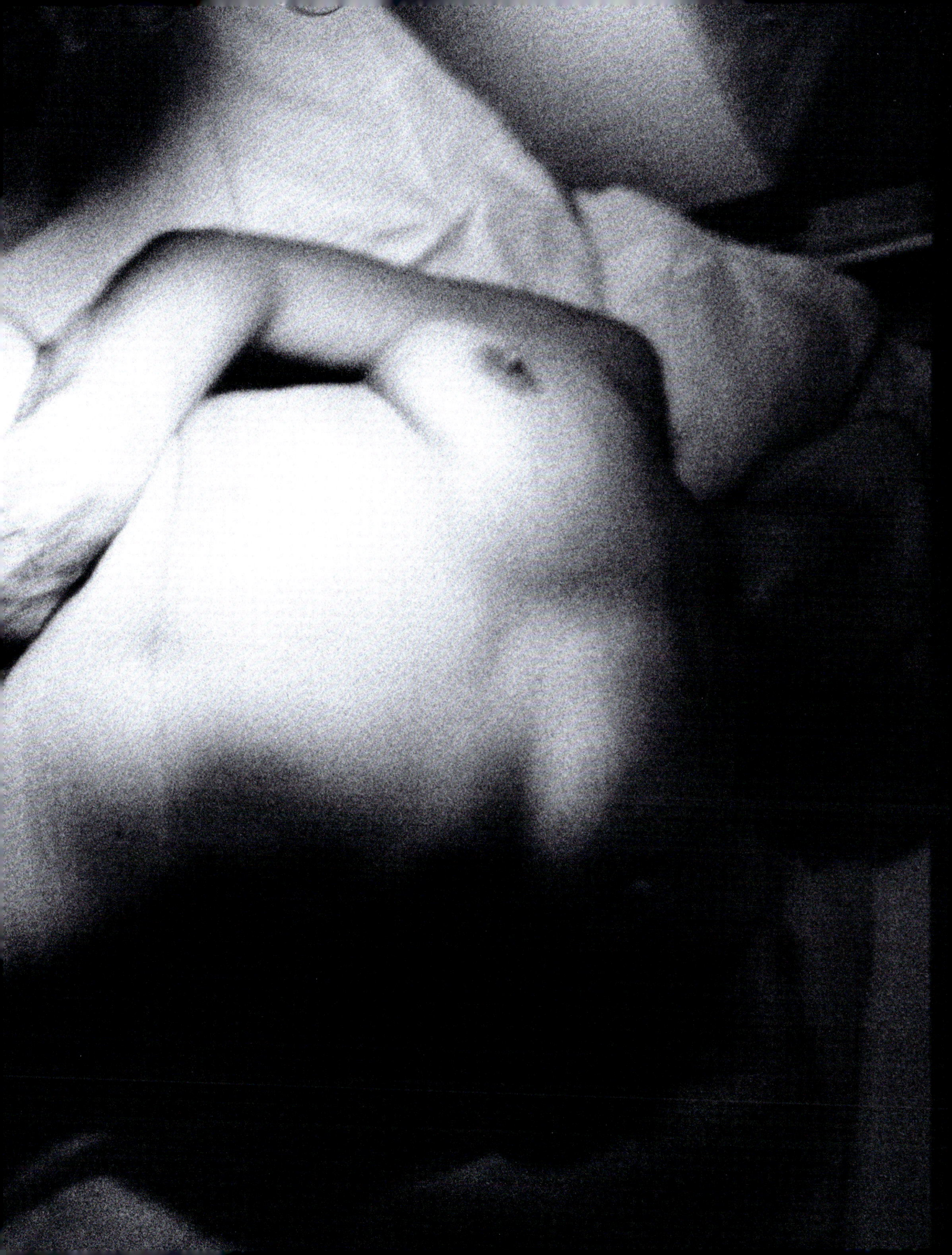

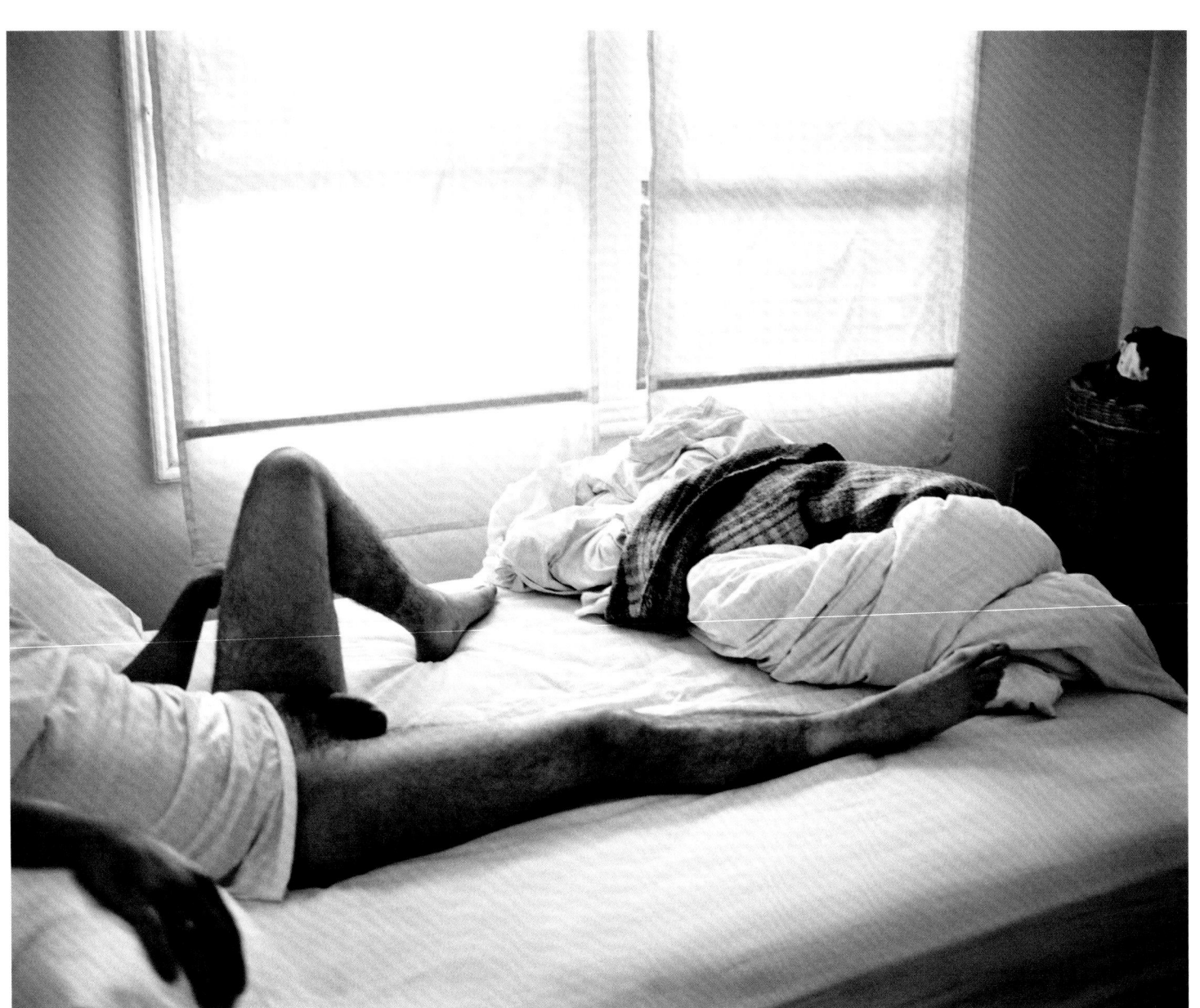

Reynaldo, Echo Park, ca. 1998

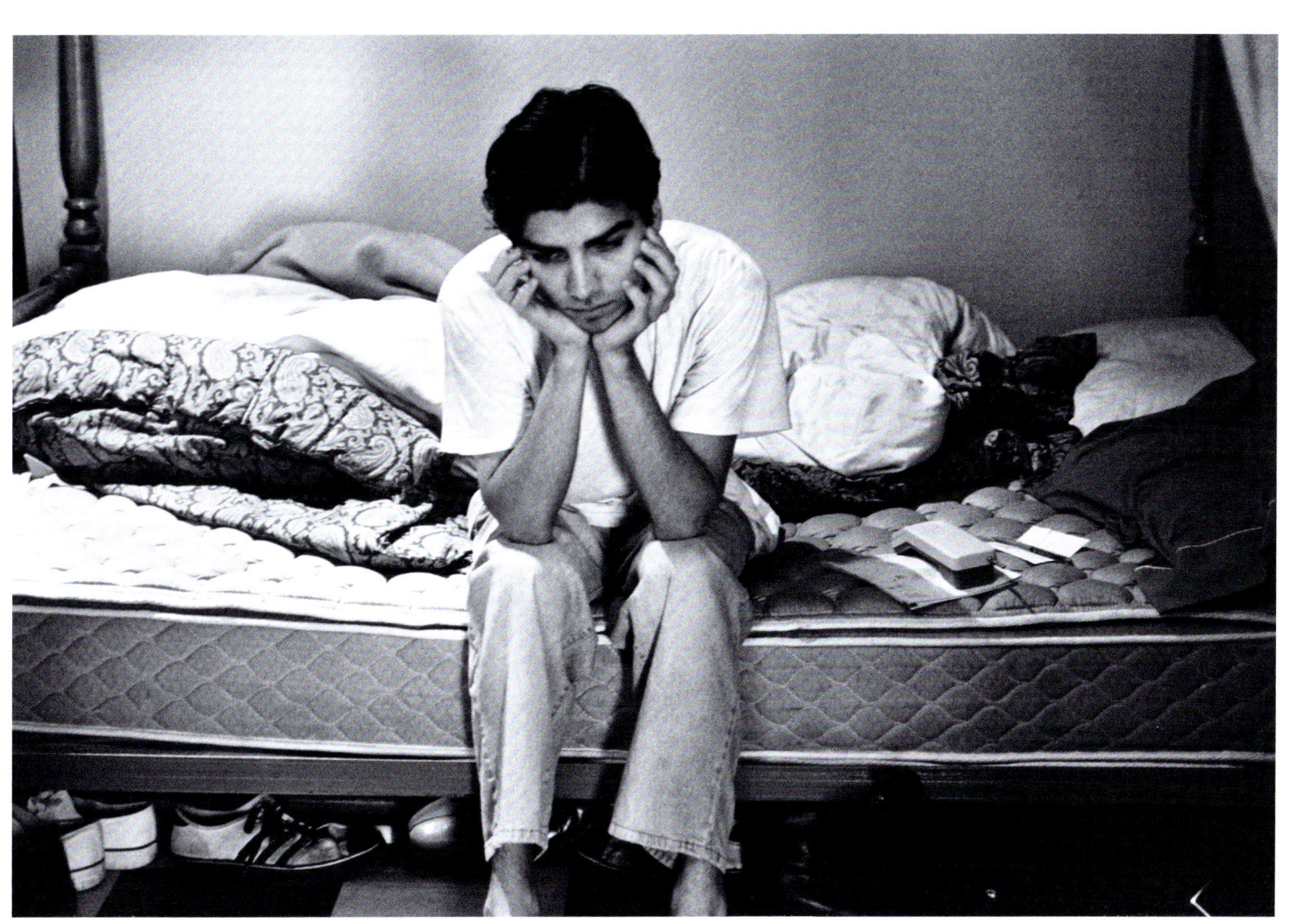

Bianco, Echo Park, ca. 1993

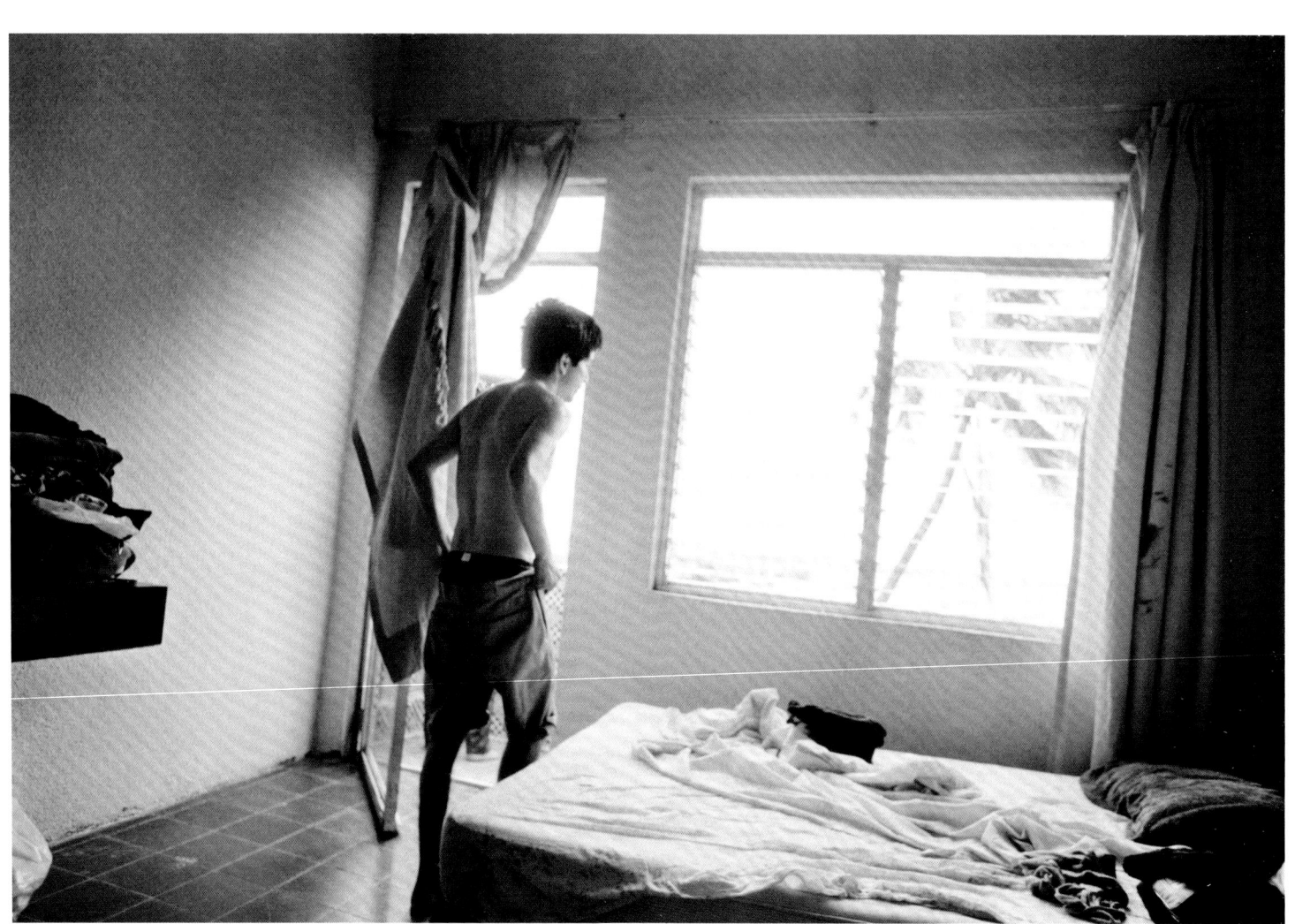

Henry, Mexico, ca. 1995

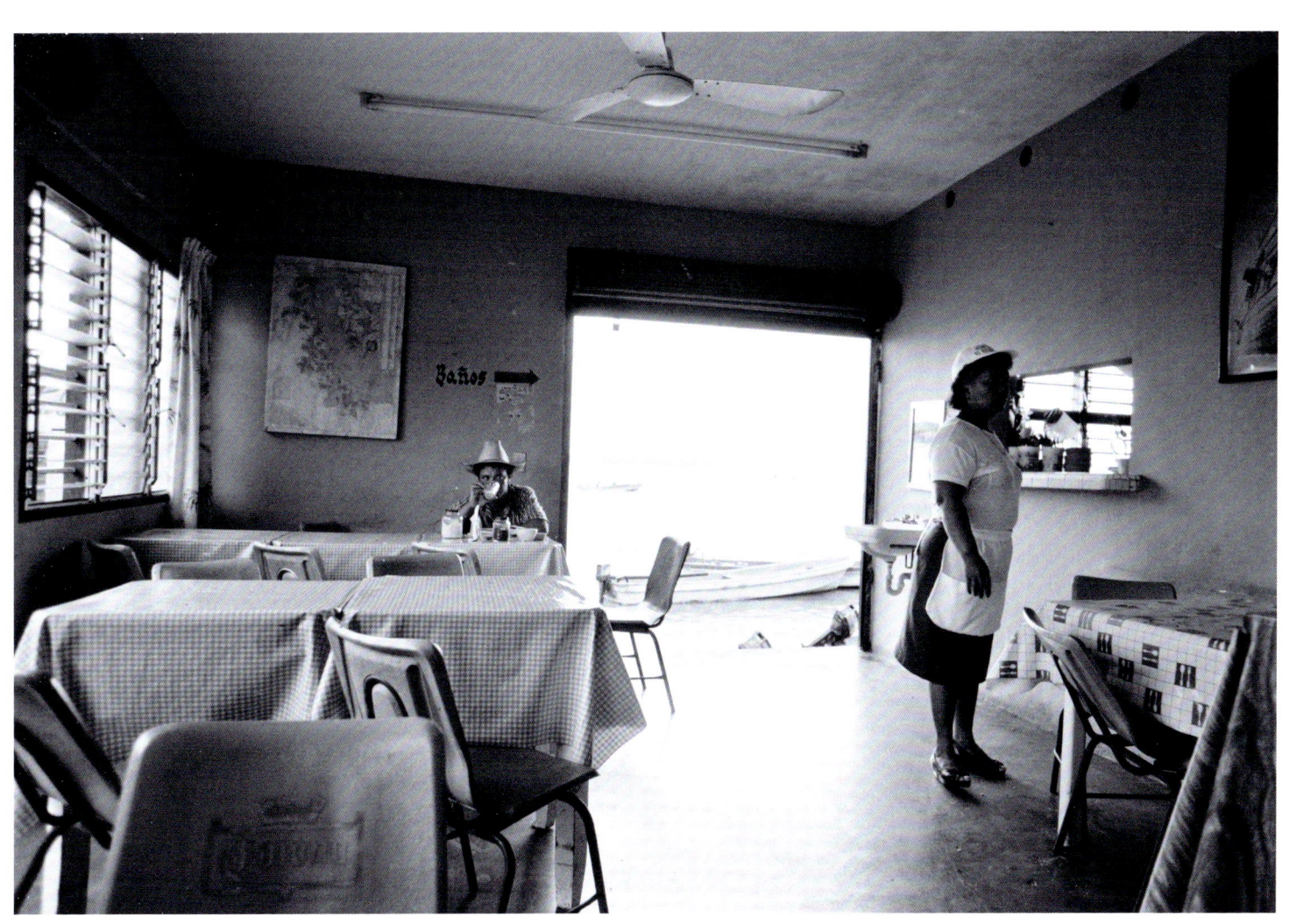

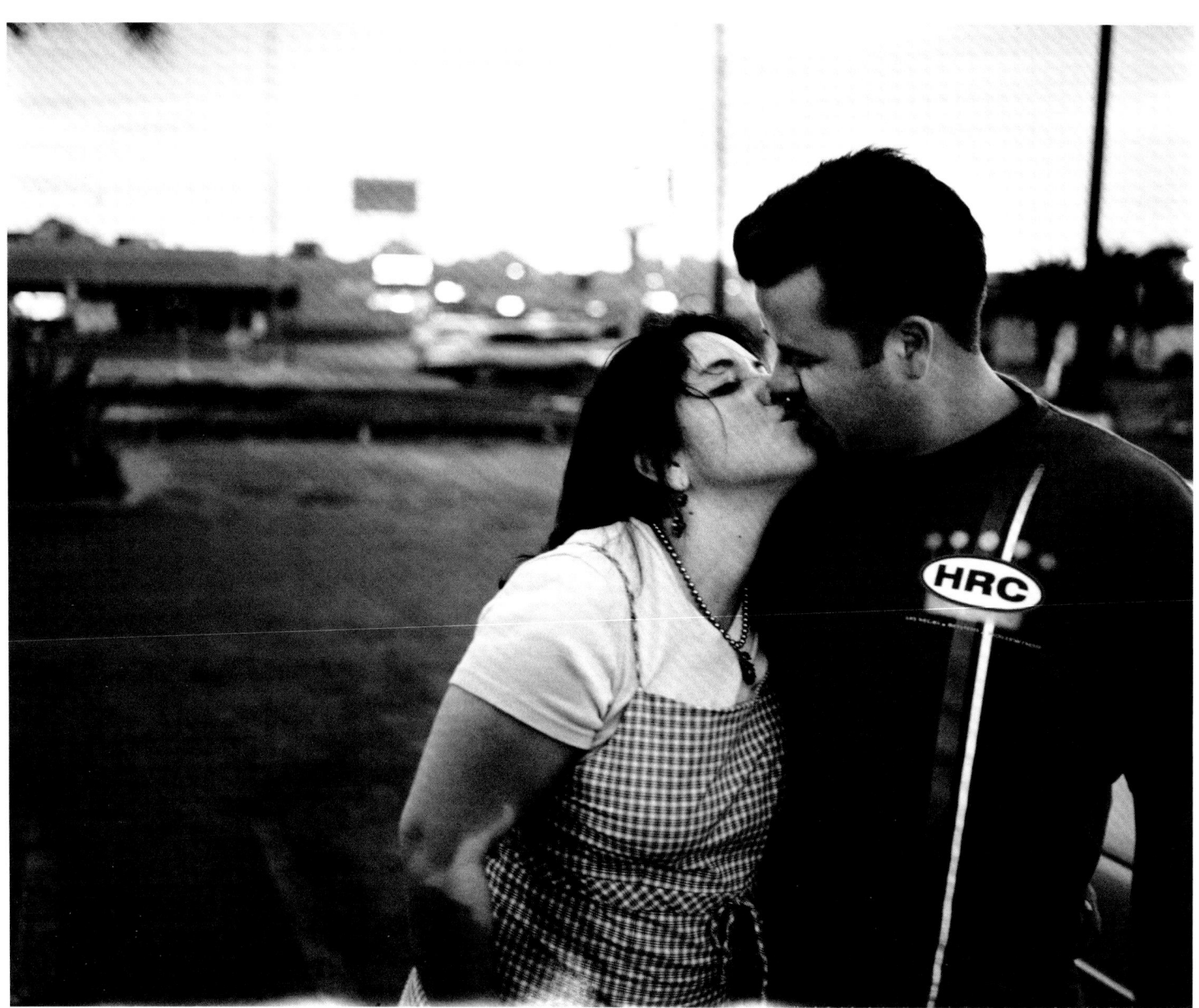

Connie, Anthony, ca. 1999

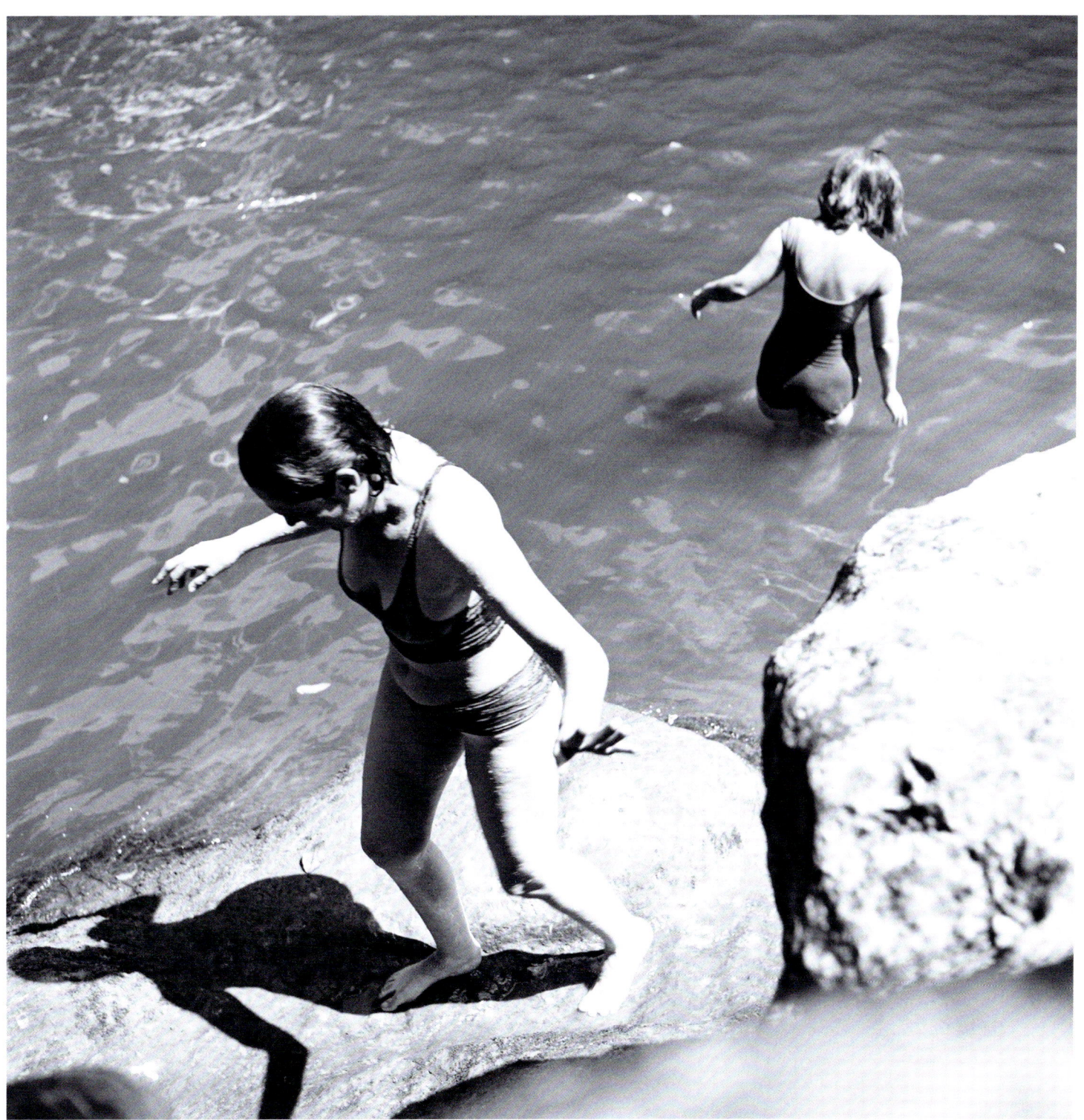

Connie, friend, Veracruz, ca. 1993

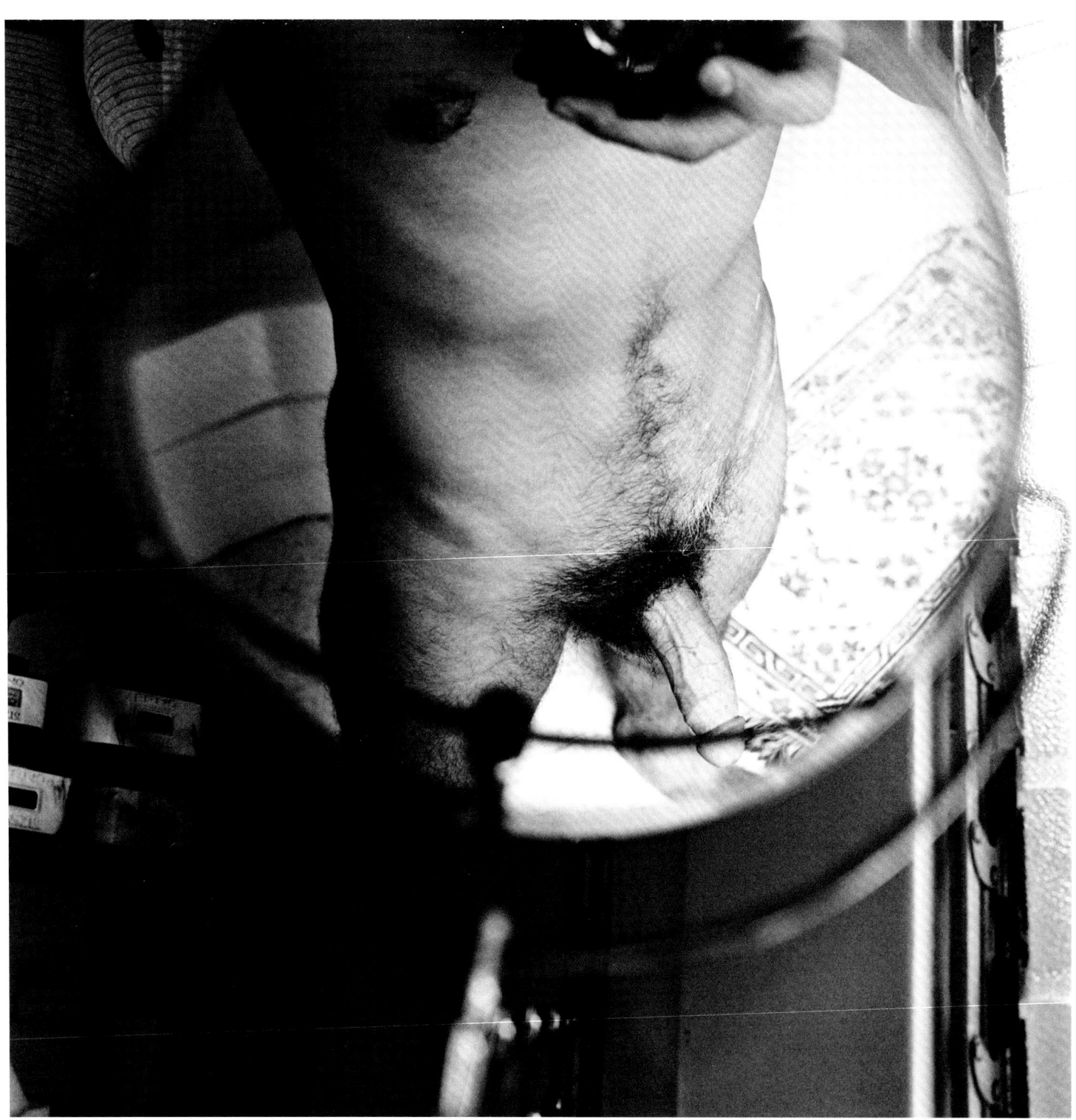

Self-Portrait, Beachwood Canyon, ca. 1989

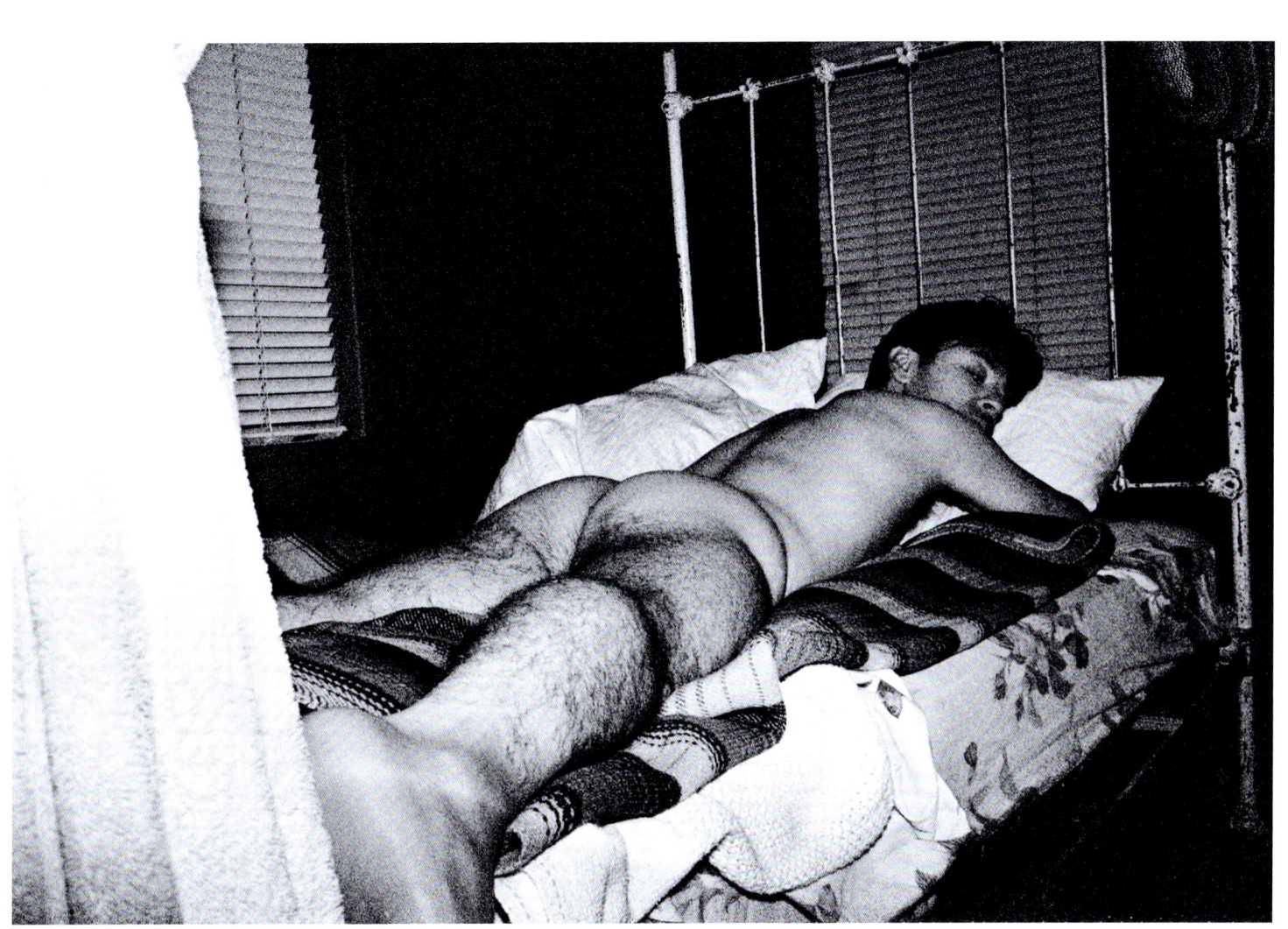

Reynaldo, Echo Park, 1995

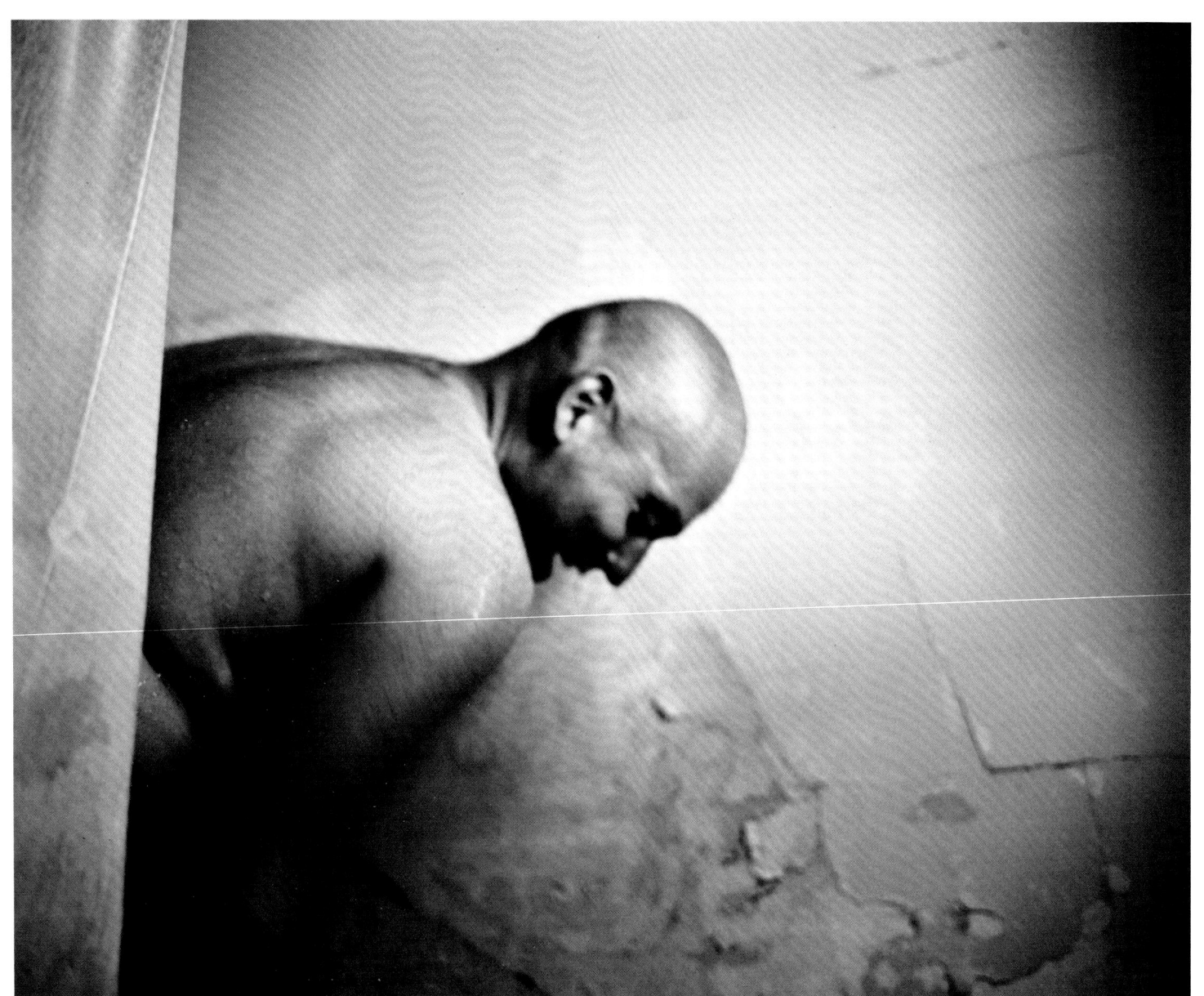

Untitled, Los Angeles, 1996

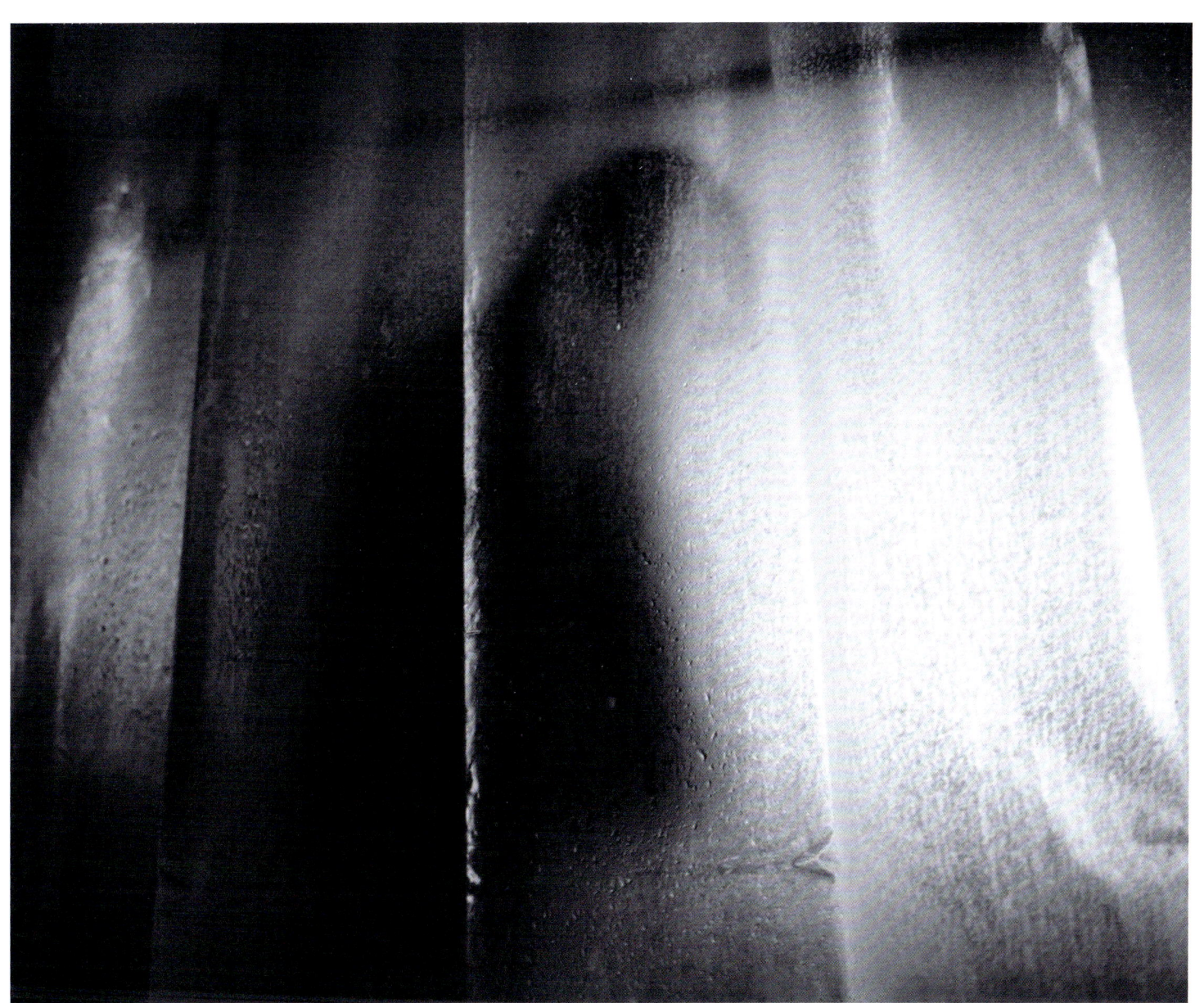

Untitled, Los Angeles, 1996

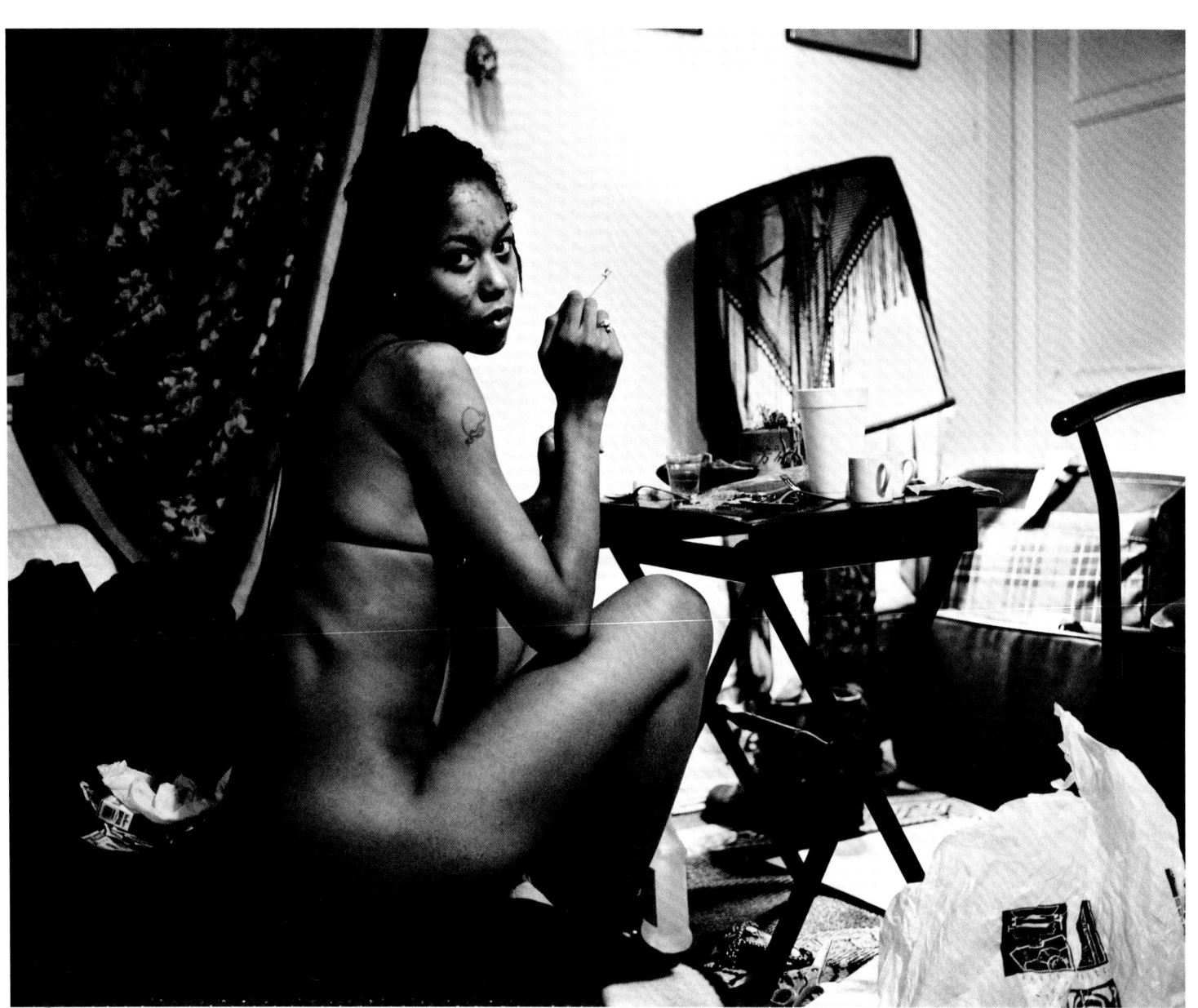

Pauletta, Echo Park, ca. 1998

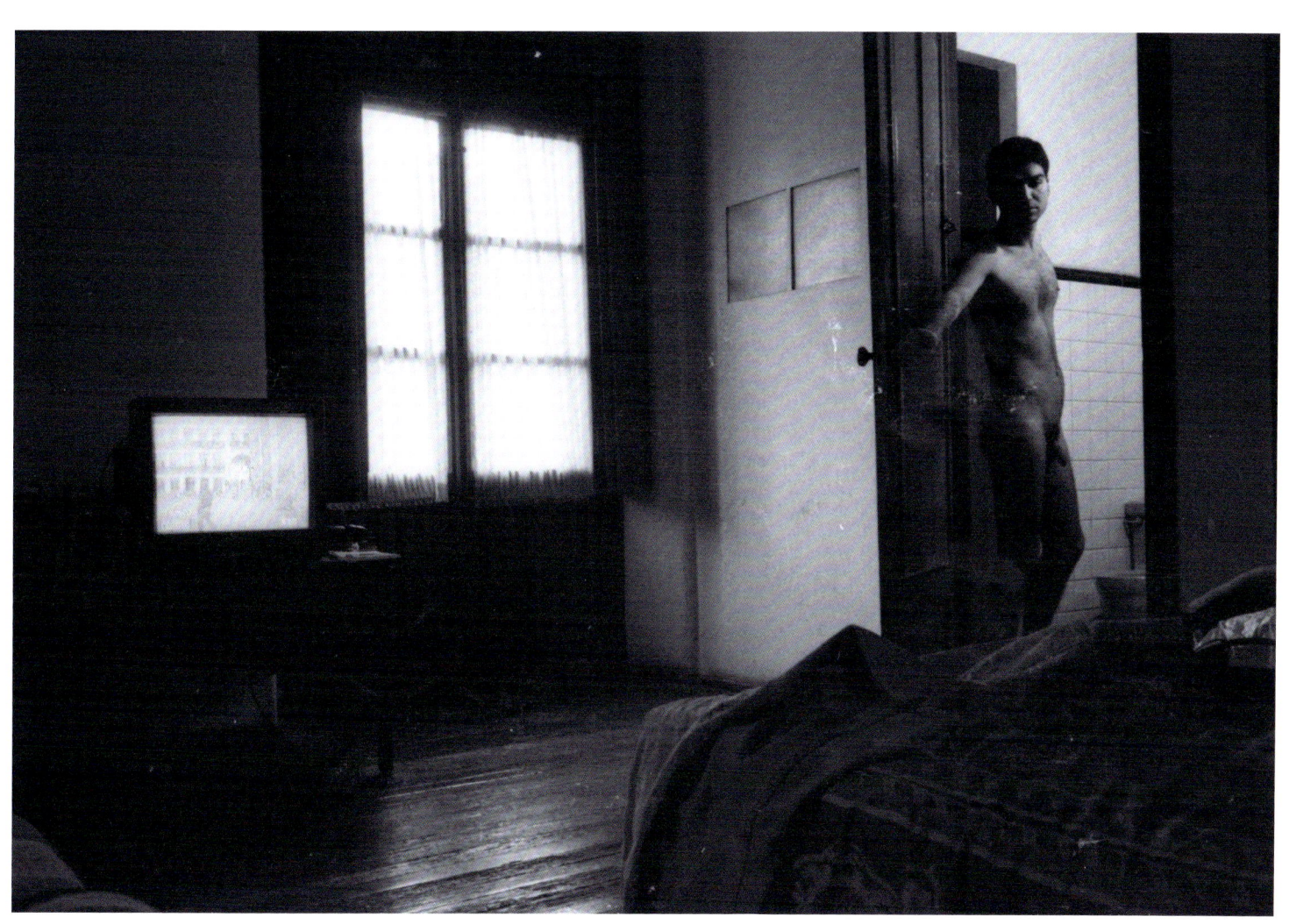

Bianco, San Luis Potosí, Mexico, ca. 1995

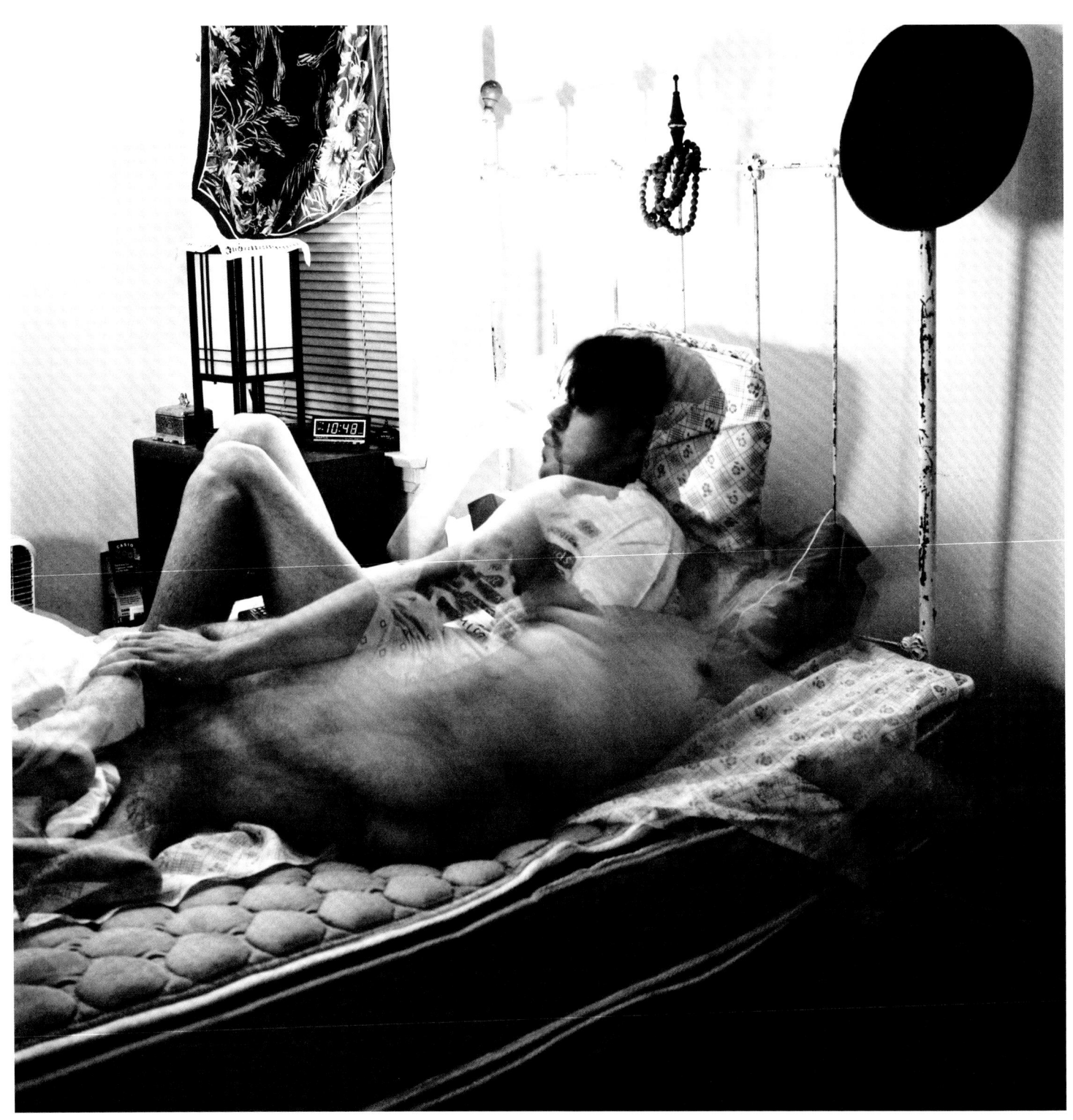

Reynaldo, Bianco, Echo Park, ca. 1995

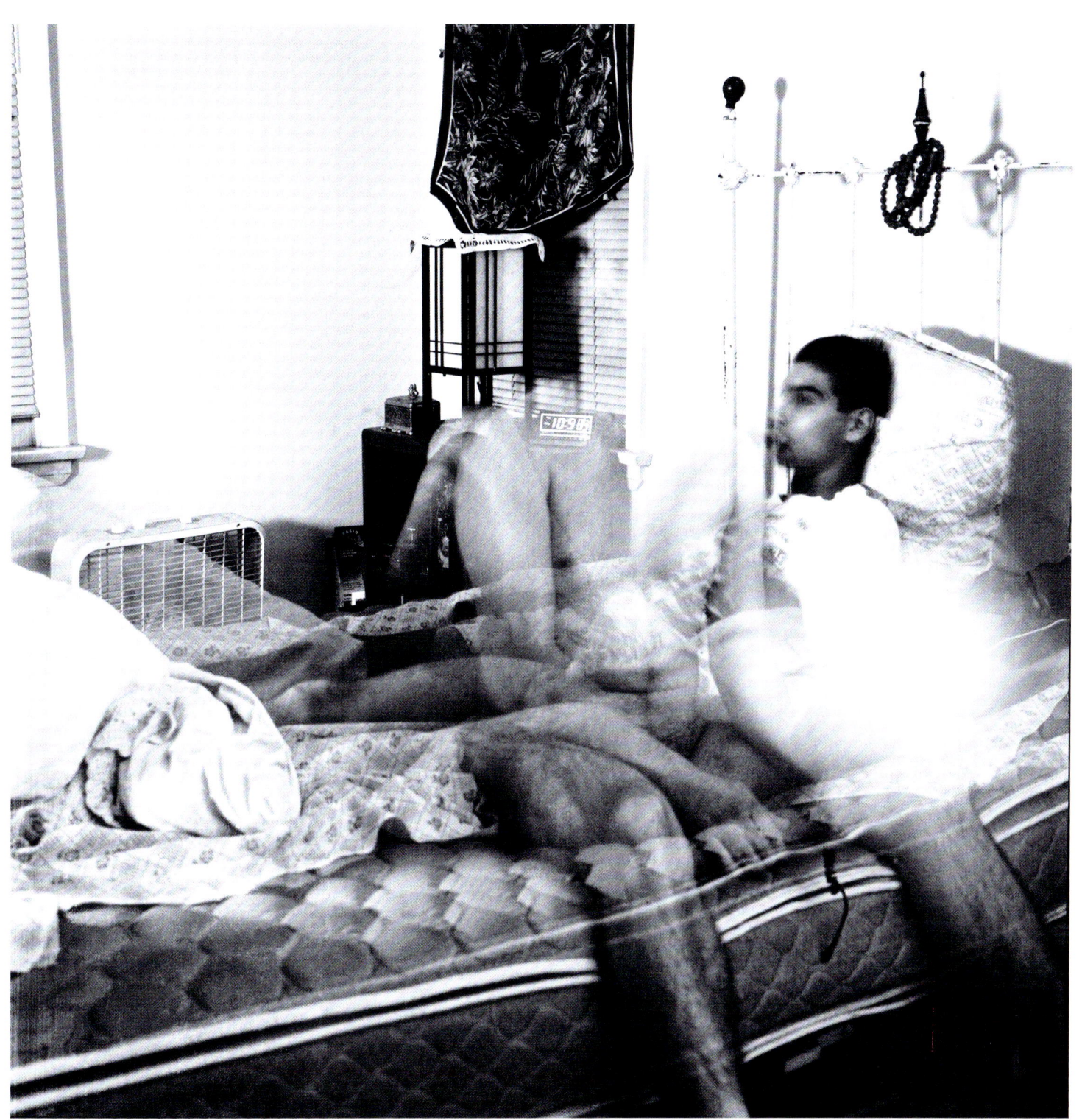

Bianco, Reynaldo, Echo Park, c.1995

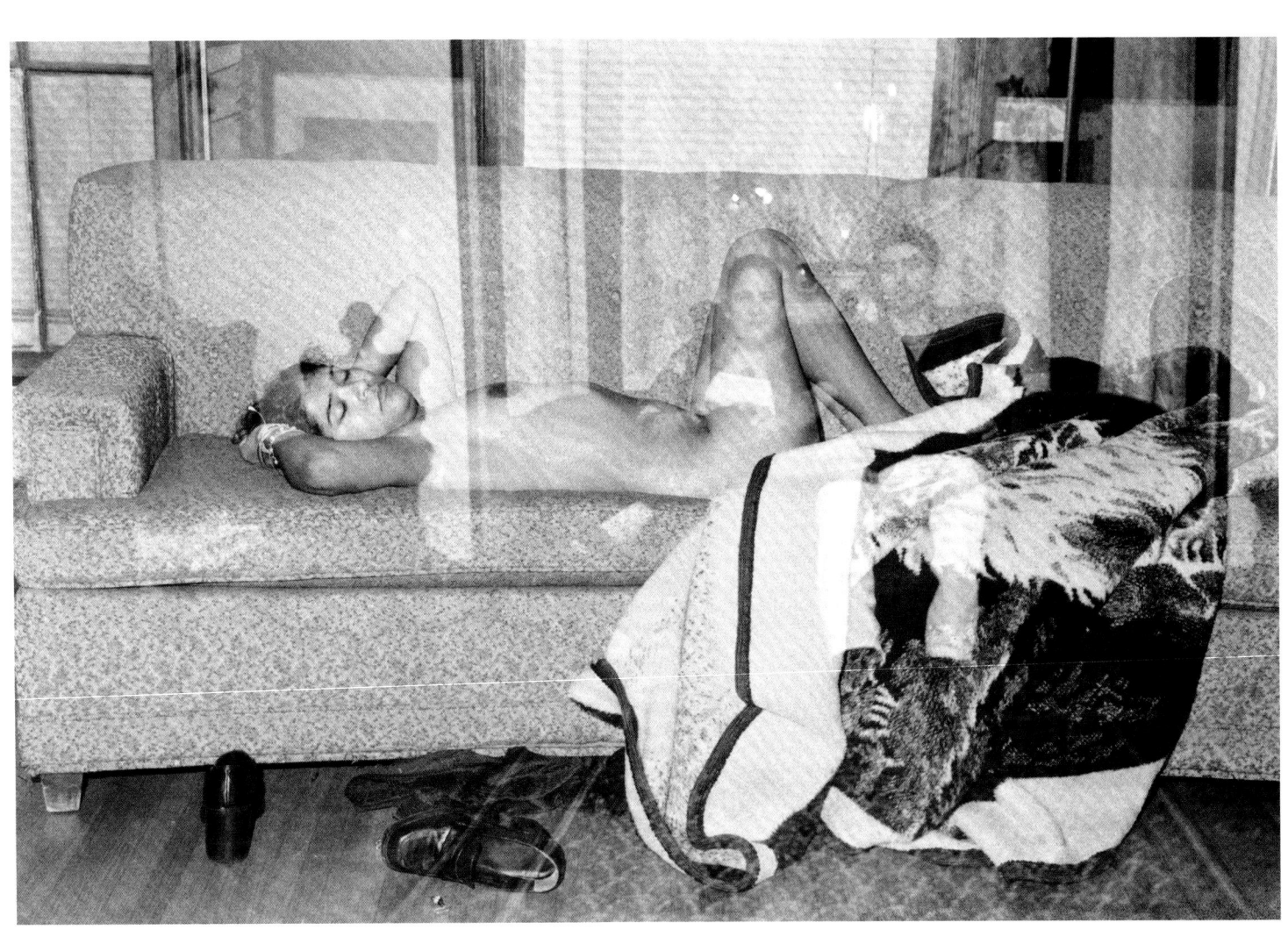

Pamela, Echo Park, ca. 1998

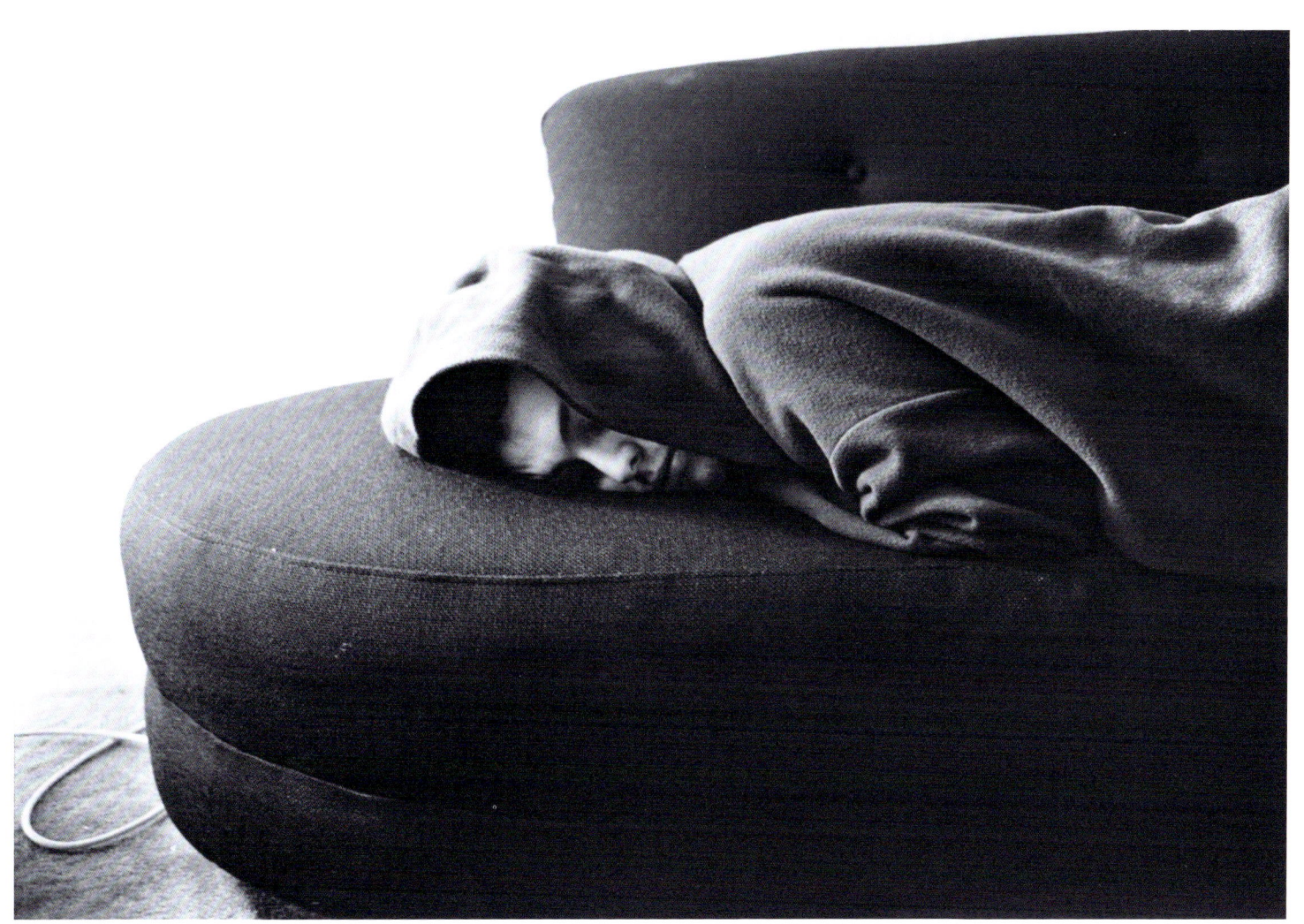

Steven, Echo Park, ca. 1991

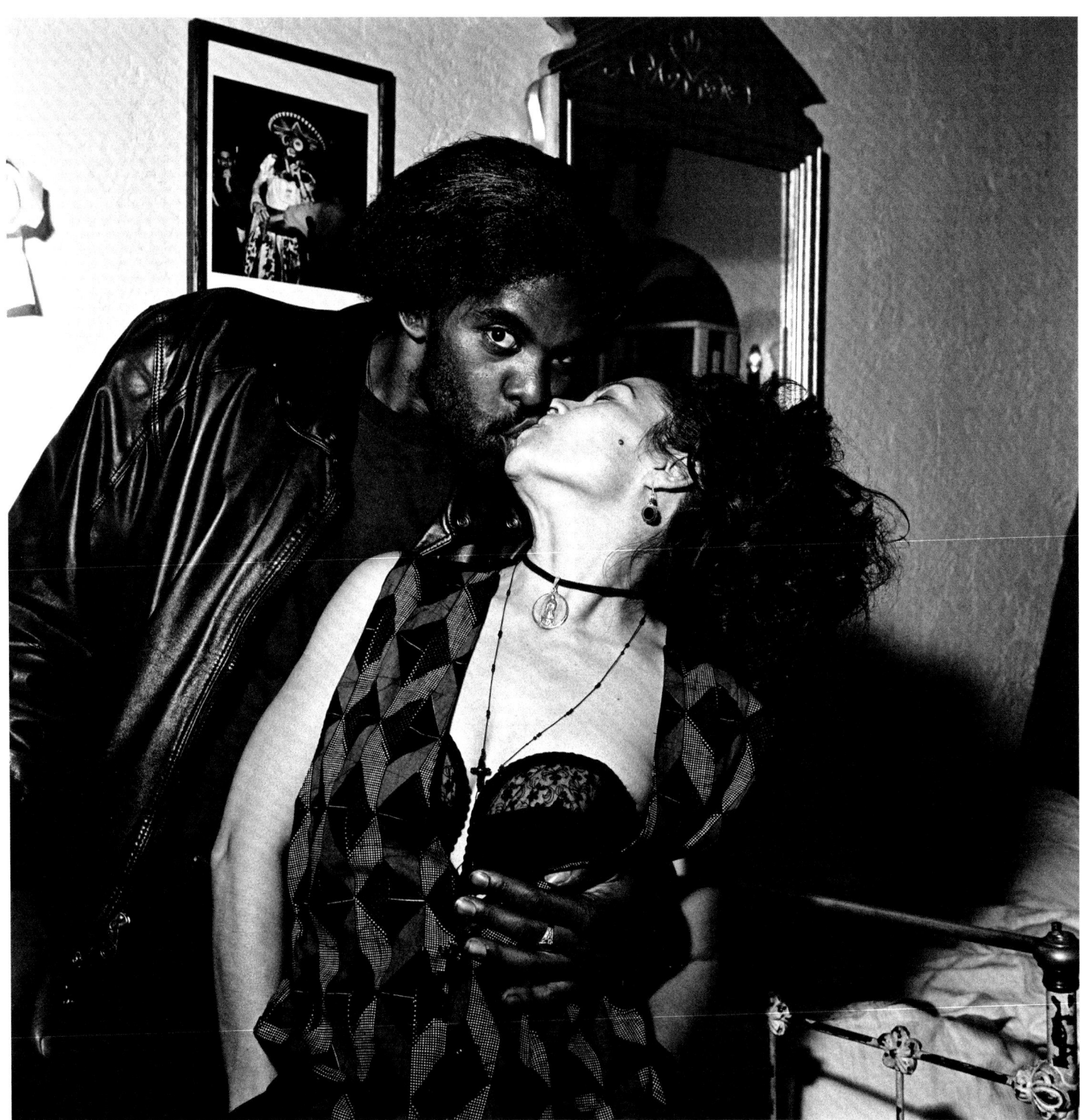

Bobbi, Sandra, Echo Park, ca. 1993

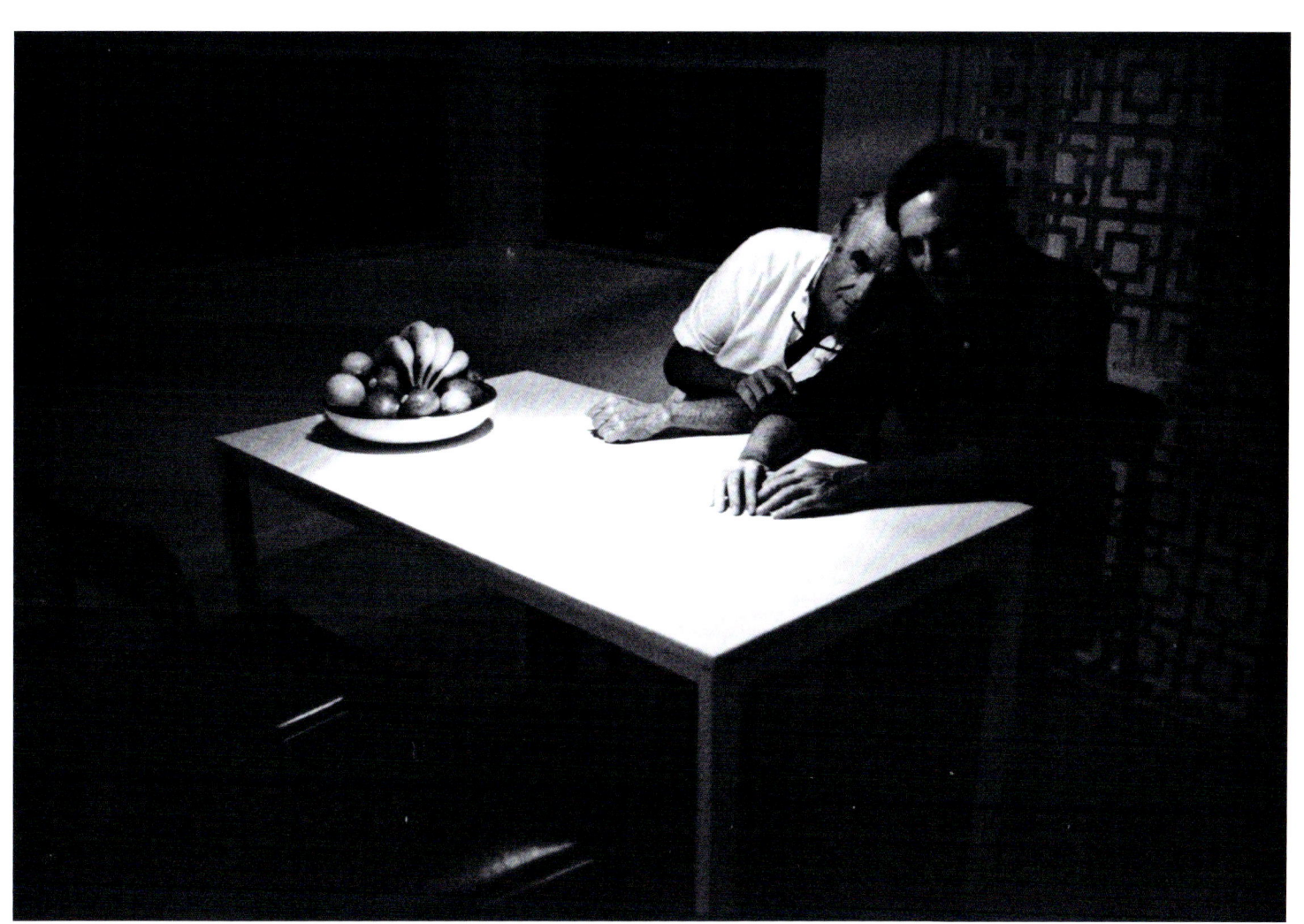

Colm, Hedi, Highland Park, 2023

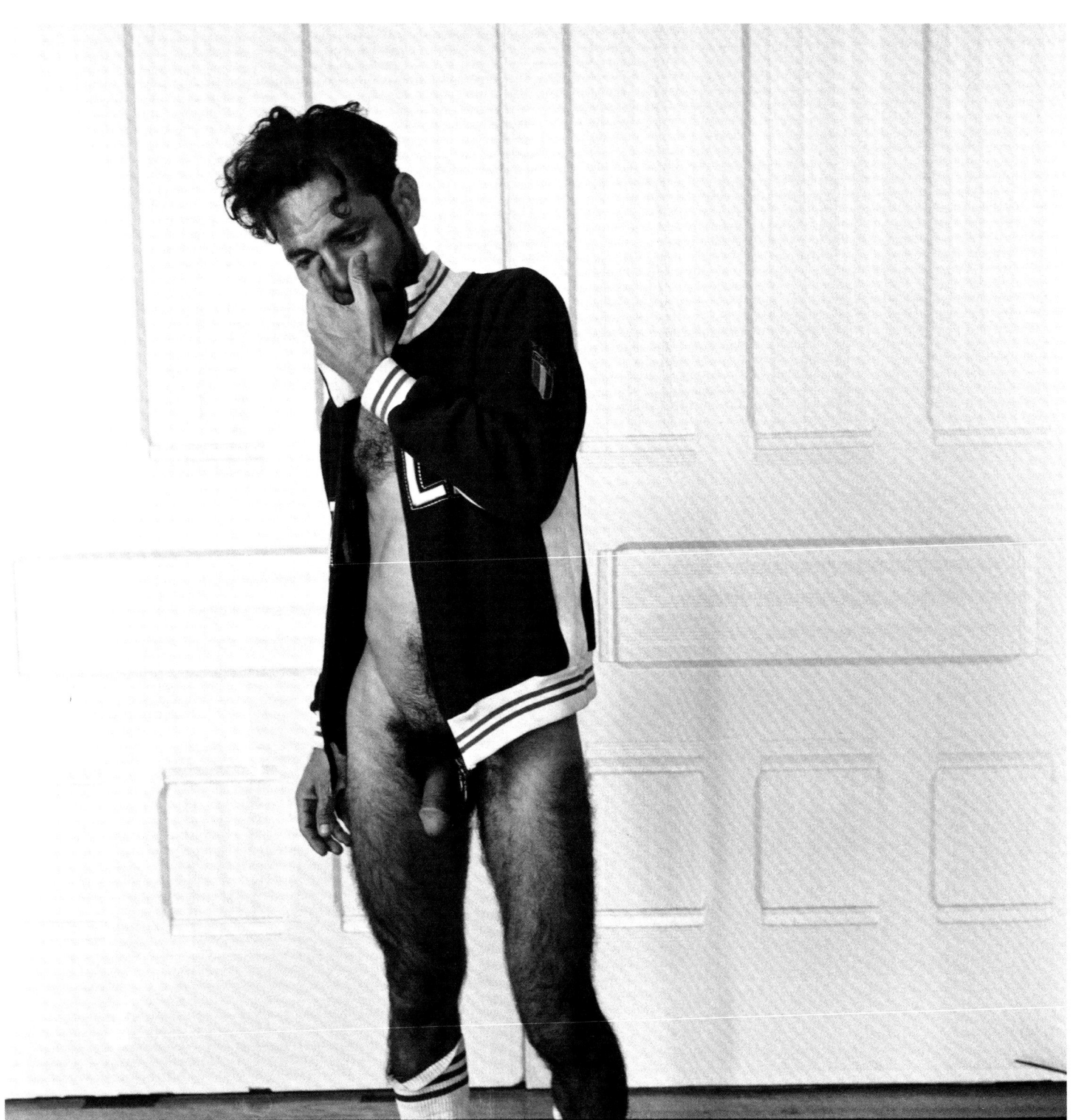

Justo, Lincoln Heights, 2015

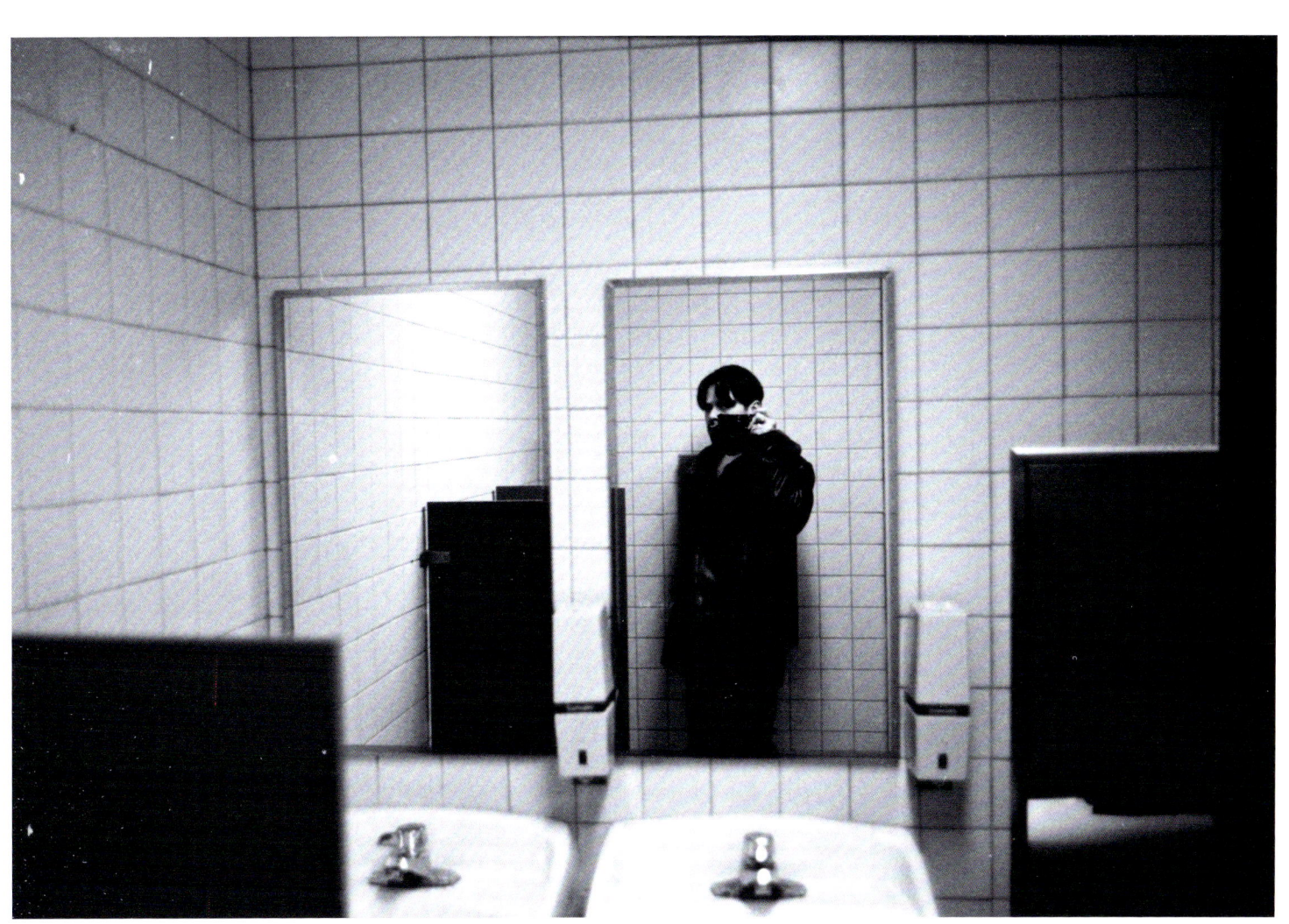

Self-Portrait, Berlin, ca. 1995

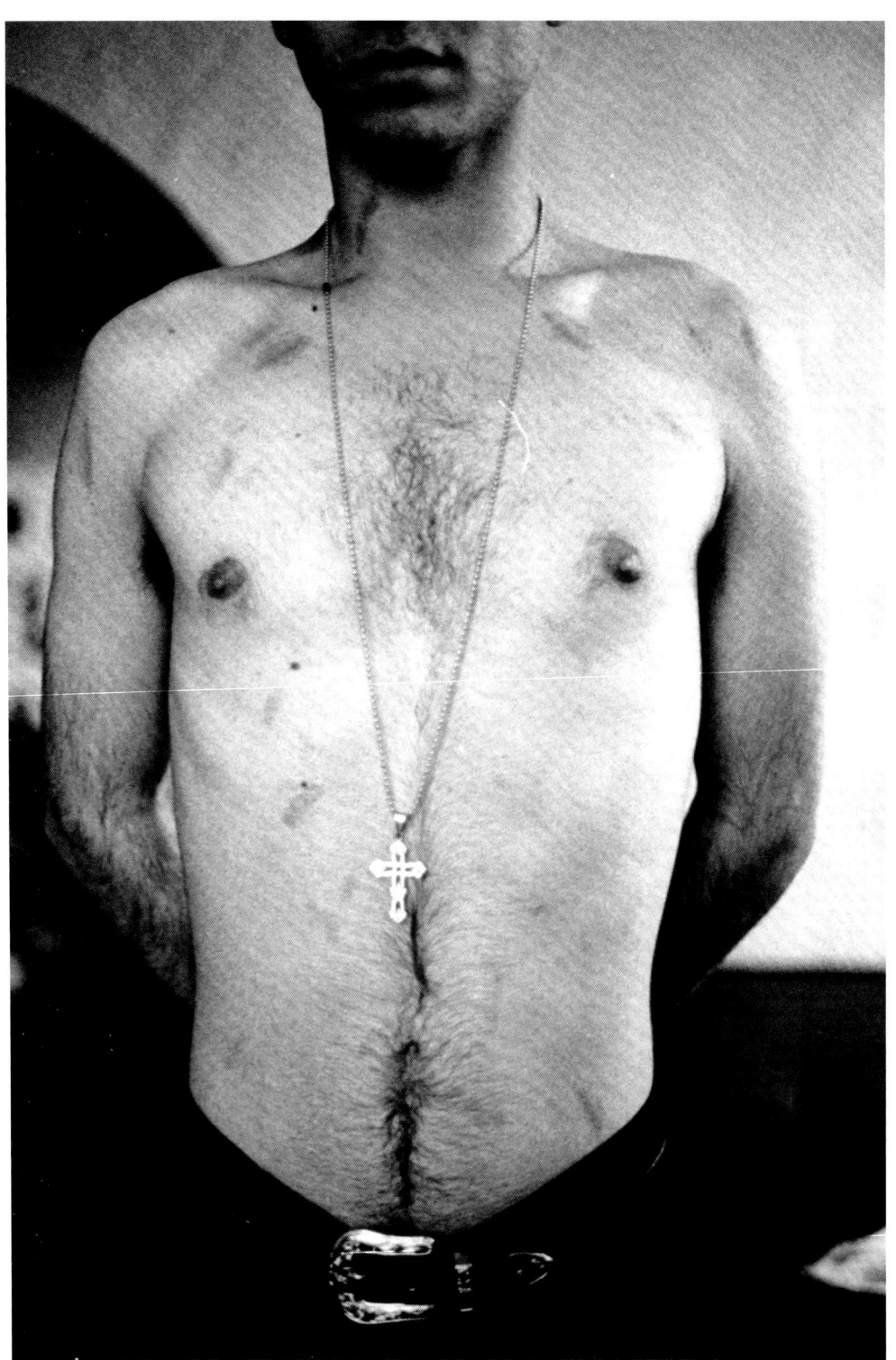

Bianco, Echo Park, ca. 1992

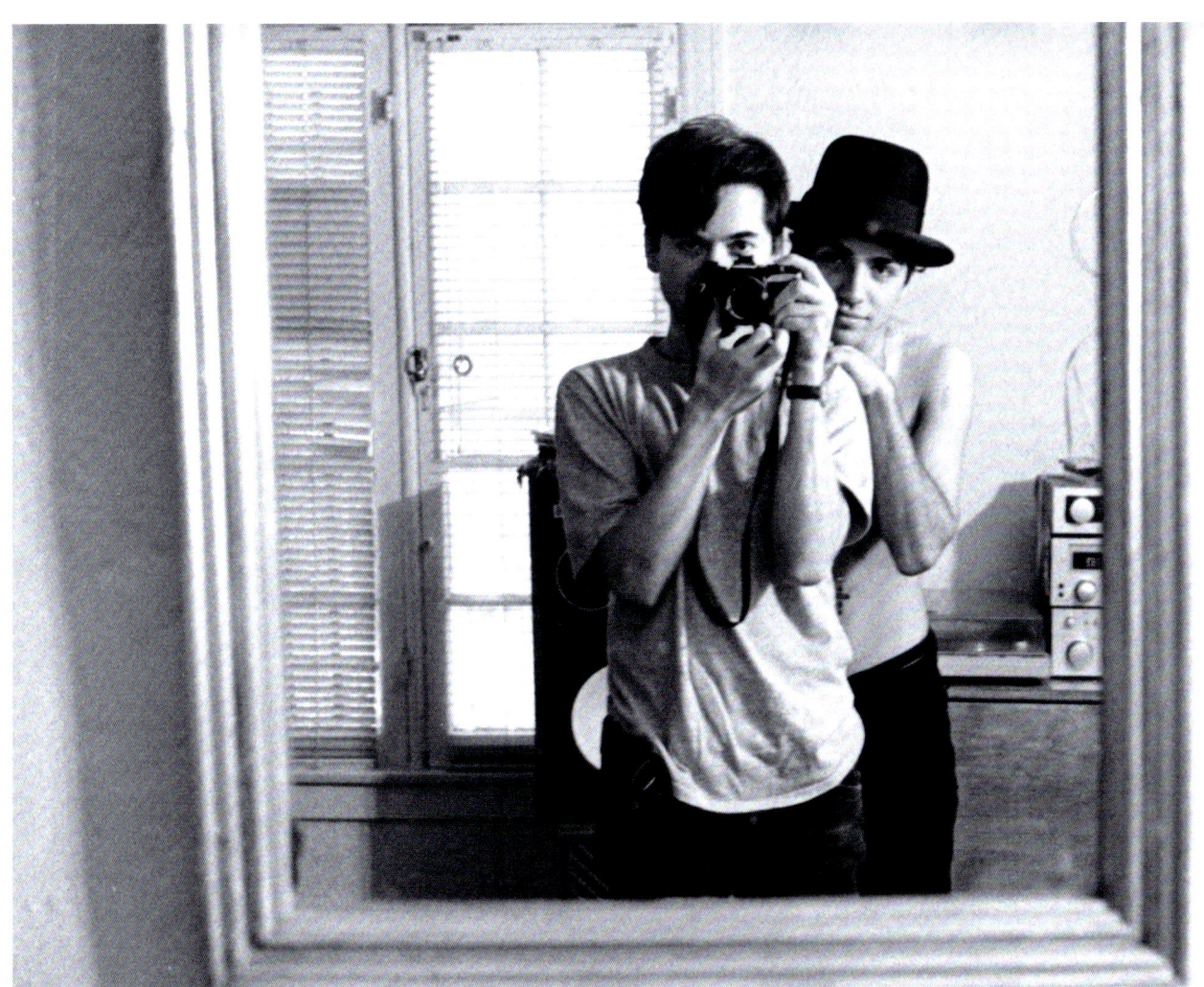

Reynaldo, Bianco, Echo Park, ca. 1992

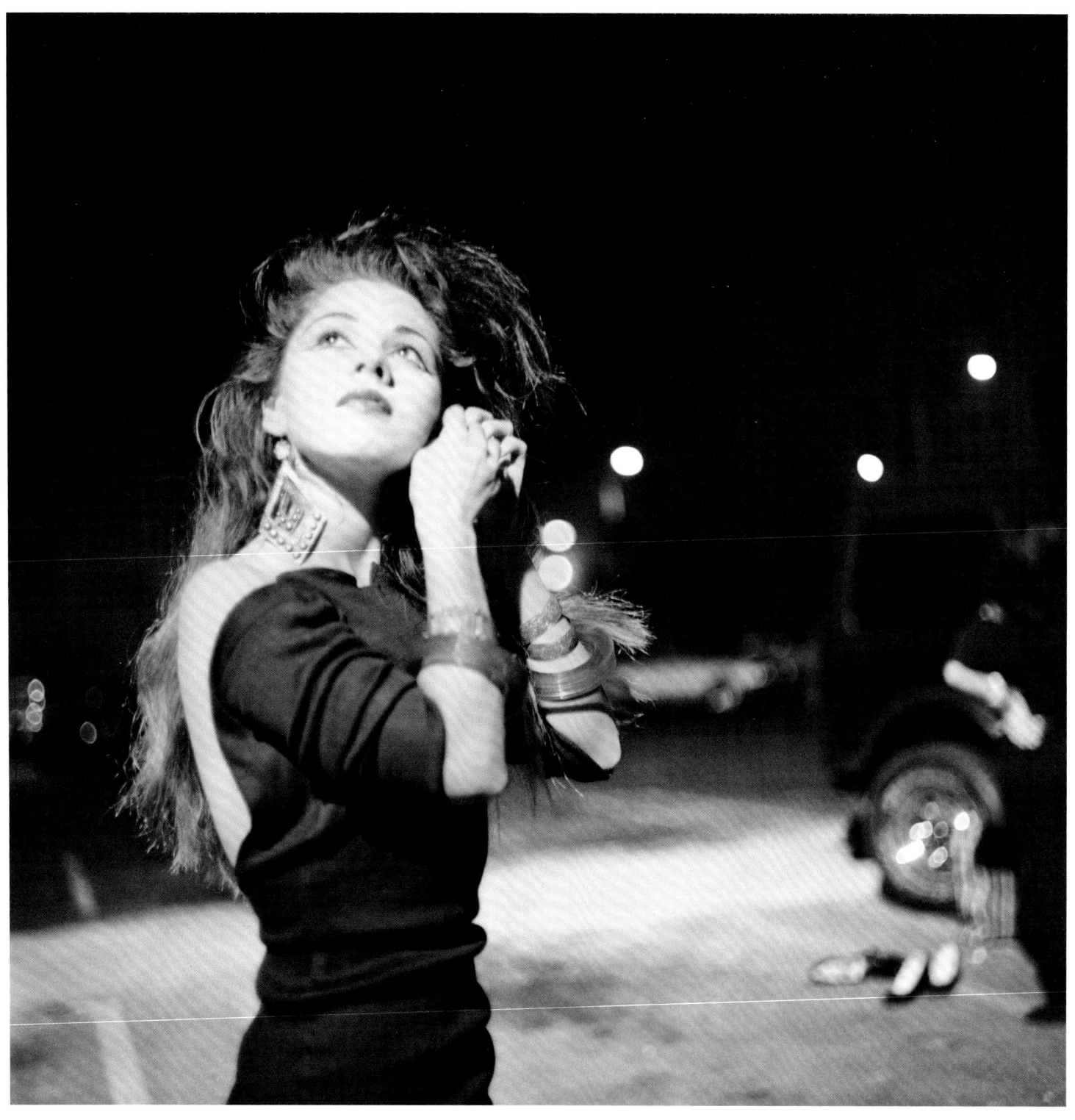

Martine, the Cha-Cha Girls, Pasadena, 1987
RIGHT: *Martha, Lincoln Heights,* 2025

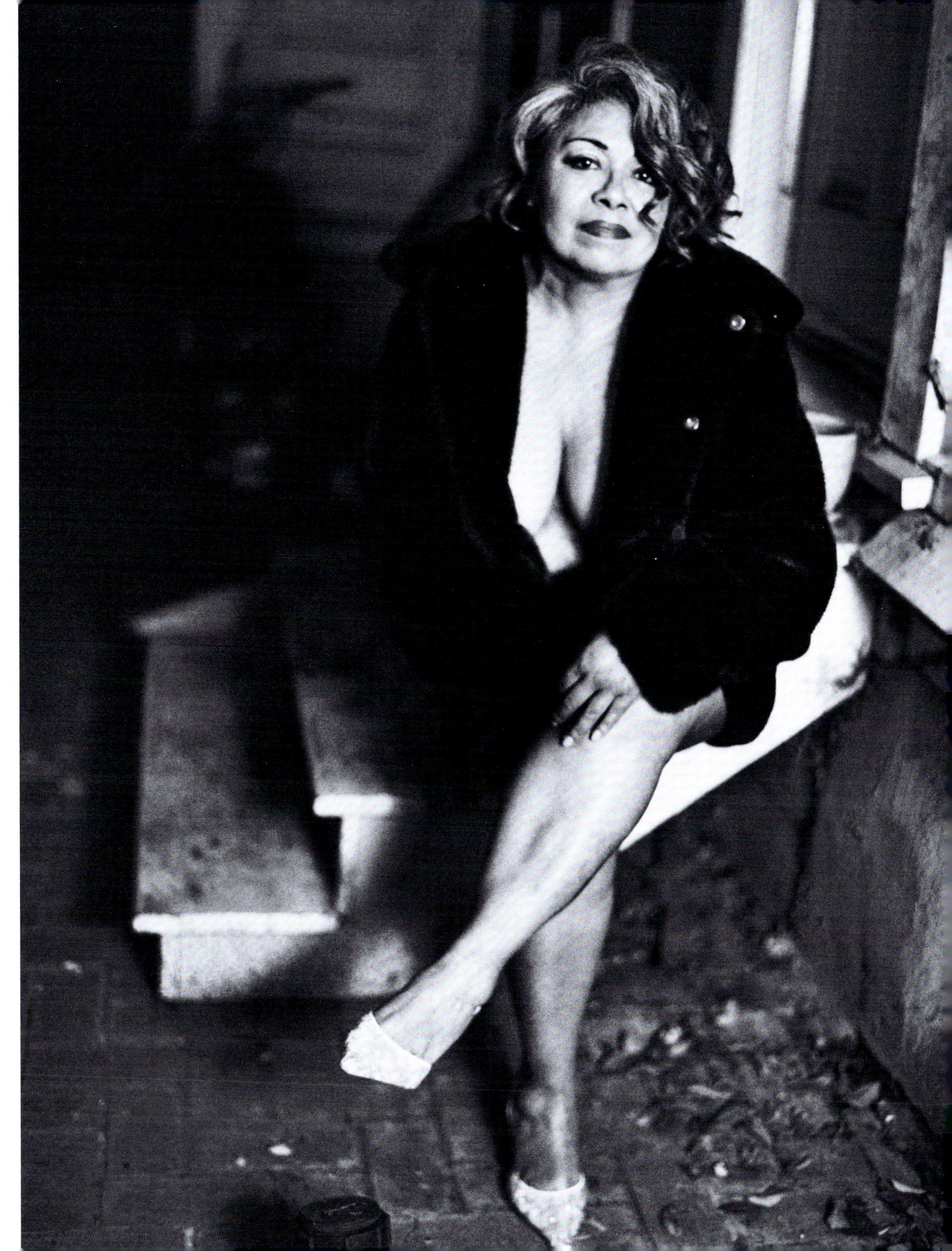

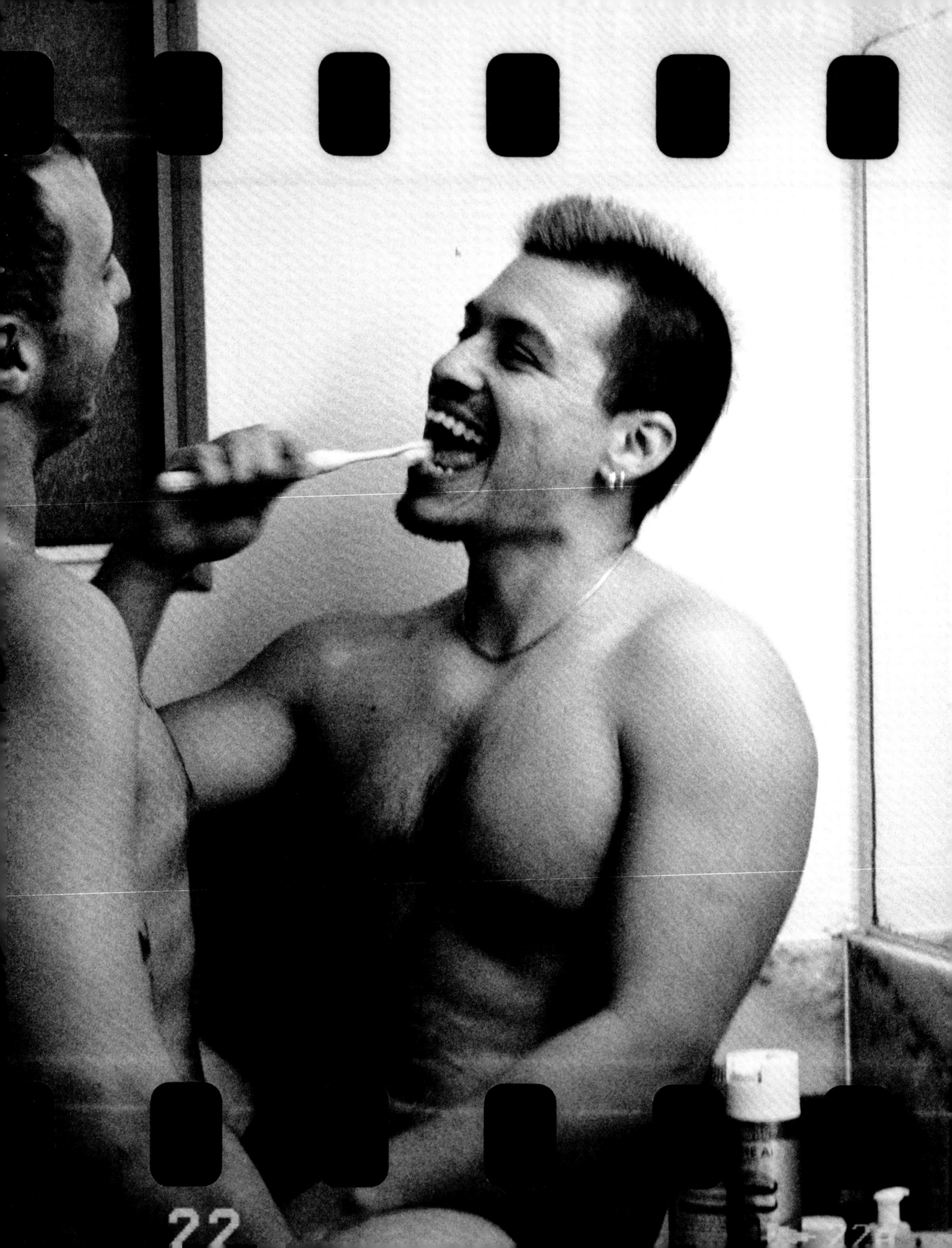

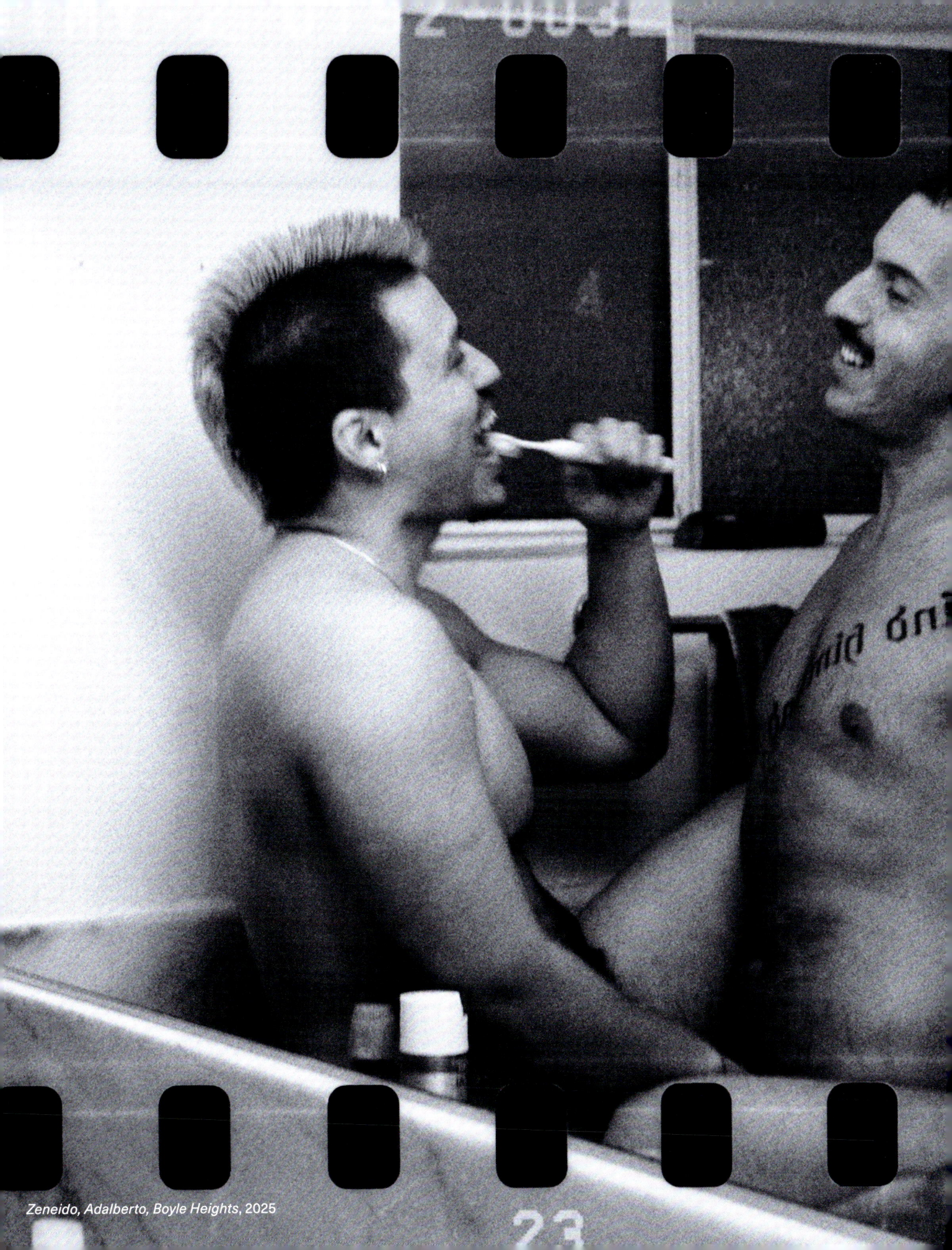

Zeneido, Adalberto, Boyle Heights, 2025

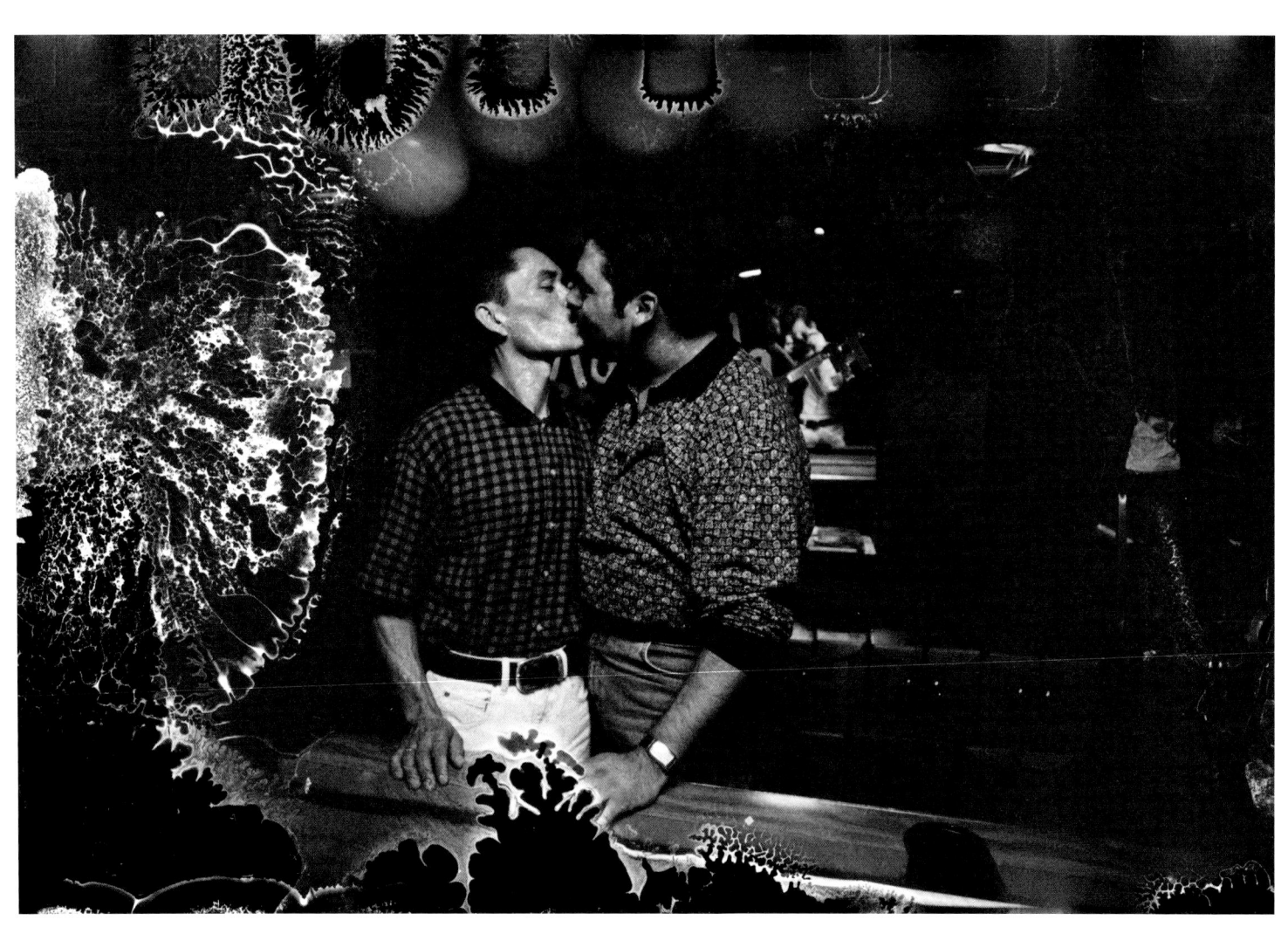

Patrons, Little Joy, 1996

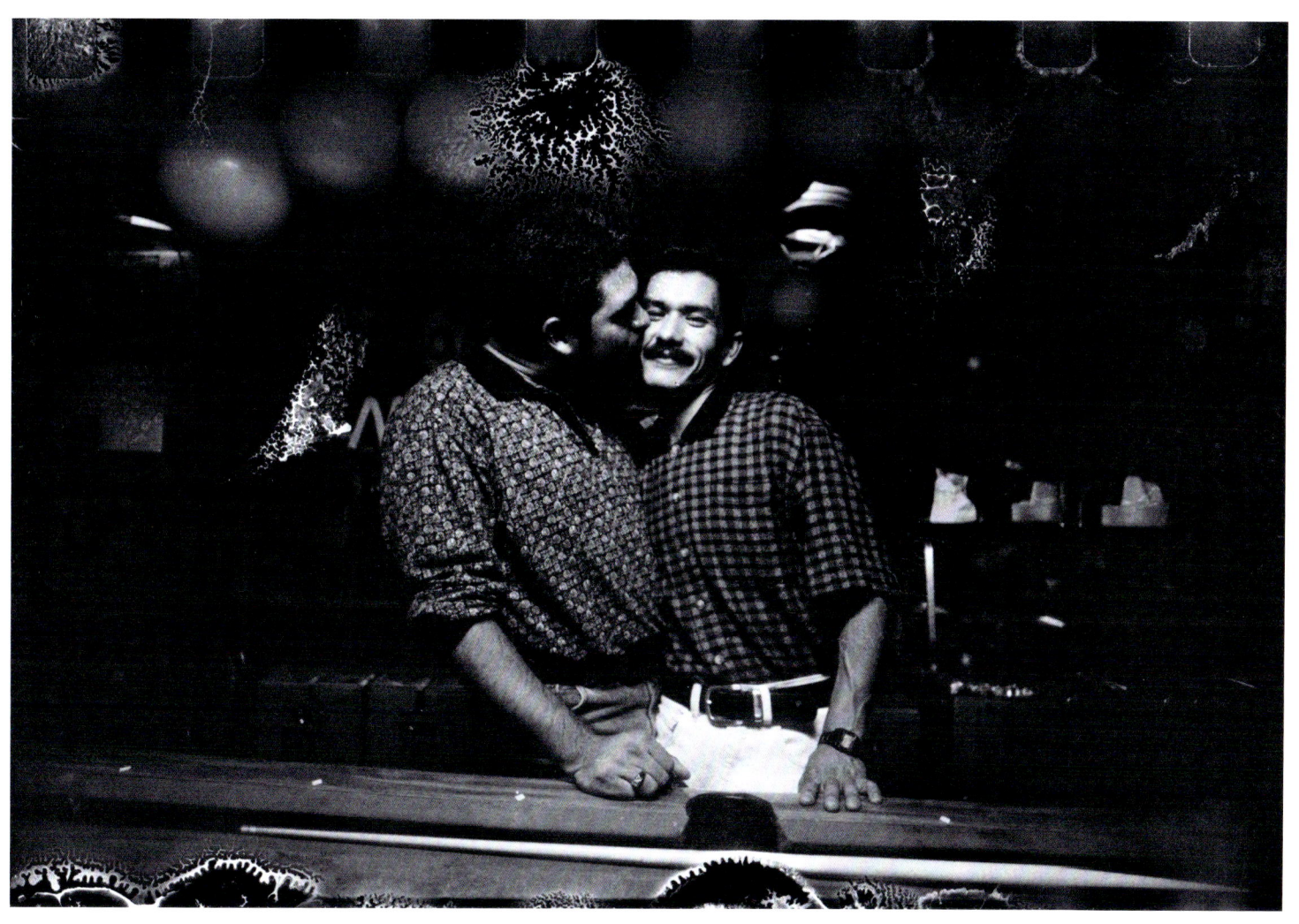

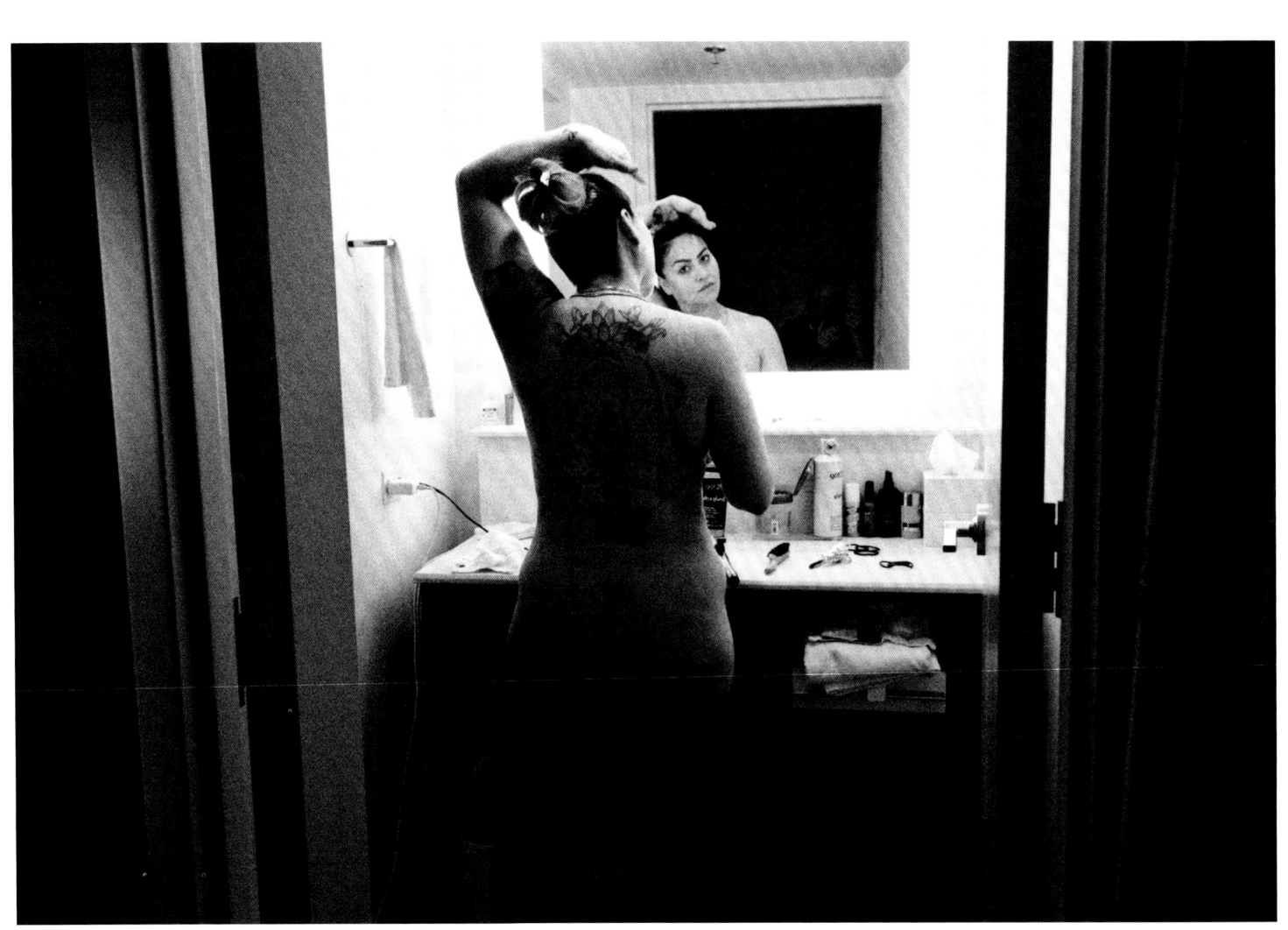

Mercedes, Austin, 2025

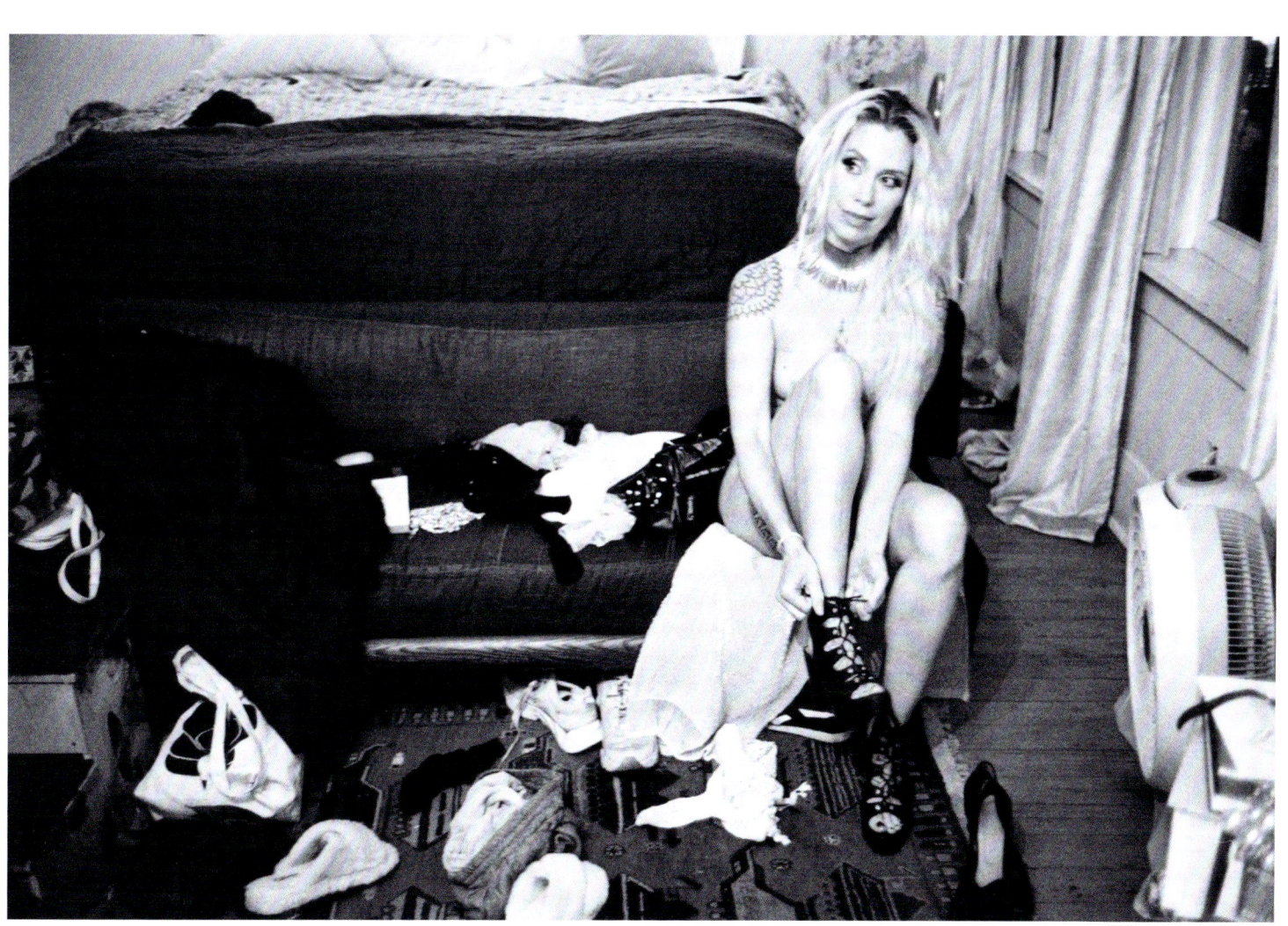

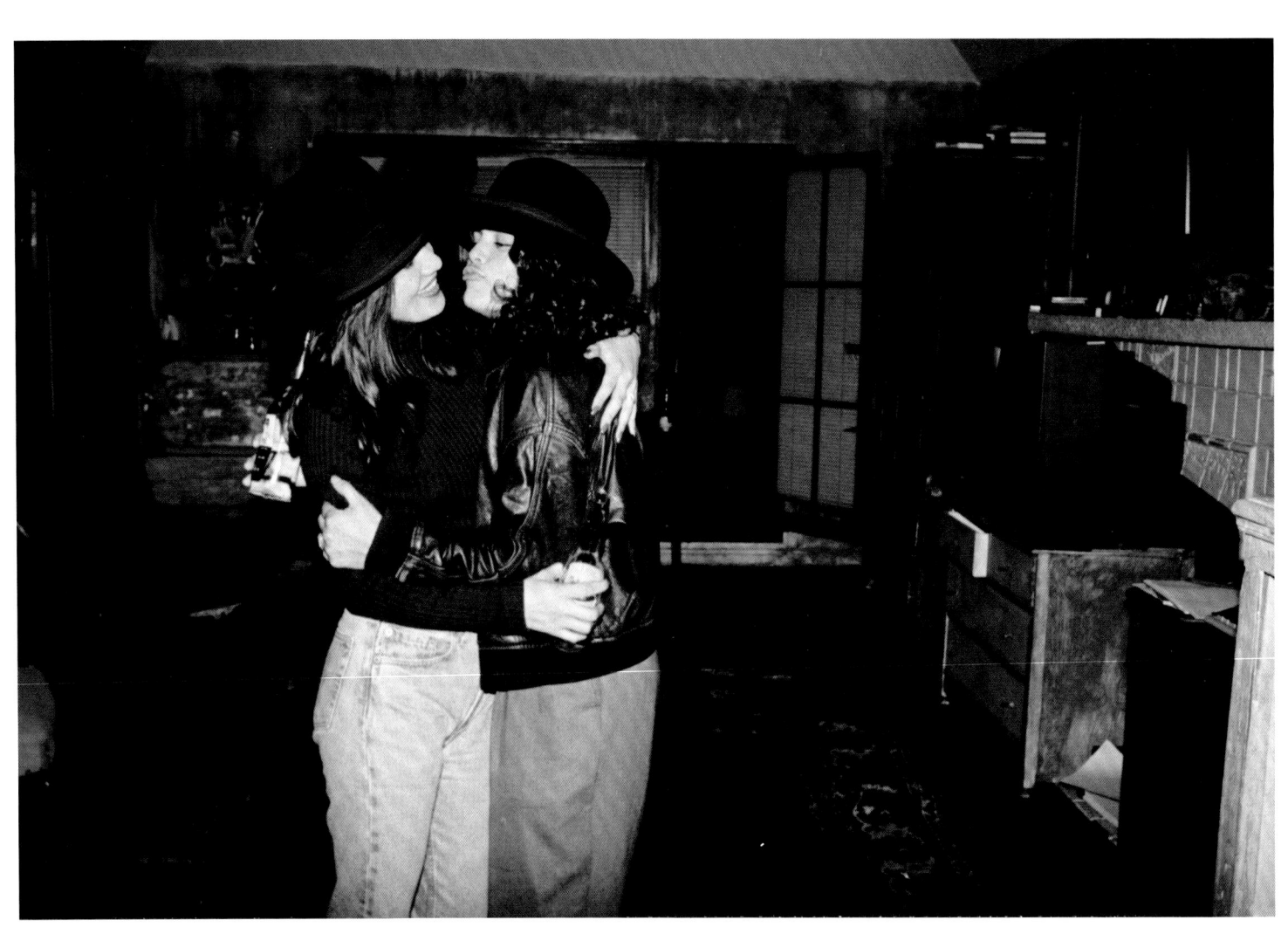

Couple, Echo Park, ca. 1997

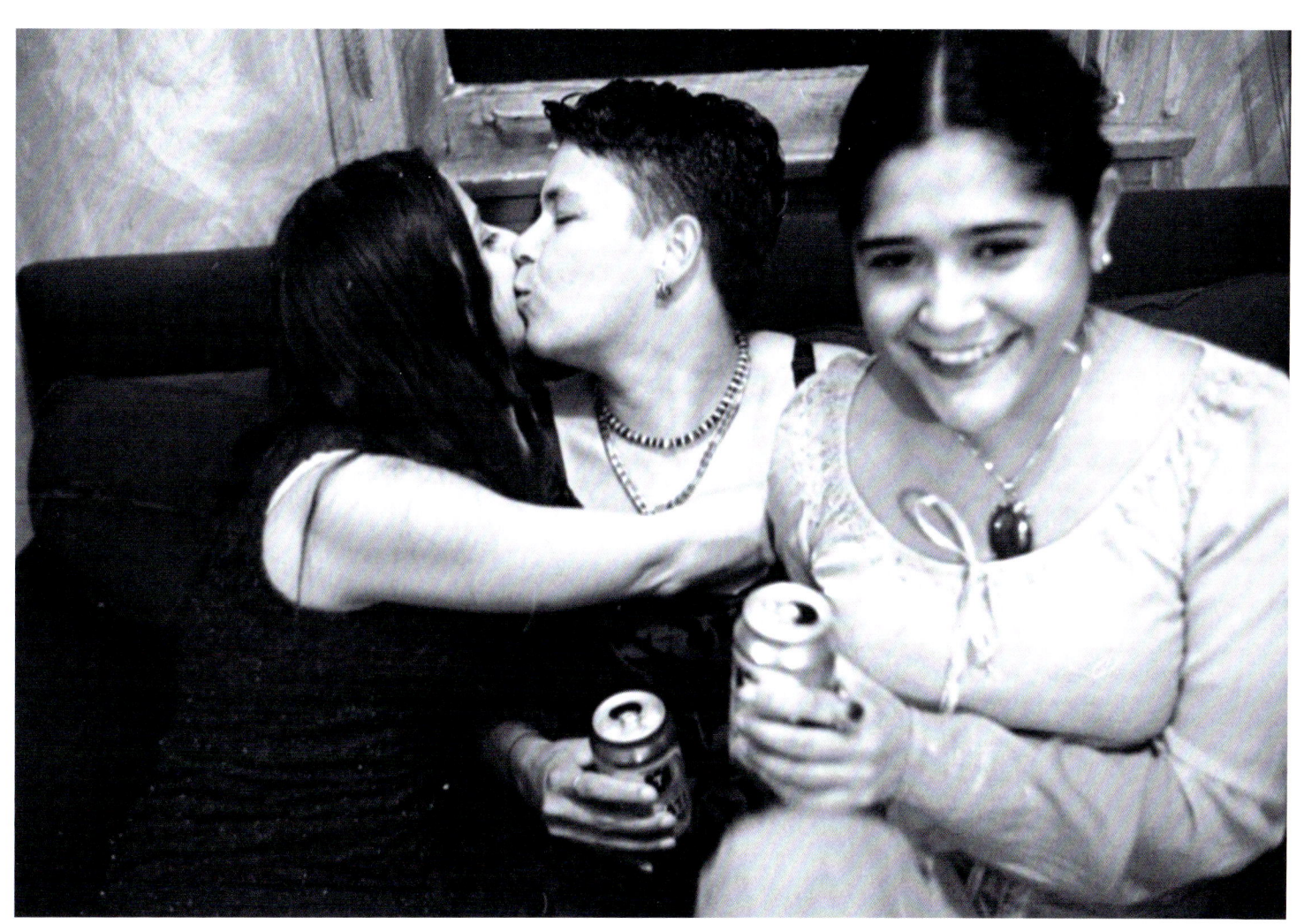

Martine, Annetta, Pamela, Echo Park, ca. 1995

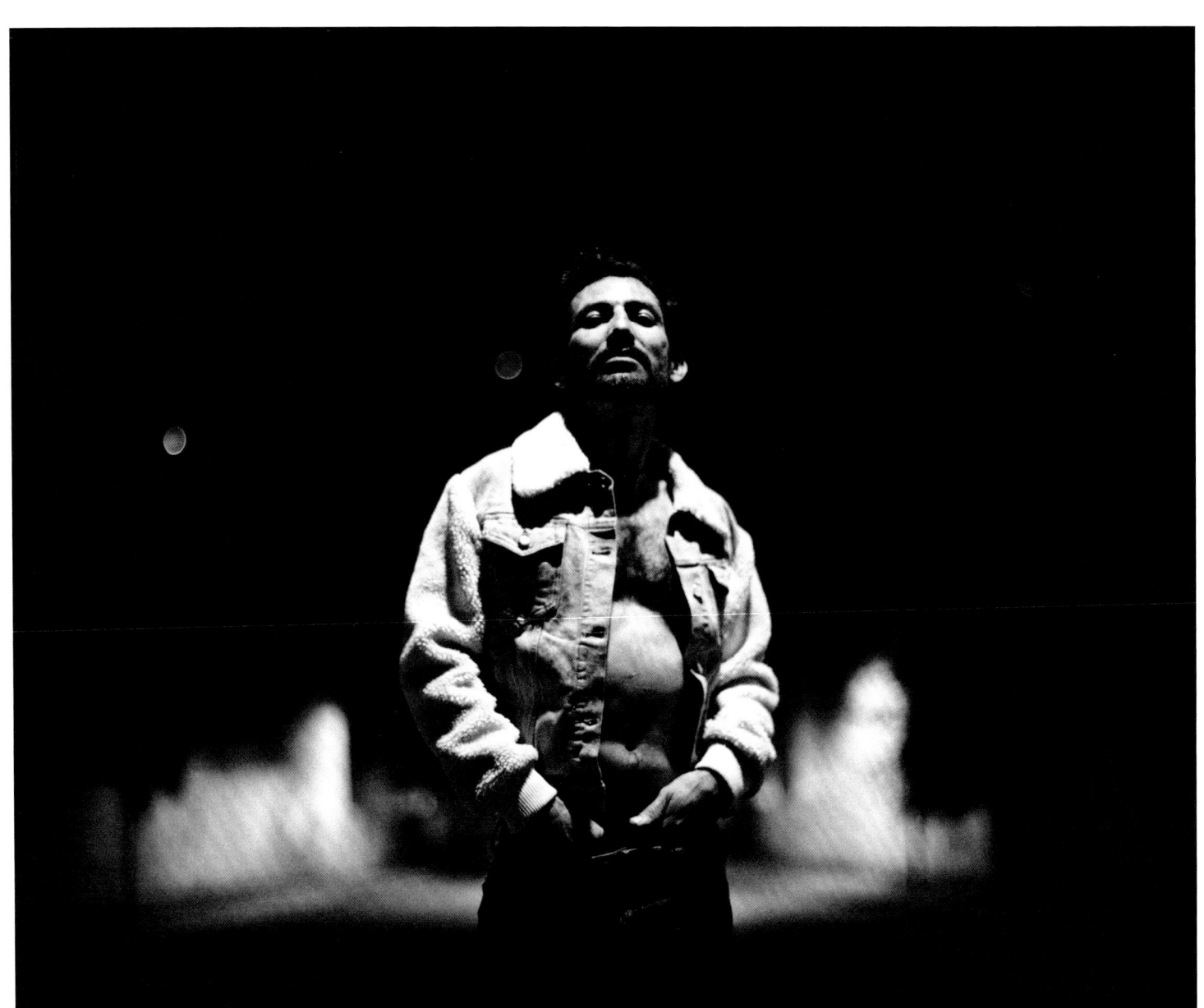

Justo, Downtown Los Angeles, 2025

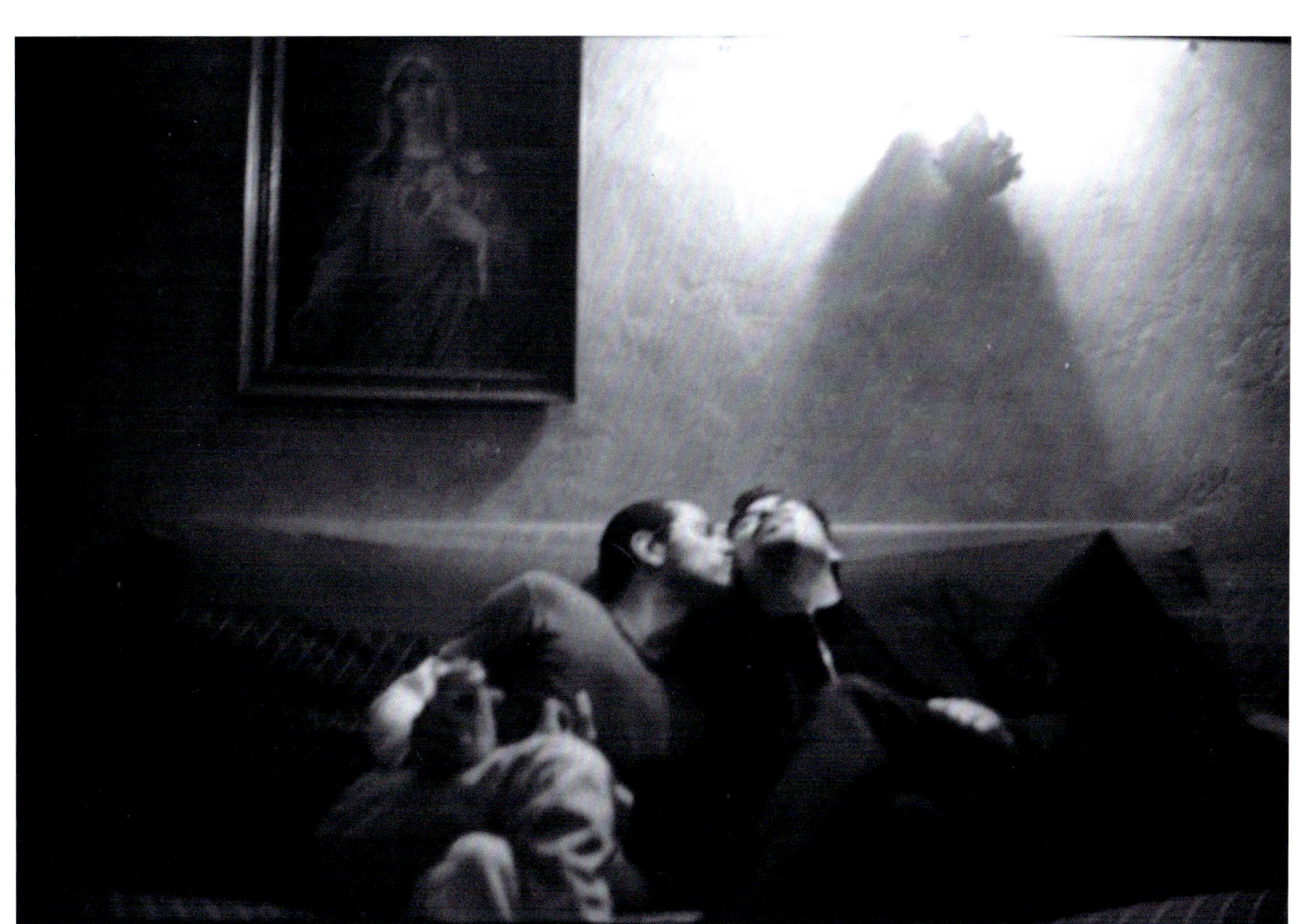

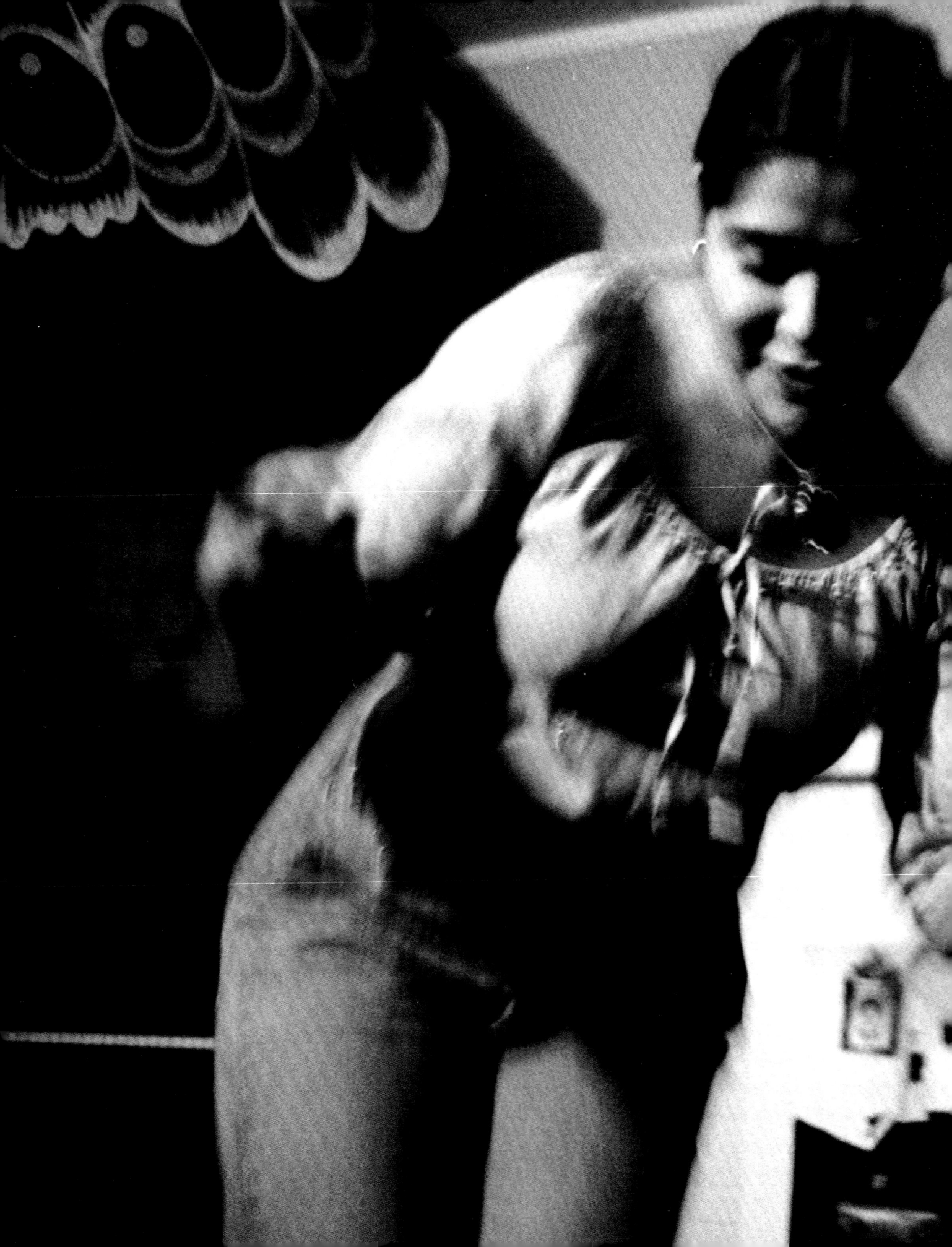

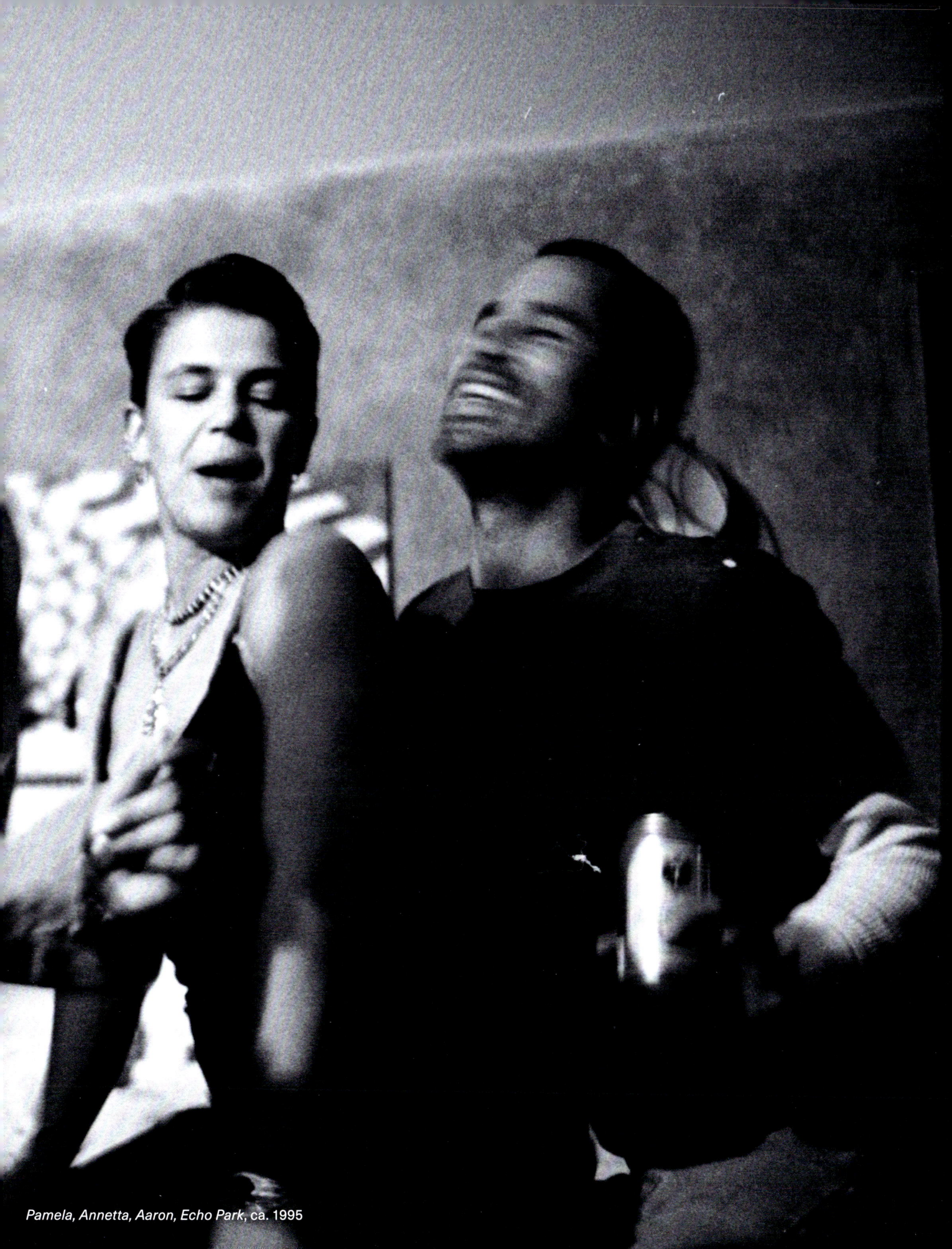

Pamela, Annetta, Aaron, Echo Park, ca. 1995

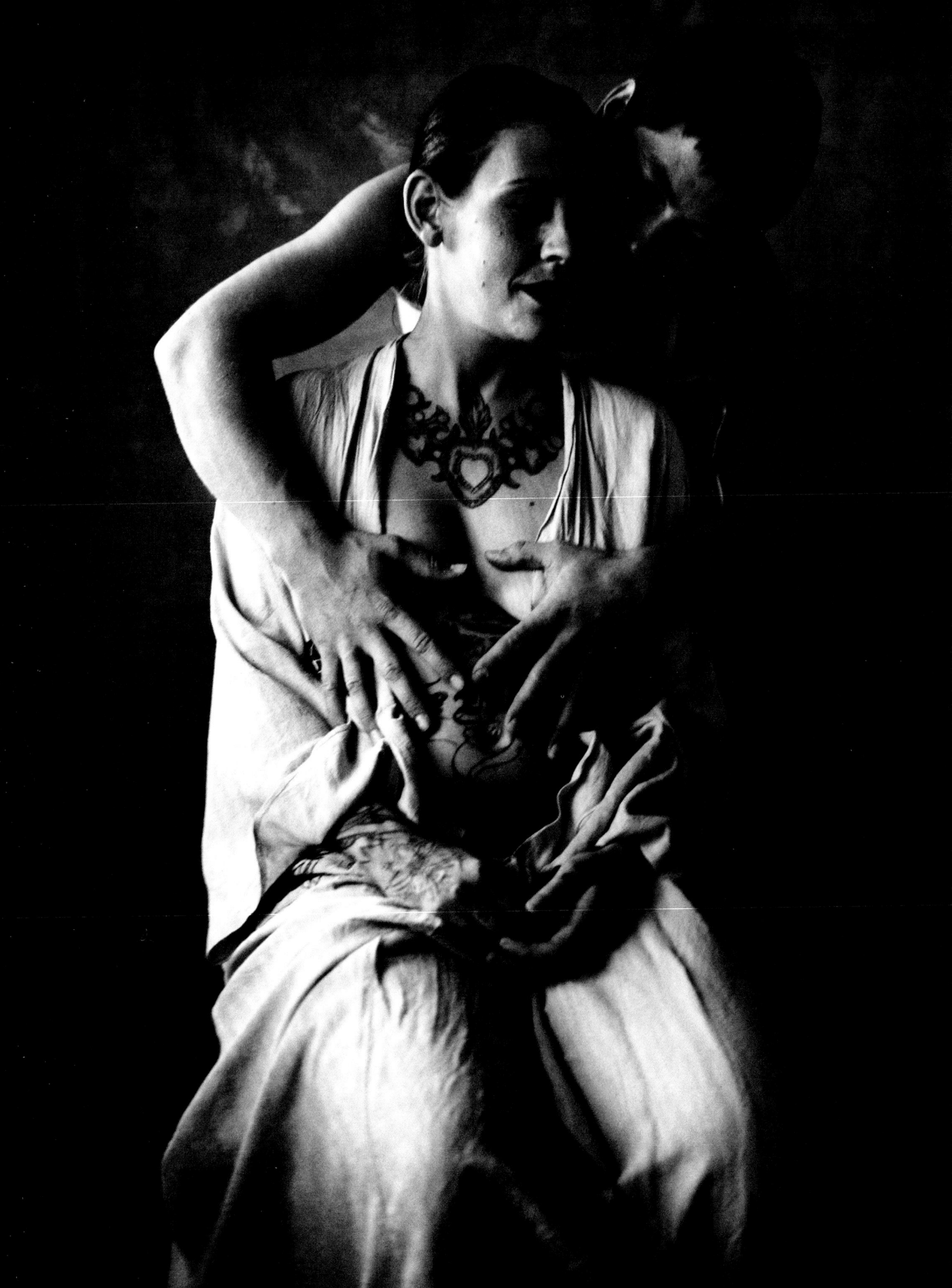

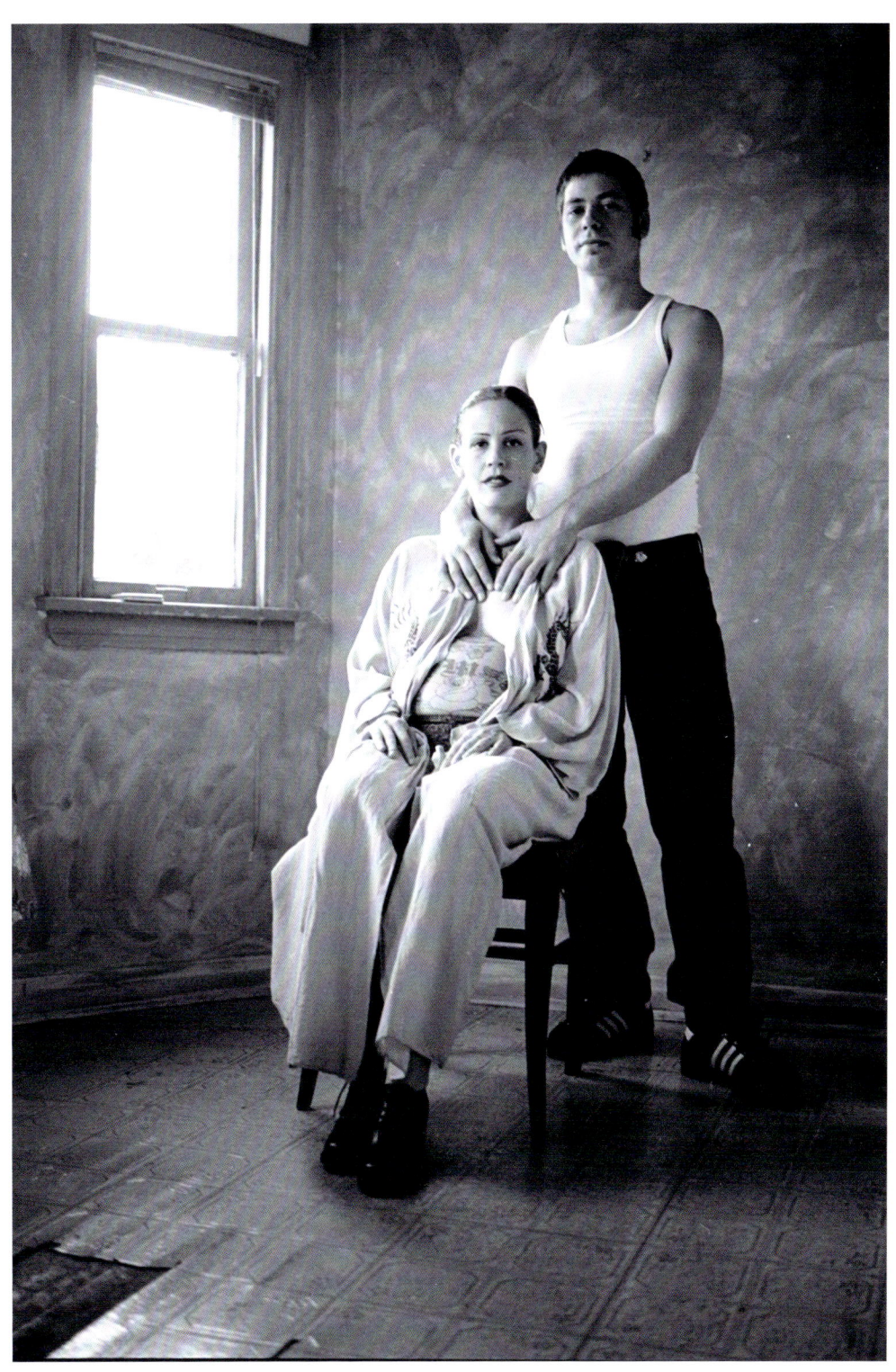

Judy, Stephan, Echo Park, 1997

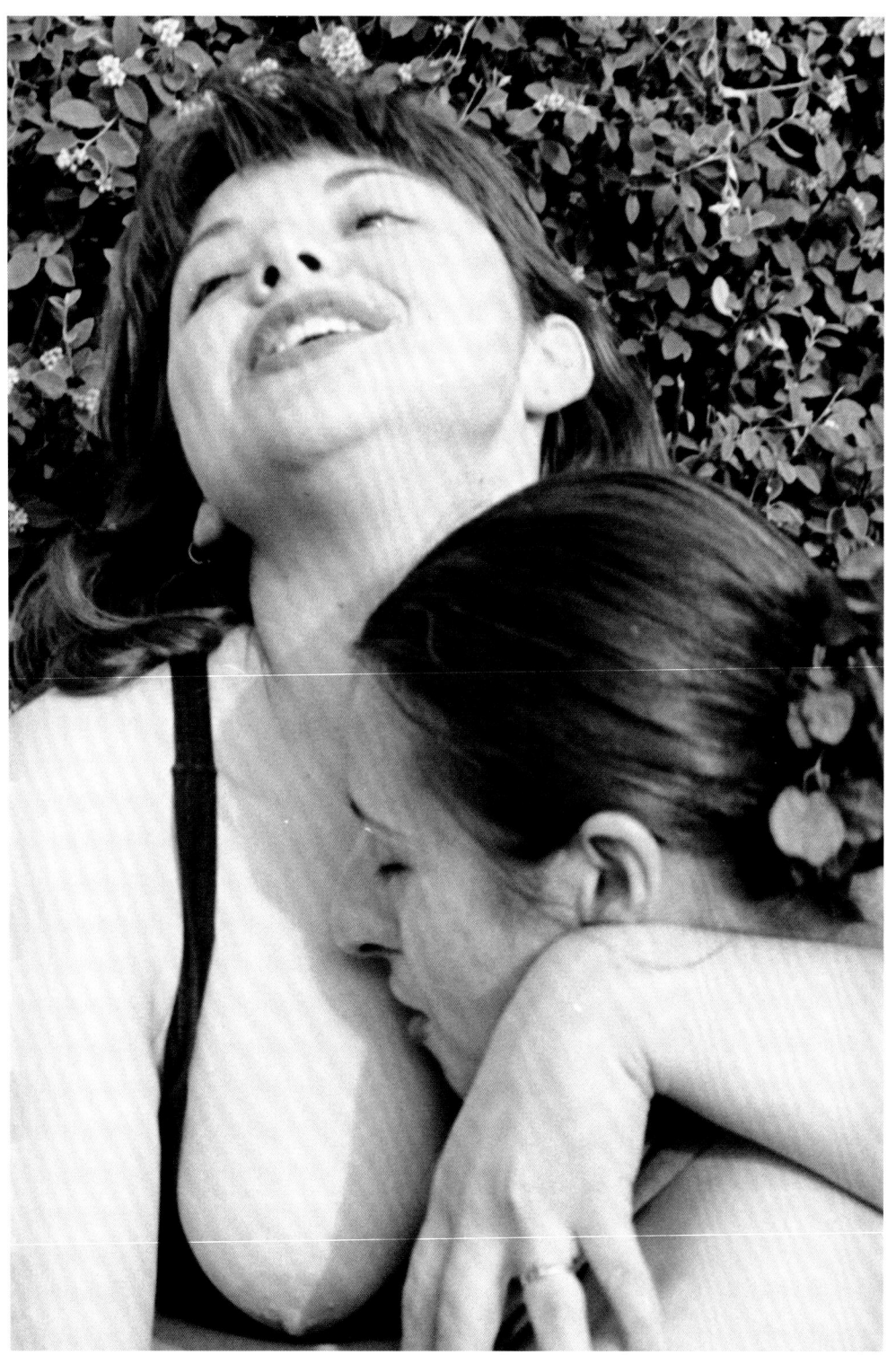

Connie, Tatiana, Echo Park, ca. 1989

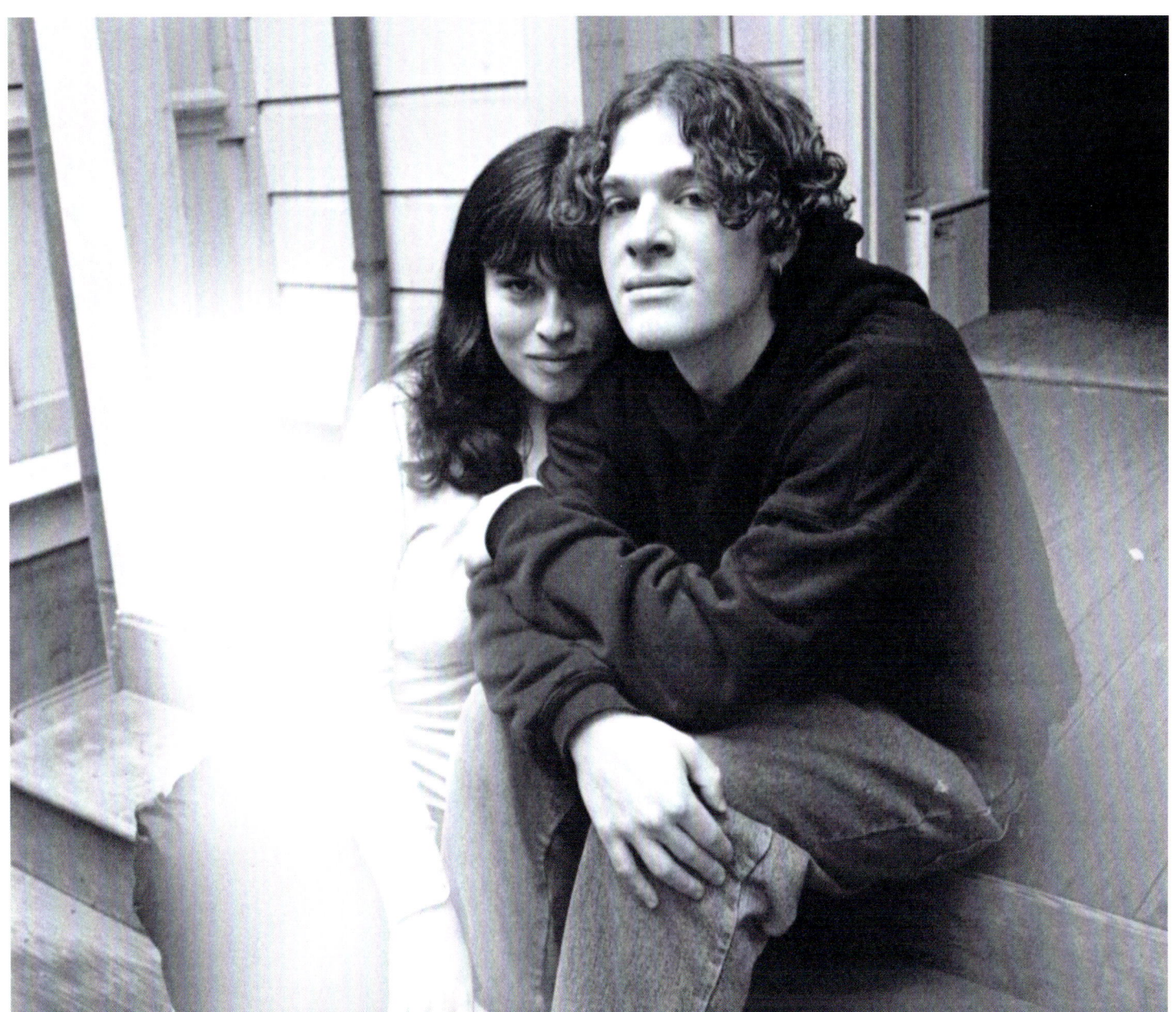

Devan, Pierce, Lincoln Heights, 2025

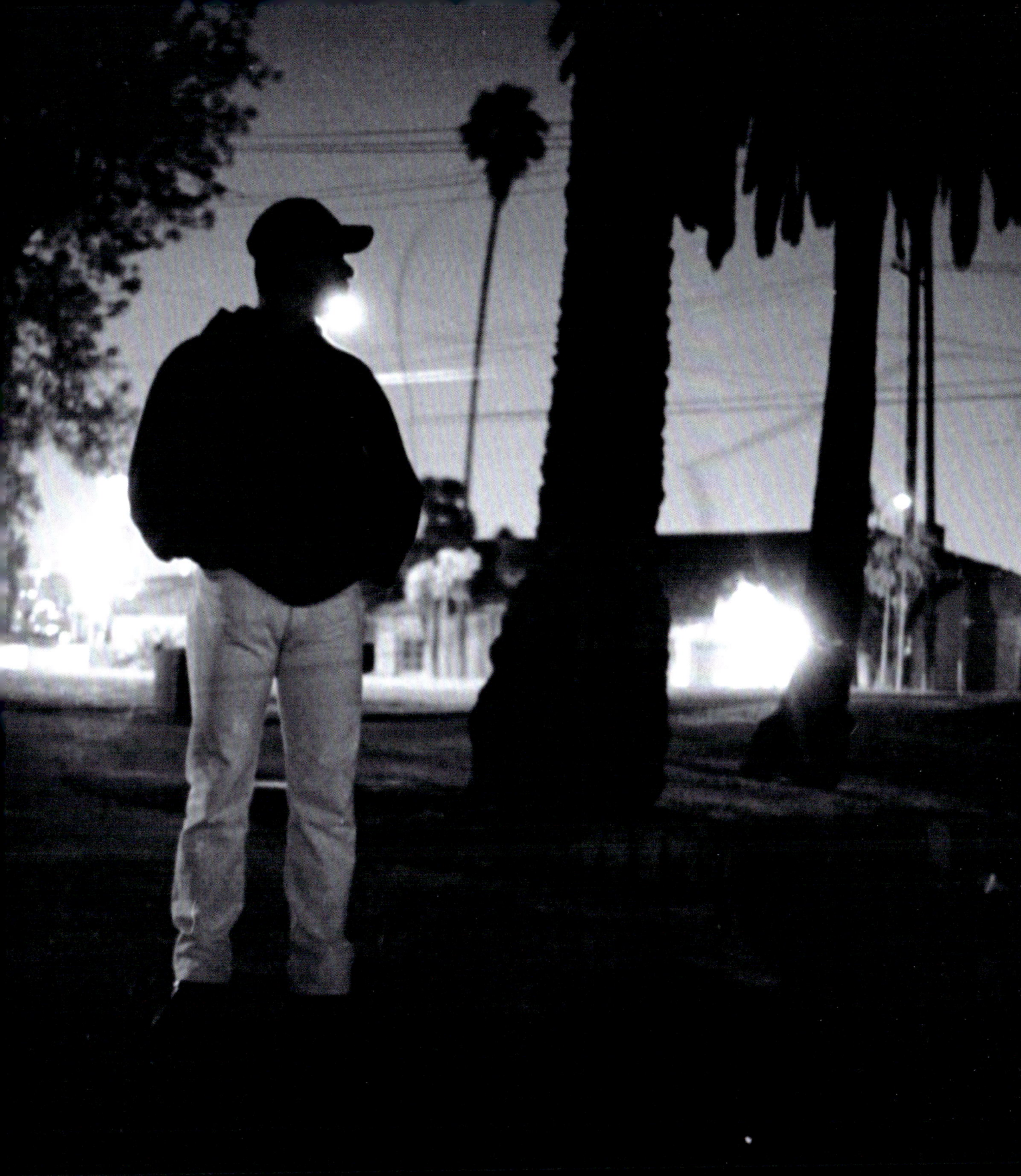

Echo Park Lake, 1995

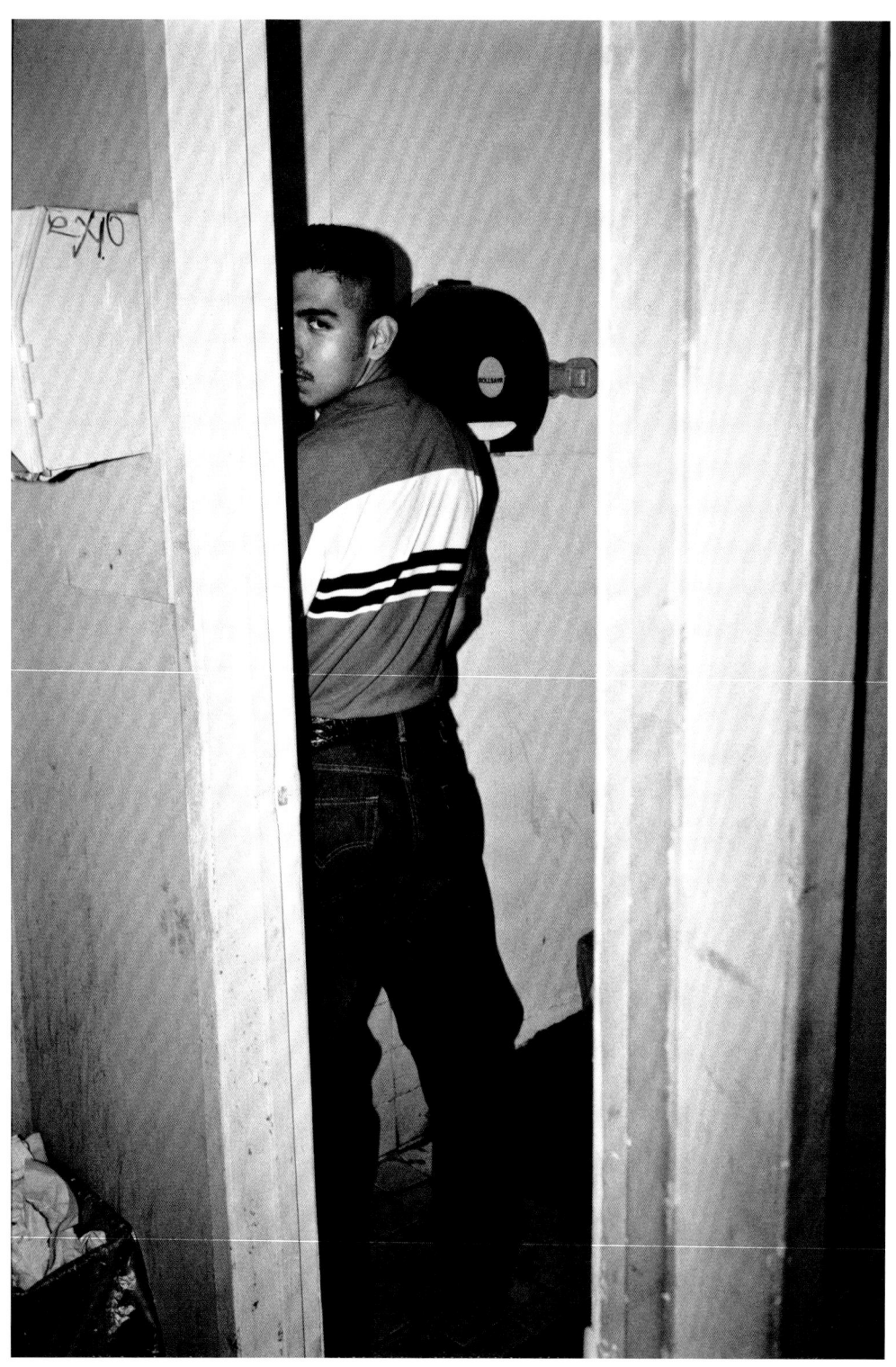

Richard, Bar, Los Angeles, 1996

I'VE LISTENED TO THIS BREAKUP SONG A MILLION TIMES
—Brontez Purnell

I'm mobbing through Bushwick, Brooklyn, in the back of a cab, listening to Lady Wray's "Piece of Me" for the twelfth time in a row, and I'm crying—very, very hard—and no, it's not ugly crying. In fact, I'm pretty sure I look beautiful right now.

There is no greater balm in the universe than a Black woman singing (I said what I said). I remember being a young gay boy in San Francisco, hanging out at the Eagle bar in SoMa, when an older white gay explained to me that he only talks to Black women therapists. He went on: "I like my health care like I like my house music—I want a beautiful Black woman telling me that everything is going to be OK." I was twenty-three and literally balked at the nerve of this man. I hate to admit it, but now that I'm forty-one and I finally—maybe—understand what things like heartbreak are about, I completely agree with him.

There has to be a reason it's called soul music, right? Perhaps because that's where it grips you the most? In my short lifetime, I feel like I've seen every nationality, age group, and social class of singer do their jarring impersonation of a Black woman singing soul, but, cultural erasure be damned, it's like Tammi and Marvin sang: Ain't nothing like the real thing, goddamn it.

Why this song? I wasn't even breaking up with anybody the first time I heard it in an Oakland bar and the opening lines cut like a knife: "You've been the best at times / You walk me through my darkest days / Why must it turn around?" A few months later I was in New York,

on what I thought would be my final rock 'n' roll tour. I had been playing music since I was twelve and had achieved two goals I'd had since I was a kid: signing to the legendary indie label Sub Pop, and opening for Bikini Kill. My lifelong obsession with music had seemed to reach its logical conclusion. I decided it was time to get a new hobby—like baking, or veganism. I was saying goodbye to a part of my life, and I felt an internal shift: What next? Eventually I ended up in the back of a cab in Bushwick, listening to the song on repeat.

I have been listening to Nicole Wray (before the "Lady" days)—a California-born soul singer with that kind of irresistible, honey-dipped voice one can only be born with, no doubt—since the 1990s, when Missy Elliott gave her a vote of confidence by rapping on her debut single, "Make It Hot." But the thing I think I love most about "Piece of Me"—and really about every soul song about heartache, heartbreak, or love lost—is that its conviction is all in the delivery. You've either lived through loss or you haven't, and no amount of frenzied vocal trilling can make it otherwise. You can't fake this: "I'll let you take a piece of me. ... And if that's not enough, / I'll let you go peacefully." I tear up as I type it.

What Lady Wray did here is both genuine and colossal. Her voice transfixes me because she's got that element of soul—hell, of singing in general—that one cannot reach by just "hitting the right notes." That is only a small part; one must also land the character one is invoking. The perfect breakup song must also be a sort of theater, where the singer becomes the character fully. The very cadence of the song, her voice, sonically pristine, still spells out a certain longing and despair. Remember the definition of *soul*: the spiritual part of both human being or animal regarded as simultaneously immaterial and immortal. I am transformed every time I hear "Piece of Me," which by the end of the night will probably be close to thirty times.

"Piece of Me" gives that throwback feel—it's *heavy*. The digital world exists in a cloud, and the music itself feels as ethereal. For all our complaints about AI "taking over music" (I would like to point out that this was foreshadowed more than a decade ago when Auto-Tune became omnipresent, condensing all emotion into that tinny computer sound), "Piece of Me" sits in counterpoise, a song mixed through tape reels and heavy wooden machinery. It feels as if the song were creating its own black hole when it was made. Who can escape the condensed emotional singularity of a breakup song?

I grew up in Alabama, and though I defected to punk rock as a teenager, I was a child of the blues. My great-grandfather, Hard Rock Charlie, played the chitlin' circuits from Chattanooga to Chicago in the 1930s. His son J.J. Malone, who came to California in his youth to play music (much like I did), worked alongside the likes of Big Mama Thornton, John Lee Hooker, and Creedence Clearwater Revival. It's in my blood to understand a very true, very sad, and very beautiful song. But who among us has not experienced deep loss yet still found a way to keep going? "Piece of Me" taps into that universal fact, reiterating the troubled paradox of both love and life: We are forever heartbroken, and forever hopeful.

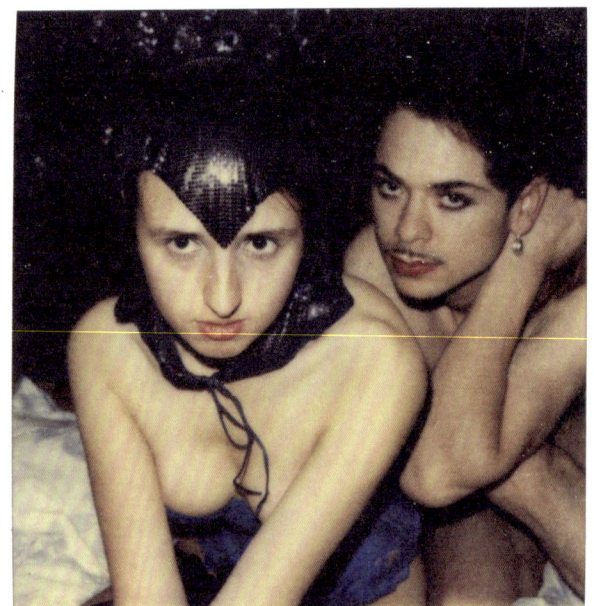

Tatiana, Reynaldo, Polaroid, ca. 1985

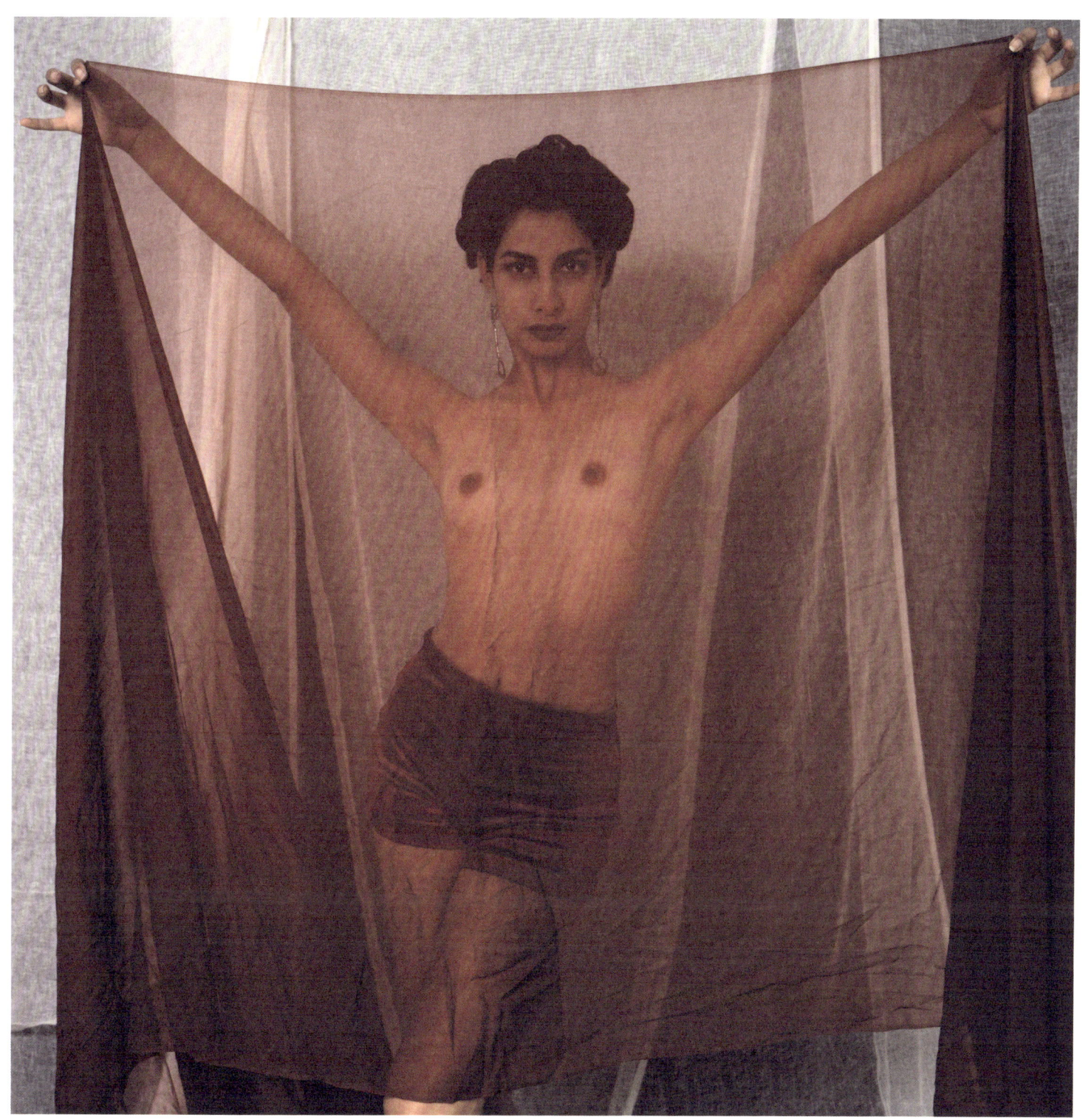

Cynthia, Hollywood, 1991

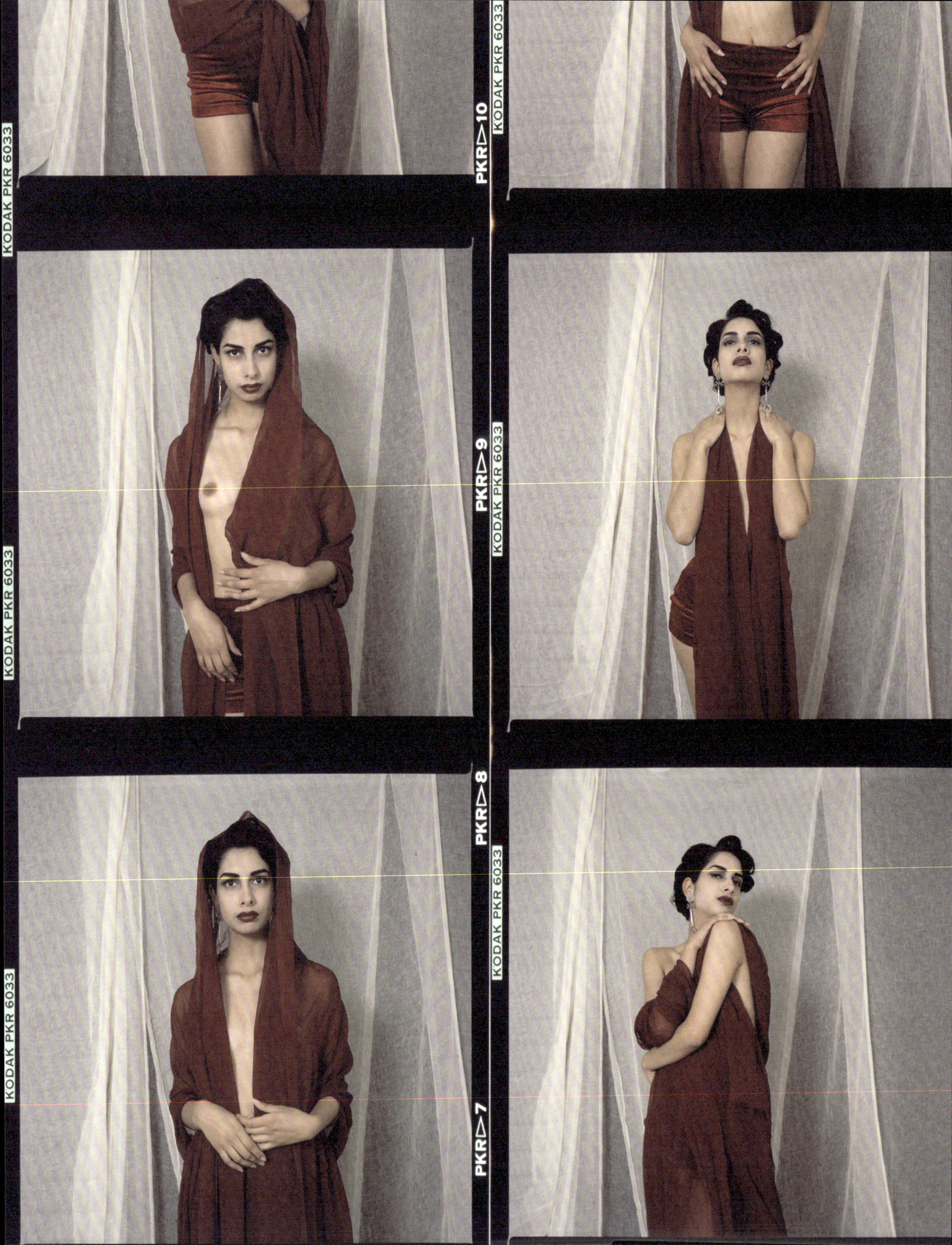
KODAK PKR 6033
PKR▷10
KODAK PKR 6033
KODAK PKR 6033
PKR▷9
KODAK PKR 6033
PKR▷8
KODAK PKR 6033
KODAK PKR 6033
PKR▷7

A NEW CAREER IN A NEW TOWN
—Hedi El Kholti

I'm walking from Midtown, around 60th Street, toward SoHo. I'm staying with Vyen, a friend from art school, and her girlfriend Christina. They are generous and welcoming, and the trip is coming to an end but I feel a little awkward and I'm afraid I've overstayed my welcome. A week is a long time to be in their small one-bedroom. I'm trying to find things to do outside. I have no particular plan until much later when I'm supposed to go to the Cock, a gay bar she insists I must visit before I leave: "You need to have fun," Vyen says imperatively, but I'm not so sure I can summon the energy. In New York I have time to kill and nowhere I really need to be. I'm stretching the minutes into hours, until I can finally close my eyes and sleep. It's windy and slightly cold for June and I didn't know what to wear. I'm passing long stretches of ugly unremarkable streets and buildings. A familiar feeling I've had while living in the twentieth arrondissement in Paris, or in LA when I first moved to Highland Park. When I'm in nondescript areas, alone, and I know nothing good could ever happen here, that I'm lost and about to be swallowed by my surroundings. I stop for a slice of pizza around 20th Street. That will do for dinner. I eat while walking, the Apartments' "What's the Morning For?" plays on my iPod, and I start crying softly, almost imperceptibly. I'm listening to the spectral slowed-down version from *Fête Foraine*, and although I don't fully grasp the lyrics, the drone of the guitar and the echo in his voice conjures abandonment and desolation. Maybe what gets me is when he repeats at the end, "Are you worn out? / Are you worn out?"

The trip was ill-conceived and had been a bust. I must have told Vyen that my life in LA was going nowhere. I had turned thirty-seven. Our publishing company had gone bankrupt despite producing a very successful book, and the freelance work I'd been doing for various publishers was coming to an end. The interviews I'd had that year didn't pan out. I got very close with TASCHEN. The editor I interviewed with, Jim Heimann, liked my portfolio, and they were about to release their version of a book I'd coedited that collected outrageous, lurid covers of men's adventure magazines from the '50s. Gary Indiana had reviewed it for the *LA Times.* It was the cover story of their Sunday literary supplement. We heard from a friend who worked there that Benedikt Taschen upon seeing our book threw it against the wall at a meeting in an outburst of rage. I naively thought that this could play in my favor. The assignment was to lay out a thirty-page mock-up of a sci-fi poster book at my own expense. They provided the images. I printed it and bound it. I'd also interviewed at the Hammer Museum, to do the catalogue of their first biennial, but didn't get the gig. The other publisher I was working with was closing and moving their content online. At that point Semiotext(e) felt like a very fragile proposition. My relationship with my partner of eight years had become noncommittal and sexless and I didn't trust it would go anywhere from there. We had peaked and it would just fade away slowly. I'd been in LA for twelve years and it felt like a cycle had completed its course. My dog had died in the dilapidated house I had moved into because it had a huge backyard for her to play in.

I needed a new career in a new town. I thought maybe I could get a low-paying corporate job in New York. I could maybe move here and start over. Turn our relationship long distance until it dissolved. A slow breakup. It would be closer to home and a rehearsal for returning to Paris, reacclimating myself to cramped spaces, unwelcoming faces, and cold weather. Vyen had arranged a meeting with a gay friend of theirs who was the chief marketing officer of Wenner Media. She chose and pressed the shirt I was to wear. It was a blue one I'd bought for the occasion a couple of days before flying to NY at Barneys in Beverly Hills. Everything was super expensive there, except on the top floor. I don't remember the brand but it was their "experimental" label. I bought two, a blue one and a white one.

I got a visitor sticker with my face on it and put it on my jacket, feeling very official. The doorman escorted me to the elevator. My mouth was dry. We met in his small, cramped office. He was about my age, give or take a couple of years. I was carrying my portfolio, a black-cardboard box that looked very professional that I bought from a friend. I filled it with books I had worked on: Feral House, Dilettante Press, and some Semiotext(e) ones too. And flyers, booklets, and press clippings of film festivals I had organized. It was heavy and I was sweating. I thought he might be impressed with my accomplishments, my taste, and that he could facilitate hiring me for some assistant designer position within his company. But he looked at my work with such contempt, the pornography and the garishness of it, and none of what I had done—the show I helped curate that traveled from NY to London and Paris, the books I had published—meant anything to him. He told me that I should start again at the bottom, by designing advertorial or direct-mail ads. He told me about his life, his partner and the weekend house they were restoring upstate, or maybe it was on Fire Island.

There was something in his tone that was almost scolding: "You need to start thinking about your future, give up the artsy stuff and enter the real world." Later when I described what happened to Vyen, I concealed how utterly defeated and disempowered I had felt. I thanked her profusely and told her it had been a great experience.

I'm walking from SoHo to Avenue A. I call my partner on the cell phone. We talk for a long time, all the way to the bar. He's loving on the phone and reassures me in the way that only he can. He tells me that I worry too much, that everything will be OK back in LA. I arrive at the bar too early and there's barely anyone there. I look at an older man intensely while he's making out with someone. He's a bit obnoxious, self-assured, my type. I move toward him later when he's alone. We start making out heavily for what seems to be an eternity. I give him a blow job on the sofa in the dark room as if this is the last thing I'll ever do in this world. By then the place is packed. I see people looking at us and I feel ashamed but I also don't care. That's how sex makes me feel, like I enter this space of desperation, like I am too eager, and that eagerness to please is the only thing I have to offer, and it's almost suspect. I go just a bit further than I need to. The shame of still replaying this old impulse I no longer believe in, looking for someone to save me, wanting to live in the shadow of someone who has figured it out, who walks the world as if they own it, who holds the knowledge to understand something I am crucially missing, something I need to learn or emulate. The smell of chlorine in *A Bigger Splash*, the scenes depicted in Hockney's paintings—a clear line and colors that don't bleed into one another, perfectly separated and orderly—act as more of an aphrodisiac than the smell of piss in a tearoom. Every hookup feels like an audition. Do I get the part?

We go outside for a break and I buy a pack of cigarettes in the convenience store next to the bar. We talk about our lives. I can't go to his place because his ex-boyfriend still lives there.

He suggests getting a hotel nearby but it feels too complicated. He writes his phone number on the receipt. I'll use it years later in a collage, placing it next to a cutout of a review of Jean Rhys's *Letters* by John Rechy that I found in a secondhand book, a photo of Montgomery Clift in *A Place in the Sun*, and the trio (Lauren Bacall, Betty Grable, Marilyn Monroe) from *How to Marry a Millionaire*, amongst other clippings. We go back into the bar. PIL's "This Is Not a Love Song" is playing. I remember how much I loved it in Casablanca in 1984. It seemed so subversive then. John Lydon's flippant vocal. I'd never heard someone sing that way. It's uncanny how it fits the moment. We're ready to go back to our respective places. I say, "Can you lead"—I don't have the energy to cut through the heavy, sweaty crowd—but he hears "Can you leave," and I see him quickly disappear without saying goodbye.

I'm back in New York a few months later for a book release. At the gallery where it's taking place, Chris Kraus hands me a copy of Heather Lewis's *Notice*. She says the author took her own life and the book is just too sad.

After the event I go to his apartment. We've been in touch. He's watching college football and seems uninterested in my presence. We are sitting on the sofa and he offers me a beer. Condensed awkward time. I deliver my usual constructed narrative, getting better at it each time. I've become adept at remaining as vague as possible, at practicing complete blandness and unreadability without coming across as aloof. I conveniently condense the years. I inadvertently touch his thigh as a signal to move to the bedroom. I'm a little high from the pot we smoke. He wants to fuck me but I am not sure. It's been a long time. I want something lighter, something I can forget as soon as I leave his place, something that leaves no trace. But he insists and I let myself drift. The sex is really intense. On the cab ride home, I feel grateful but I am not exactly sure why. Back in the studio where I'm staying, I start reading *Notice*. I stay up all night reading

it. It's frightening and exciting in equal measure and I recognize something of myself in the character. I copy three sentences from the beginning in my diary: "What the extra need is, the thing besides money? I've never pinned it down. I know it's there, though." And even if no money is exchanged tonight, it feels transactional, and never finding out what is exchanged resonates right then. Shards of past experiences left hanging suddenly resolved.

On the phone he tells me bluntly I'm too old for him. But still he comes to visit a month later for a weekend. I drive to the Four Seasons on Doheny to pick him up. We go to an Italian restaurant in West Hollywood. A pitcher of vodka that tastes like water. Back in the room, we're listening to Sade's *Lovers Rock*. It's the only thing I find in the stack of CDs they provide that I can endure. We have sex. I accidentally spill some amyl nitrite in his nose while he's fucking me. I can't sleep. In the morning I drive him to Highland Park. He wants to see where and how I live. Exit the freeway at Bridewell. Garbage-strewn streets, mattresses in vacant lots. It spells destitution. He walks into the house and I see it through his eyes, another familiar feeling. The ride back to West Hollywood is nearly silent.

I'm listening to Kate Bush's "Moments of Pleasure." I think of him. She sings, "The buildings of New York / Look just like mountains through the snow." I didn't experience them at Christmas in 2004. He disinvited me. I search in his emails for his description of how magical the city is that time of year but I don't find anything. There's a gap and I deduct that it must have happened on a phone call. But I do find the email when he tells me not to come after I have purchased my plane ticket: "I'll make this short without going into too many details, but J. and I are trying to make a go at our relationship again. We've been spending a lot of time together. Therefore, I think it wouldn't work out if you visited me for the New Year's holiday. I feel bad as I do like you, but I am in love with Jeffrey. I'd prefer we didn't contact each other, so as not to confuse the situation. I'm really sorry to have messed up your plans, but from my perspective, it's the right thing to do."

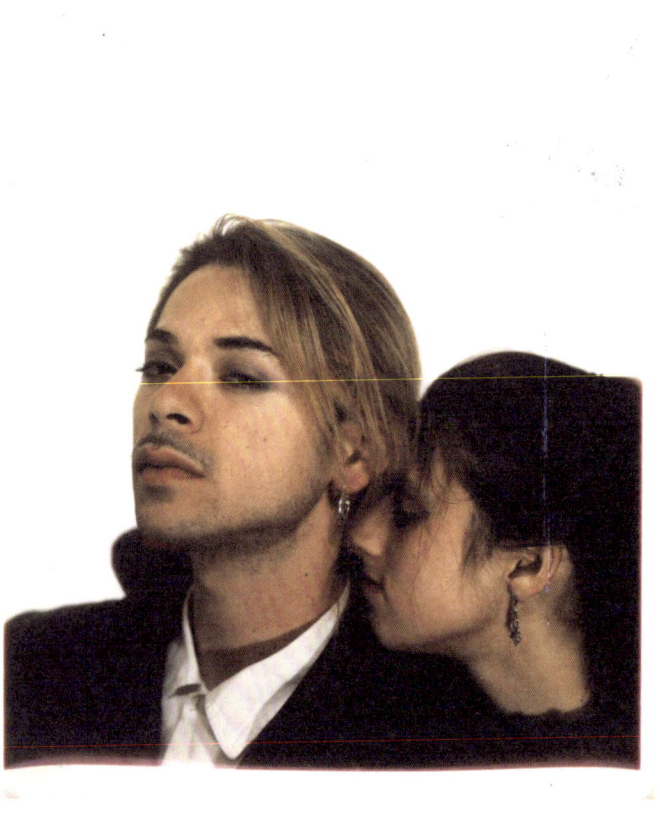

Reynaldo, Tatiana, ca. 1985

QUE SUEÑES CON LOS ANGELITOS, YA QUE ERES UNO TAMBIÉN
—Raquel Gutierrez

Ernesto had begun to make these yard sales a daily act and I couldn't bear to look out my window facing a street strewn with his long-sleeve shirts, backpacks, wallets, leather belts, and the scuffed dress shoes he had probably worn to the job he had just lost a few weeks back. It was a year before the housing market would crash and I would, myself, stop being gainfully employed.

He looked thinner. He admitted he was struggling with addiction. A clear-eyed admission. He worked in public health and he was more than familiar with the conditions that undergirded his habitual use. There was no need to skirt around it. He had been dating someone and it ended. And something needed to absorb the shock. I pursed my lips and nodded sympathetically. Drugs were fun. We did them in the club. That fun could follow anyone of us home. Disrupting the boredom that comes with ache. Or a way to hide from the world that determined how we could afford our lives.

He worked in HIV prevention. Case management? Peer counseling? I had no idea except everyone I knew seemed to do one or the other. Being queer was never a barrier in that field. It was a space where so many could be respectable. Upstanding. I always wanted to party and everyone I knew who worked in HIV prevention always knew of good parties. It was a professionalization of pleasure, but I was always the amateur. It never occurred to me to say anything to Ernesto about moderation. Meth was addictive and I tended to stay away from everything that wasn't fertilized by shit.

My addictions were harder to discern but often came burdened with a U-Haul punchline. The sunk-cost fallacy strong-armed me into remaining entangled with the wrong people.

If you have ever enjoyed a queer social life in Los Angeles, much of that pleasure was likely derived from the networks that enabled your ability to have good housing. Once you have a place to lay your troubles, then everything feels possible. I had a friend once connect me with their coworker whose fourplex had an upcoming vacancy. That was Ernesto, and I had jumped at the chance to make a good impression on him just so I could live in a neighborhood adjacent to the neighborhoods I could once afford on my own.

I insisted on living with someone who had wanted to break up with me despite her overpowering fear of abandonment. *Me gusta la mala vida.* That tension pushed-pulled us toward the apartment in question: a 1,200 sq. ft. one-bedroom Spanish number with a lavender-tiled bathroom, no yard, and a garage space we couldn't use. It was not ideal but it was cheap and near our favorite watering holes. Silver Platter. Silverlake Lounge. Remy's on Temple. Little Joy. Akbar.

What haunts me now is not failed cohabitation but the image that comes in and out of focus of the man who was our neighbor. Ernesto was from Mexico. He spent much of his adulthood in Silver Lake throughout the 1990s. The kind of queer man raising a SOLO cup to Chaka Khan performing at the Hoover Stage many Sunset Junctions ago. A regular at Le Barcito, Cuffs, Woody's, Circus of Books. *Siempre en busqueda.*

Ernesto was a decade older than I. We would entertain a neighborly smoke, recounting the week's shreds of gossip, and he would recall his failure to buy an old Craftsman on Micheltorena for $150K. This was just before one of us brought up our landlords who lived far away in the San Gabriel Valley but who would threaten us with eviction if we parked our cars in the wrong place or if we—God forbid—had pets in our apartments. I had two huge pugs—a bonded pair who were the products of a lesbian divorce. I could not resist them—they were a source of unconditional love when love had become too hard to earn. I was struggling to keep these dogs from being discovered.

I remained on a sinking ship. And I woke up every other morning with a hangover and an inability to remember important events, like the landlord coming to check on the broken toilet in the first-floor apartment below me. Or that was the pretext. He knew about the daily yard sales. I answered Ernesto's call that morning reminding me that George was on his way over and he had forgotten to lock his door and was afraid the old man would snoop around and find the drugs he had out on his coffee table. I said I would take care of it, as I had my own panic to contend with and nowhere to stash my dogs.

The intimacy of that necessity brought me such shame. Needing help brought me anxiety. In hindsight I could have asked many of my friends to help me out, but I was disempowered the way a Brown LA butch often is—the butt of jokes, the site of twisted desire. I was full of bad ideas back then. Hiding under Ernesto's bed with my two cream-colored, wrinkly faced dogs, panting into oblivion. A little Ziploc bag moistened in my sweaty palm. I was careful not to let the pugs lick my fingers.

I was always embarrassed around Ernesto, even when he was too zonked out to notice the humiliation I carried at knowing he had overheard the scores of heated arguments that transpired that first year, next to his apartment. I nodded out of custom every time we passed each other on the staircase to our apartments. Our walls barely holding the intermingled wreck of our intimacies.

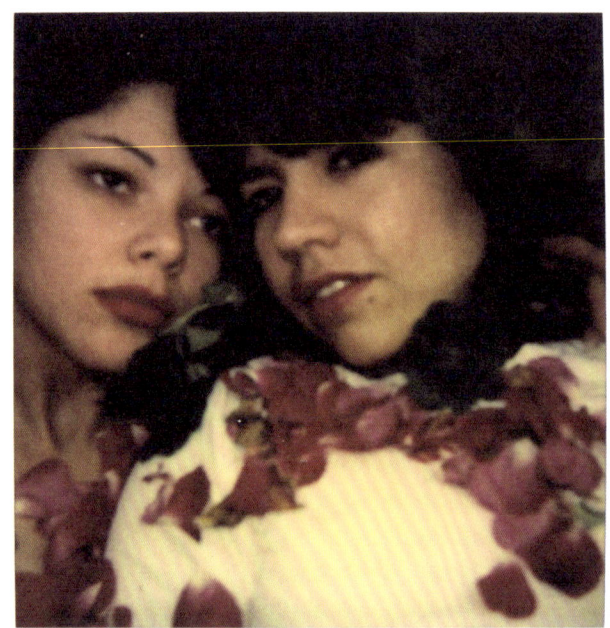

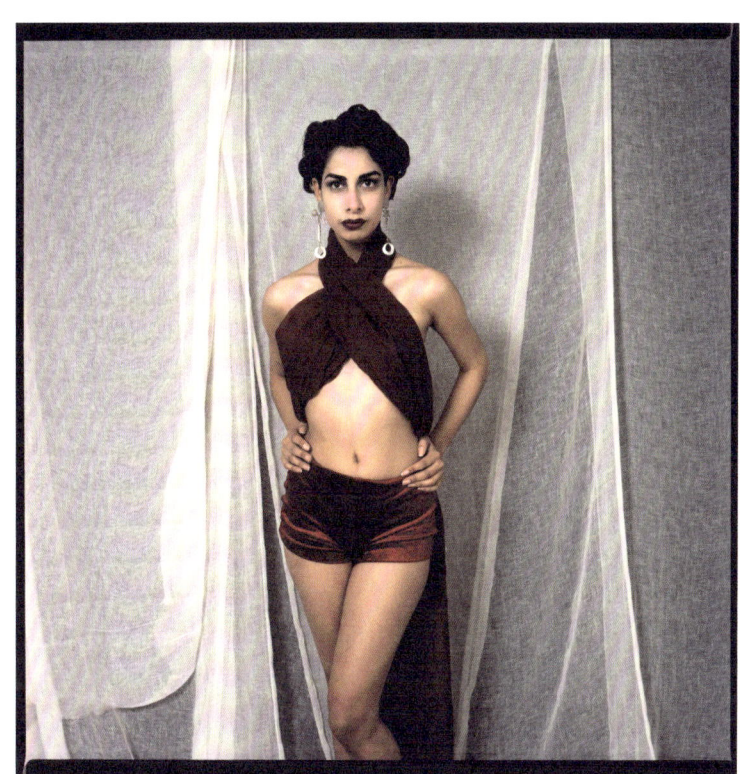

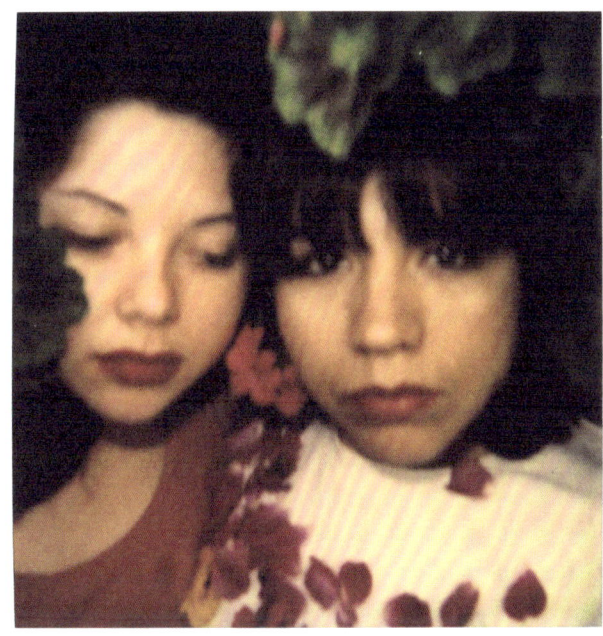

LEFT & ABOVE: *Connie, Cindy*, Polaroids, ca. 1987
Cynthia, Hollywood, 1991

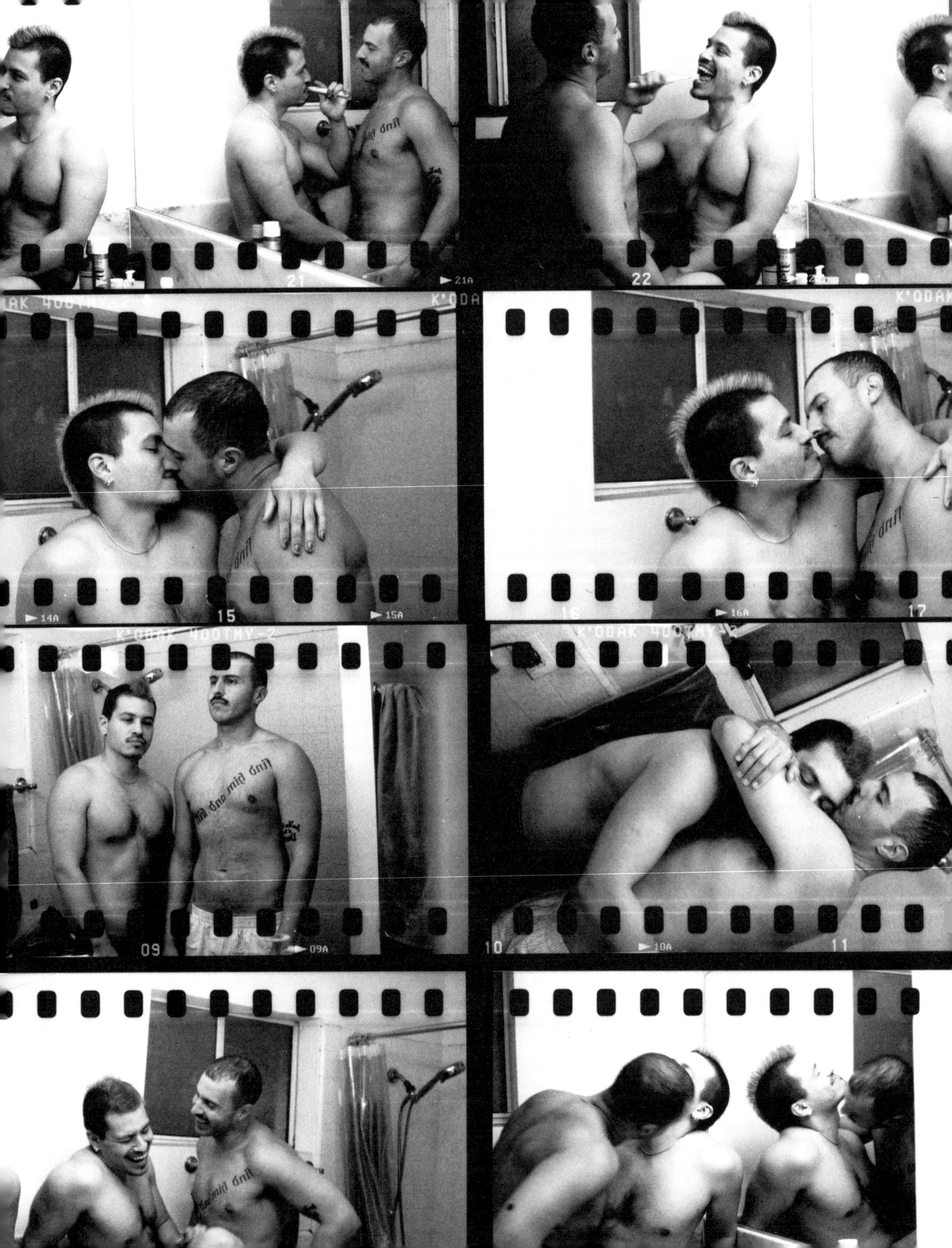

SPUN
—Justin Torres

Whose is the night-long breathing
That keeps a man alive?
— A. E. Housman

An early heat wave has me up just after dawn, out on the balcony in my skivvies, watering the tomato plants, the pepper plants, the bougainvillea, and thinking about the morning light in Los Angeles, and the way the poppies slant to catch the sun, as if leaning out for benediction. I squat before my potted herbs, worry the leaves, looking for signs of growth, signs of damage. The news filters out from the kitchen radio, all of it bad. They do not speak of the real ongoing genocide, but a long segment on a fake, white, genocide. A young man calls up from the street, *The more you stare, the better they grow!* It takes a moment to understand it's me he's addressing: teasing me about my little garden. I rise and mumble a too-soft reply. The look on his face tells me he's only pretended to hear, or maybe he's only now clocking that I'm in my underwear. He's cute, though young, with wide-set eyes and a half-suppressed smile, and I'm not sure if he's laughing at me or flirting. I play the line again in my mind, *The more you stare ...* Everything feels small and insufficient, tending my little seedlings, worrying about distant atrocities, gazing dumbly as the news comes in. The broadcast moves on to the weather— tomorrow a drop in temperature, the return of the marine layer. Something about the combination of watching the handsome kid vanish around the corner, and that phrase, "marine layer," finds me standing in mist, in memory, up

north with my ex, who loved to talk in weatherman phrases, marine layers and microclimates. We stand on a hilltop and watch great whorls of fog roll in. The low clouds swallow the Golden Gate Bridge, and soon enough we're enveloped in fog ourselves. What looked so sublime from the outside—clean and bright and gentle— inside feels only gray and damp and indeterminate. That would have been some twenty-five years ago. We'd left New York more or less on a whim, but with no intention to return. He'd inherited a minivan from his mother, and we'd crammed in all our worldly shit, so that the side and rear windows were entirely blocked and it was impossible to know what was coming up behind. All across the country, we stuck to the slow lane, saying a little prayer whenever circumstance forced us to merge. We arrived in June. I was twenty-one, and he was twenty; we'd both dropped out of school. He was strikingly gentle, with an open face, and strangers often spoke to him kindly, commenting on small things. That never happened to me. We knew nothing much of the world, and nothing of the local climate, which, to our disappointment, was not at all summerlike. The June Gloom, everyone called it. That was when his weather fascination began, the West Coast seasons so unlike the rhythms we'd known, and he loved to pull me up a hill to watch the low clouds of fog and the sun setting on the Pacific, and he'd name the distant trees, new to us—sequoia, valley oak, blue gum eucalyptus. We'd soon learn that we arrived shortly after the dot-com bubble, whatever the hell that was, had burst. This bursting was much discussed in those early months, and from what I could glean, was seen as a net positive for the poor and the punks facing displacement, though nothing could stop what the internet was doing to media, running the local rags out of business, devastating revenue from the back pages, where the escorts paid to post a brief caption, a phone number, and a photo. I miss the simple analog anonymity of those photos—an under-wear bulge, or a naked torso, or a head in profile, face turned toward the shadows—and how much was left to imagine. A few of the new friends we'd made were part-time escorts, and they had funny stories about the transition to digital hooking, where suddenly clients de-manded snaps of the full trifecta, face, cock, and hole. Finally, September came, and with it the heat, and we found ourselves in the true, deep, fogless days of summer. I don't know why I am remembering all that now, in my undies, on this balcony, except that maybe the sun on my skin always makes me horny, or maybe the angle and intensity of this California light on my middle-aged body stirs some memory of that younger body, driven by restless desire. Another memory: my boyfriend and I lying, groaning in the heat, a very rare day in the high nineties, fantasizing over an AC unit, or a swimming pool, and him saying, *We're too poor not to sweat.* A sweet memory, colorful—we'd finally found a room we could afford and painted the walls canary yellow. We lay on the mattress, not touching, too hot to fool around, but then too naked not to. He pulls my hand over to feel how hard he is, and soon we work ourselves into a sheen. When we finish, he rolls over to show me a magazine (was it *SPIN*?) stuck to the sweat of his back. It must have been lying open on the bed. He shakes and shakes and the magazine stays stuck, the pages flapping around, and I shout with laughter. We make a game of it, purposefully pressing our slick cocks into torn-out magazine pages and then prancing out into the kitchen, to startle and amuse the room-mates. It would have been shortly after that

day that I posted a silly little ad on Craigslist, in search of a man with a pool. I thought I might have a swim and make a little money. Did I really think just behind every grand Victorian was an in-ground? No one had a pool, at least no one within walking distance, but still I received some offers to cool me down. One man promised to crank the AC to the mortuary setting, which tickled me. I replied. His place was a studio, not a particularly spacious one. On the television, a quad split of talking heads barked in commemoration of the one-month anniversary of the planes flying into the World Trade Center. The screen cut to the images, on a loop—impact, collapse, faces covered in ash. *What have we learned?* they asked. *How has the world changed? Who else must pay to make us whole?* We didn't have a television at home—the eight of us, little punks crammed together in a railroad apartment—we had drugs and books and a shared computer with dial-up. I hadn't seen the televised images since those early days of aftermath, and so I found it all surprisingly naked, the bloodlust of these pontificators, the insistence on guilt by proximity, the demand to bomb the entire region, invade nations, the hunger for collective punishment, for revenge from wherever, whomever, the disregard for the innocent, all of it morbidly mesmerizing. (All the news is bad, and it's come around again.) Eventually the man noticed my distraction and clicked off the set. Then sudden quiet. I noticed him noticing me, looking down to my mis-matched socks, which I feared must seem intentional, and I slid one foot on top of the other. I was shy back then, but also pretending to be more so. The decor was the next thing I noticed, how the floral-patterned curtains actually matched the bedspread, and this made me wonder if this man, who was probably in his forties or fifties, did not actually live there. If, perhaps, it was a bed and breakfast. But no, too much clutter, too much mail shoved into a carved-wood organizer, a decorative object made functional. All his furnishings were plush, the sofa overstuffed, an uncomfortable amount of fabric for such a tight space. I wanted to ask, Had he inherited this place from his grand-mother? Or had he eaten her? I tried to think of some joke about the Big Bad Wolf, but instead I pointed toward the top of the curtain and asked, *Are those called "cornices"?* I knew they were not. They were valances. *No clue*, the wolf said. And so I launched into a long story about how back in New York, I worked briefly as an errand boy for an interior designer, and how one day my boss took me on a long drive. I don't remember where he said we were headed; the whole time he spoke glumly, obsessively, about the various stresses in his life, basically just money and family, both of which he seemed to have plenty of, until we arrived at an empty lot, a pullout spot, which seemed to be almost underneath the Verrazzano, and I thought, *He's either going to blow me or kill me*, but instead he started talking about how truly awful I was at every aspect of my bullshit job. A job, he said, for a simpleton. He cataloged my ineptitude, all the times I brought back the wrong swatches, missed orders, spilled drinks, and he kept going until he was laughing so hard tears came into his eyes. I had always found him to be stretched and dizzy and overwhelmed; I had just assumed he hardly noticed me fucking around, but as it turned out, I had not escaped his attention. *I'm firing you*, he finally said, *that's what this is*. Only now, on this balcony, when I must be the same age or older than he was then, do I realize that he liked me, that he was amused and almost proud of my disinterest and complete lack of ambition. I thought his world was bullshit, and he liked me for that, and I realize I've come to feel that same appreciation for the young people I meet. Anyway, I recounted all that to the Big Bad Wolf and he liked the story, he said that he was fond of the personal touch. I told him I'd have preferred the blow job. Or a better job, or a raise. *At least he didn't murder you*, the wolf said. And I looked at him with comic suspicion. *It's never the ones you suspect*, I replied. Then

he wrapped his fist around the pretend handle of a pretend knife and pretend stabbed me, several times. We fucked. I remember thinking, *He's good, this dude.* Simple, straightforward instructions. Verbs, gently modified. *Take off. Don't rush. Unbuckle. Slide down. Step out. Turn, halfway. Bend, a little less. Show me. Get there. Look right here, kid. I want you to look. Look here.* I did not believe I was worth the money he was paying, and I worried about his finances, or maybe "worry" is inaccurate, but I speculated about his finances with some concern, some empathy. I did not understand how and why he lived in that place, the cream carpet, the close attic air, the wallpaper. I thought I was too thin, toothy, ugly, both too crooked and too smooth. Each time a client first got a look at me in the flesh—sliding into the passenger seat, or scuffing my shoes across the doormat, or breathing heavy at the top of the stairs, or shaking rain from my hair in the vestibule—each time, I thought, *He must be disappointed*. The angles and the poses of the photos I posted made me look slightly more than I was. Now of course I realize they were just glad to find me as young as I claimed online, and glad to find that I looked even younger still. I never thought, *I could charge more*. And then I'm back on the balcony, out of the reverie and thinking how I should chase down that kid who passed by and teased me about my gardening—the pluck!—and I should tell him to demand more, whatever it is he's selling. I wonder where he is headed, so early, and it occurs to me that he's probably high. I remember that little half smile, I remember it for myself. Probably not early for him, but very late, the end of a long night. *Demand more*, I'd like to tell him. From the wolves. From all of us wolves. Today will be a scorcher, day three of a heat wave. Our house is old for LA and built to stay cool. Very soon, I know, I'll need to go inside and escape. Either that, or take to the street.

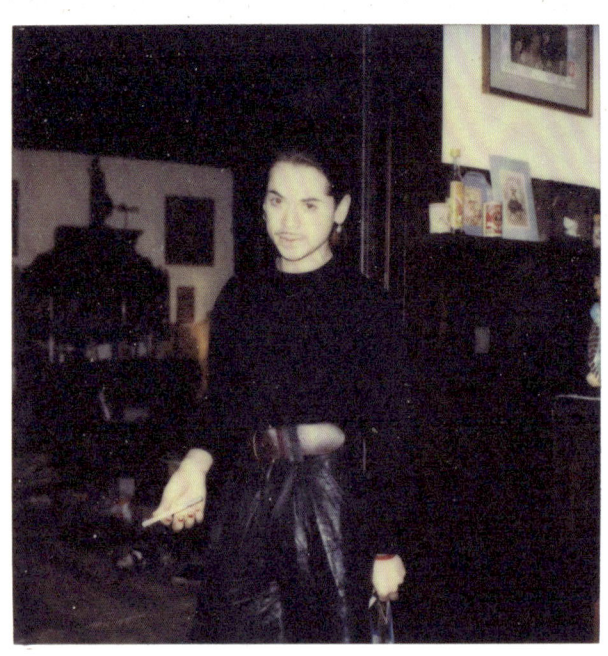

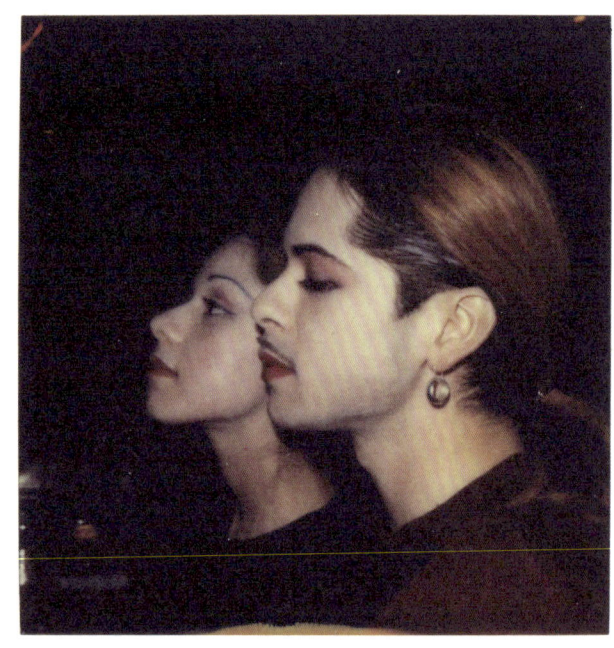

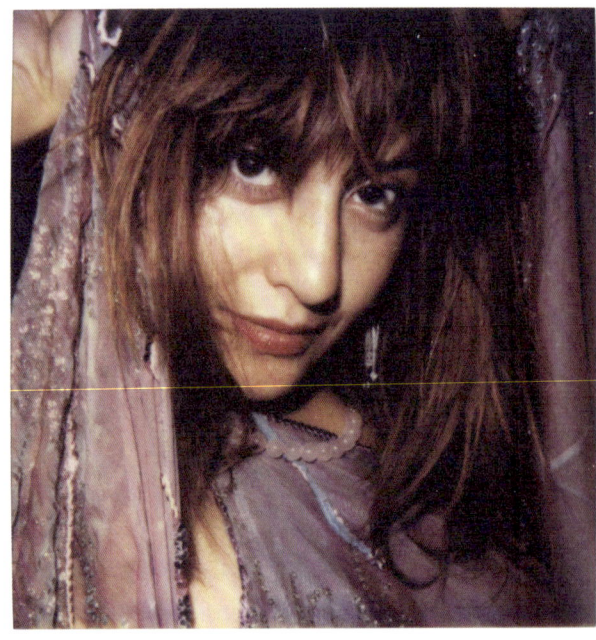

Reynaldo, Martine, Patricia, Polaroids, ca. 1985
RIGHT: *Connie, Echo Park*, 1997

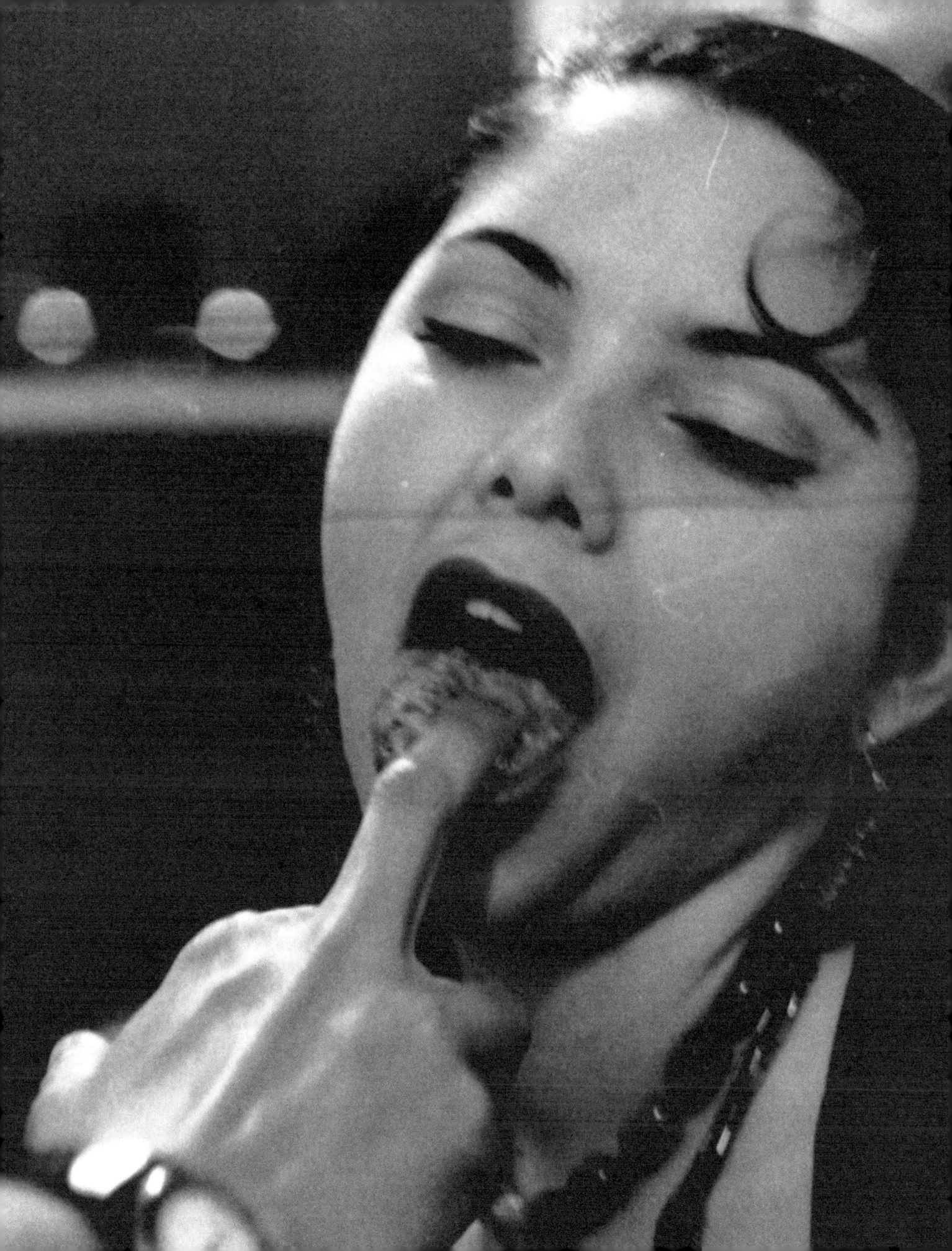

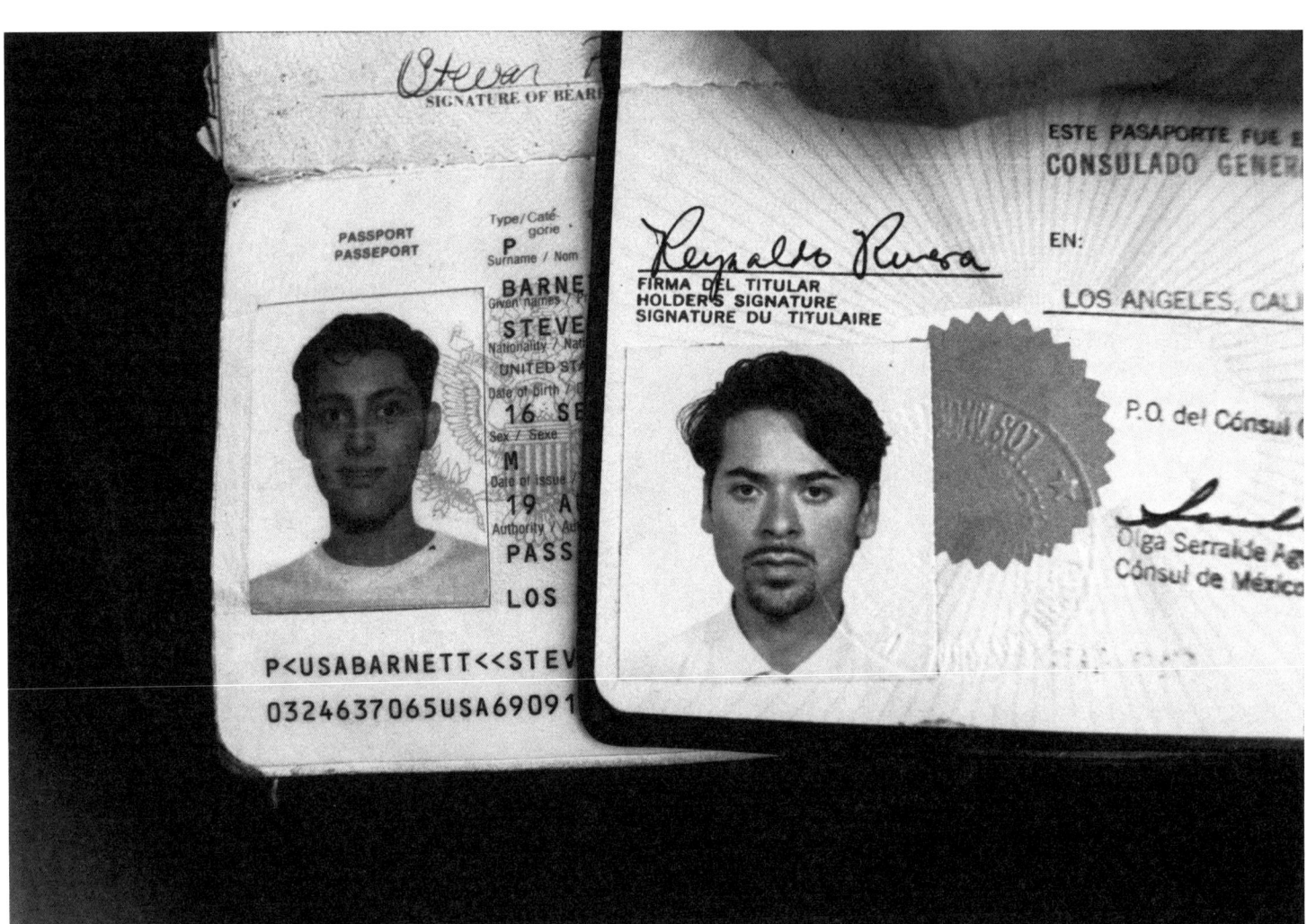

Steven, Reynaldo, Passports, 1990

SIGHT
—Gil Cuadros

At first I think it must be the fires and the winds, miniscule ash floating through the air and into my eyes. Or the dry Santa Anas pushing down the hillsides, raising the temperature till moisture vanishes, making the edges of my eyes blood red. On the freeway, driving to my doctor, I see clouds of black smoke billowing off the mountains, strange aerial formations of crows and seagulls, twisting and turning like a swath of fabric falling in air. These are the signs, clues written in some ancient script, and I want to know what it all means. The doctor looks at me, her hair pulled back away from her face, as if she were asking,

"Can't you read this language?" She is obviously frustrated, her fingers snap against each other, disbelief in their sounds. I must look ridiculous, sitting there, a smile across my mouth. She pulls out a model of a large eye the size of a bowling ball. She begins to disassemble the eye, the cornea, the retina, the optical nerve. I push the parts away from me; I can see that everything, everyone in her office has a glow around their bodies, some with colors more distinct, others thin and wavering. Even more unsettling, some people leave trails of light, a residue that takes a long time to dissipate. Occassionally a trail will curl upward, a large snake the color of ochre, poised as if ready to attack any nearby person. The doctor wants me to understand, says without this medication there is no hope; without this medication you are sure to lose all the sight that you have; the small discomfort you'll experience will be worth it compared to the alternative; what is one more drug to you? She is telling the truth, I can see it being said in the gold light that temporarily covers her body, can taste it under my tongue like a hazelnut liqueur. I tell her, "No, thank you." That is all I have to say and she starts shaking her head. The bones in her neck pop; she tells me I am foolish. By the time I near home, the drive has become more dangerous. My peripheral vision diminishes, the crest of my forehead, the crown of my head seems to ignite. My other senses revel in new-found power, guiding me through a maze of streets, using the scent of jacarandas and freshly cut,

96

large-leaf philodendrons, the feel of bumps on the road, the dampness along my arm that means I've come into my underground parking space. People seem entranced with me as I step into the lobby of my apartment building; there is vague recognition but no recall of my name. I hear a few whisper, "Who?" They look at me as one would a religious painting, a lamentation. I am temporarily blinded by the various colors spewing out from their bodies, can see one man is covered with nothing more than white static, while another woman has tendrils of bluish light connected to everyone she's near. For a moment the inside of my chest seems hollow. I smile briefly; by now I am used to people not recognizing me because of weight loss, the waste of my muscles, but this is different. An elderly woman holds the elevator for me, her arm braced against the closing door. A warm tingle runs down my throat, informs me that she is not well, some perceived similarity with myself. I face her and smell lavender, old wool, sweat like eucalyptus oil. Her hair is white, I know, but I see tumors instead, the stench of black rotted fruit, dappling her brain. Her heart is erratic and I feel as if it is my own and that I am the one who will fall soon. I want to touch her. I sense the elevator aching to lift us up. She is saying something to herself, I hear her say the word "God" with the warm buzz of bees and wooden flutes in her mouth. I feel my palm near her shoulder and her body begins to change, slippery as mercury. Now I can see an amber light emanating from

97

her stomach, her head. She is unsure of why she feels better, but she takes it like a gift of inestimable worth. In my room I lie back, close and open my eyes and all is darkness. My ears hum, and the woolen blanket beneath my fingers seems unbearably rough. For a second I think I have fallen asleep, and now it is late, the street lights are turned off. Somewhere in the house, my roommate watches TV. Miles away I can sense my folks readying themselves for sleep, the rustle of their bedsheets, the sounds they make using the bathroom. My brother far away in another state begins to open a can of beer; I hear him spray the fluid across his hand. It used to make me sick, the thought of my family, but now I see it as a legacy I will not understand till much later. Through the window, a man watches me: he is white, bright as if a hundred candles were burning inside him. He sees that I am ready, calls more of his people to the window. At first I pretend not to know what he offers, can taste meat in my mouth, blood on my lips. There is no judgement on whatever I do; he is just there for me. Before I go, I want to tell my roommate what he needs to take to stay alive, the astragalus I have in my closet, this new experimental treatment out of Korea. I want to call my ex-lover and explain that I really understand why he had to leave me, his heart battered like bronze from all the other deaths in his life. I want my mother to know I know where all her anger comes from, and if I could just touch a certain spot on her body, near her breastbone, it would all be

98

released, she would always be warm after that. But I have come to the end, thoughts of the world seem woven of thread, thinly disguised, a veil. I let the angels consume me, each one biting into my body, until nothing is left, nothing but a small glow and even that begins to perish.

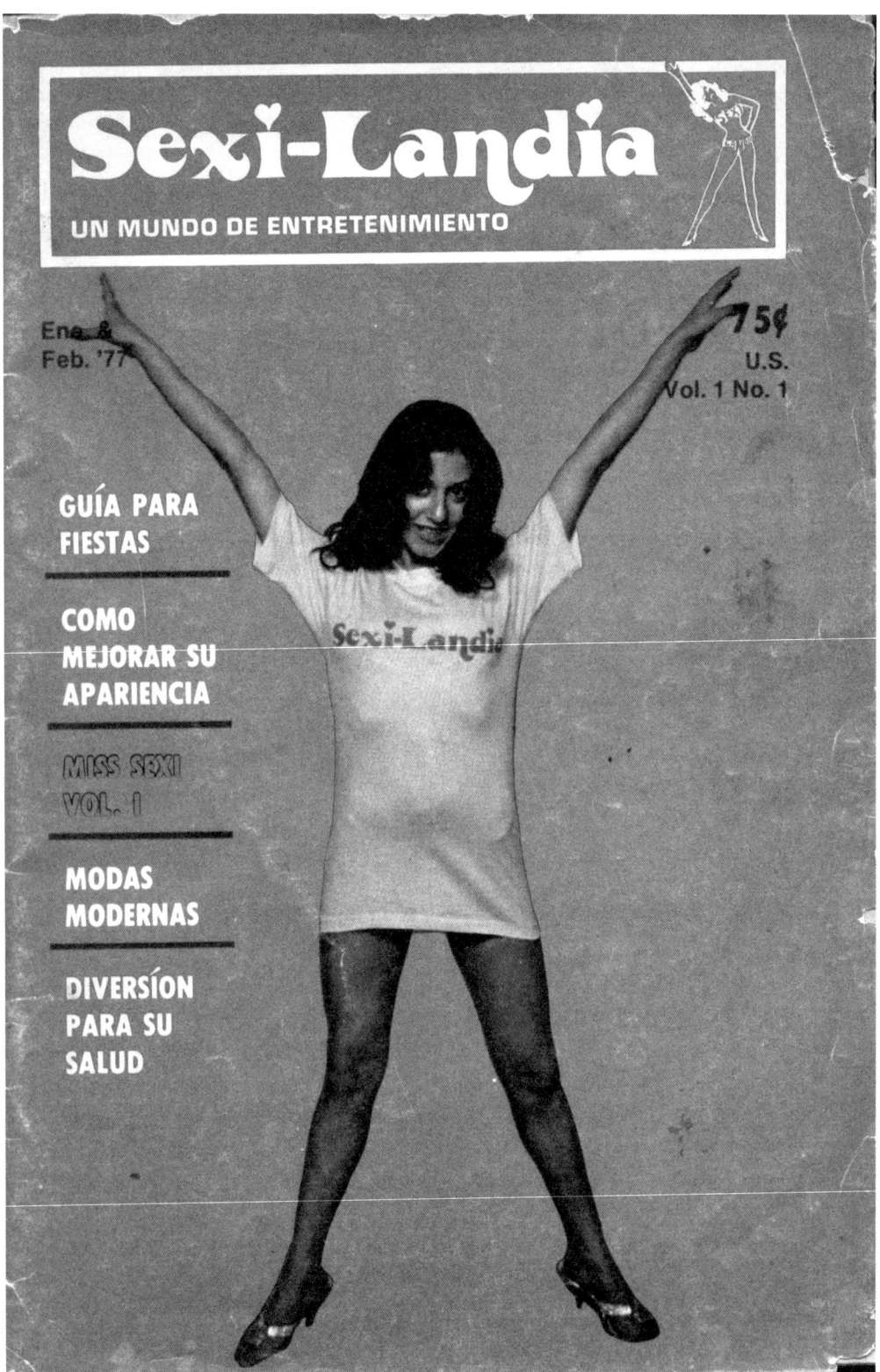

BLUE
—Lauren Mackler

We're moving at a clip, taking one of those long, meandering night walks through the streets of Pasadena that Reynaldo Rivera treks every night without fail. "Monika told me, a long time ago, that the body can't feel pleasure at the same time as pain," he recalls. "She was speaking on behalf of masturbating. She was saying that back in the old days they would masturbate women during childbirth, because the body cannot feel pain and pleasure at the same time." We pass derelict mansions and lush, fragrant gardens. Rivera is an amateur of decorative eras and is fascinated by architecture. He's listing his life's love stories to me with occasional interruption for an anecdote about a building. People rarely walk around here, much less at night, and once we veer off the main streets, we are alone. Rivera is talking about pleasure and pain because he is meditating on their overlap. Do we seek one to avoid the other? Does one inevitably lead to the other, like two sides of a lever? "Hope is a four-letter word," he muses while walking. He is making this list because he's articulating his position on love—love is hope, love is pain, hope is poison—and ultimately trying to clarify the photographs that compose this book. He calls them his Blue Series.

The photographs in Blue were taken between the 1980s and the present, though many of the older images are difficult to place. At their core, they are sex photos, a mix of raw and erotic shots taken candidly during sex, or right before or right after. They were taken for pleasure, many as acts of self-capture, and often left undeveloped or tucked away for decades. "Never meant to be seen," Rivera says, with the whiff of a promise unkept. Until recently they had never been printed, save for a few pinned to his darkroom wall for self-use. It was only about three years ago that one—the picture on the cover of this book—slipped out of a pile of old prints, and Rivera decided to look for others. But the more he considers it, the more the Blue Series grows, and what it comprises becomes looser. The series now mingles sex acts and

acts of self-presentation… It erodes boundaries between lovers, friends, siblings, and some near strangers. There are couples making out with the kind of abandon that flavors the early days of love; there are people getting ready for a night out, relishing the privacy of the moment and the salacity of their exposure; and then there are more posed images, staged in the streets that Rivera calls his studio, where he is aiming to do something less spontaneous, more intentional regarding representation. In this book, the photos are organized in step with how a life is lived—bare intimacy alongside public performances of love. He is in it too. There are also self-portraits and moments of handing his camera over to his lover or friend. There are many reflections and many more pictures by Rivera, which can be glimpsed on his apartment walls within the photos, like a hall of mirrors, in infinite regress. The images swell with confidence, they exude a feeling of ownership over one's body, and over the other. And to Rivera they are a personal collection. In 1971, the Peruvian singer Lucha Reyes—"my patron saint," Rivera often claims—first sang "Propiedad Privada." Through the song, she embodies the longing to own—to brand, even—one's lover: to inflect a person and a place with impossible permanence. Reyes describes a green, jealous flame, burning, and a possessiveness that fringes on murder—the desire to feel (steal?) her lover's breath. And death does feature here too—the little death of an orgasm, and the big death—since many of Rivera's subjects, fixed on the page in peak moments of pleasure, have since died.

I've been looking at the series for years now, images buried in folders, on shelves in Rivera's many rooms. An image for Blue might be solitary on a sheet of negatives that otherwise carries birthday parties, improvised fashion shoots, protests, dinners, and nights out on the streets of LA. During Rivera's recent survey at MoMA PS1, a reviewer for *The New York Times* asked whether these images had a right to be put on display. She was questioning the consent of the people within them and the scenes that might be better served by being left unexposed. From Rivera's perspective, posing *is* consent, and each subject is double cast as the main character of their own story and as an extra in Rivera's. (Rivera's first love is cinema, and the stark spotlights of silent film, alongside the ethically complex character of noir, are always present in his shadowy images.) But her question is valid. Does consent evolve over time? Is consenting to Rivera in the intimacy of a room the same as consenting to us—the viewer/voyeur that we are—decades later, in the pages of a book? Does an image innately accrue universality and publicness over time? The subjects of these images are visibly complicit, and likewise Rivera implicates himself, turning the lens on his own vulnerabilities—naivetés and infidelities—in ways that muddy a clear moral stance on the exposition of others, and taken a step further, raise the question of who else might be telling these stories, if not those involved.

In 1969, Andy Warhol premiered his erotic film *Blue Movie*. The film depicts an ordinary afternoon spent by two lovers in a daylight-drenched New York City apartment. Viva and Louis Waldon talk to each other about their lives, about the ongoing Vietnam War; they shower and have sex before a camera that they almost wholly ignore, save a few furtive glances and a climactic interruption. It's a portrait of intimacy, really, more than sex (though Warhol had set out to call the film *Fuck*, alongside his other monotopic films *Sleep* and *Eat*). Supposedly, it is titled *Blue* because Warhol mistakenly used tungsten film to shoot in daylight and one of the sex scenes of the film emerged with a prominent turquoise hue—though it's likely also "blue" because this was a fashionable euphemism for the coarse or the obscene, especially in literature and film. The film ran for a week at the Garrick Theatre in NYC before it was banned, the theater's staff arrested, the reel confiscated for being irredeemably pornographic.

The law dictates what is obscene, but it cannot define what is erotic—a perception as subjective as color. The erotic here—in *Blue Movie*, in the Blue Series—is not the synthetic bodies and calculated images of advertising or entertainment, it's the messy, wet, candid physicality of real bodies and relationships. What was broadcast in *Blue Movie* was also a method. "Perpetual documentation was the zeitgeist," Chris Kraus tells me about these years in NYC. In 1969, once the new technology of portable cameras was made available on the market, artists and citizen journalists took to recording life and reporting from the ground. The camera, as media historian Deirdre Boyle would put it, was "a witness and a weapon." Another example, contemporary to Warhol, is filmmaker Michel Auder (Viva's partner shortly after *Blue Movie* was released). Scholar C. Ondine Chavoya describes Auder's work as an "anti-spectacle approach to chronicling lives," one that complicates the notion of the "video voyeur" since the camera is often set up and left rolling and the filmmaker occasionally enters the frame. This is a step away from Warhol, whose chaste outsiderness to the intimacy he is directing elides him from the scene and gives the more conventional impression of a study, even

if a sensual study of the erotic. Rivera's camera is an extension of his body, and the Blue Series, fluid as ever, is a hybrid of both types of practices, the insider (Auder's, and others') and the outsider (Warhol's), a mix of naturalistic depictions of life and then some artifice too: the way one primps for the mirror, the way one performs one's own life, how Rivera may actually be heavily directing a session.

*

"It helps that he's hot," a friend says while I'm trying to intellectualize the swell of feeling I have when I work on this series. "The images are just pleasurable to look at." But what differentiates the Blue Series from the simply pornographic is that these images are not about selling eros—though they may arouse the viewer, they are less about an exterior performance of desire and more about an interior one, or how one sees one's own desirability. In that sense, they find kinship in the legendary Bruce of Los Angeles's crisp depiction of the male figure through his 1950s bodybuilder series, or Myriam Boulos's contemporary live-wire scenes of queer Lebanese life. They also echo works of other "participant observer" artists: Peter Hujar's direct, tender portraits; Brian Weil's enigmatic, scratched documents of the queer communities he embedded in; Dash Snow's lustful, chafed Polaroids of friends. These are artists who lived and died alongside their subjects—who were present in their scenes. Like these atemporal examples, the images in the Blue Series are also situated within the intimacy of queer family, something that is within and beyond sexuality, and involves another kind of parenting and coming of age.

"My experience of sex was tainted by death," Rivera continues, and it's hard to look at these images and their subjects without talking about AIDS, even though that is not Rivera's priority and the series has been enlarged to contend with more than that—with a wider range of illnesses, even. But as Rivera puts it, "A man my age cannot tell his coming-of-age sex story without the impact that gay cancer had on everything. I started having my sexual awakening with AIDS, we both came up at the same time. In 1979." Rivera and his sister Herminia spent formative years of their childhood in San Diego de la Unión, where they had very little adult supervision and were mostly left to themselves. "I knew, since I was a very young child, that I was different, and that what made me different was dangerous and could get me killed." He describes being dragged by his feet through town by other kids for seeming queer. "When AIDS happened and they said it was something that happened to gay men, I thought it was already in me. That it could come out at any time."

In 1994, two years before his death, writer Gil Cuadros published *City of God*—an intimate, first-person account tracking his life as a gay Latino man living in LA from childhood through the early stages of his disease. It begins in a lucid, flowing prose and unravels into fragments and poetry as he cares for his lover—achingly watches him die—and as organized thought and language begin to fail.

Rivera used to regularly gift Cuadros's book to friends, seeing in it a mirror of his own experience and objectification—his feeling of disposability in the eyes of society and more upwardly mobile lovers. Cuadros's writing has an uneuphemistic clarity, it has the distance of reportage, unsentimental to its subjects and events, even one's own death. It describes being confronted with stereotypes and apathy from the larger world, even the medical practitioners whose work was to help him and yet who treated him like his illness was deserved, a consequence of perversity, justifiable. In the story excerpted here, Cuadros contends with his own physical deterioration, specifically his loss of sight. He notes the betrayal of the body as it makes his illness (and imminent death) public and forces a disconnection from his neighbors and the outside world as they disappear behind the shroud of cytomegalovirus (an opportunistic infection that takes advantage of a weakened immune system and affects the cornea). The outside world is nonetheless there, and *City of God* tracks the degradation of a city alongside the transformation of sick bodies—he compares his own infirmity to a larger, architectural loss of community. His book is titled for a city that can only be partially portrayed, seen through the funnel of a growing alienation and blindness. Halos rise behind stranger's heads, an image that one associates with near-death narratives or religious experiences—the sense of time is troubled like that of those living between worlds. The book offers a vanishing.

When asked why the series is "blue," Rivera's response is often "because *I Am Curious (Yellow).*" *(Yellow)* and its companion *I Am Curious (Blue)* are Swedish semidocumentary erotic films in which an actress, doubly playing herself and an activist, sleeps with her director and others on-screen while navigating questions of social class and resistance in the Swedish society of the 1960s. Rivera misremembers it as a coming-of-age story: the yellow chapter, he thought, was foreplay, the blue one contained the full sex act. But it doesn't matter. The

idea of it, the memory, is more important—the sexual-intellectual conflation of high porn, the ethos of fact and fiction intermingled. And so are the titles: Rivera revels in wordplay and often repeats phrases for their idiomatic quality, refashioning their meaning. The precocious character in the films is a good double for the young Rivera: a character navigating the politics and society of her time, floating above the fray and rather youthfully concerned with herself, her own pleasure. The films break the proverbial fourth wall and sex happens unromantically, in step with life and politics. Like the Blue Series, *(Yellow)* and *(Blue)* contain a lot of photographing, looking, and filming of the filmmaking process itself. This process of making (a photo series, a film) mirrors the associative quality of Rivera's mind, his stream of consciousness, his way of connecting words and anecdotes. His cultural repertoire is wide-ranging, self-sought and self-taught, moving fluidly between high and low, united by a single metric: himself.

Some of the earliest photographs in this series are, unsurprisingly, self-portraits in mirrors that mark a liberatory sexual coming of age—a desire to capture himself in defiance of the taboo surrounding nudity in Latino culture. Rivera describes a sudden awakening in his early twenties: the body that had once been a source of shame became a source of desire—his own, before anyone else's. His camera offered a means of othering himself, of stepping outside and seeing his own body anew. These early images press up against the strictures of his Catholic upbringing, confronting the shame and prudishness surrounding desire. They become self-affirming and self-satiating.

In a video Rivera shot in the midnineties, some of these self-portraits are printed in an improvised darkroom in his small bathroom and pinned to the walls. Rivera films a close-up of the sink, the photos, then himself masturbating to the images. After climax, he picks up a pen and continues—as if uninterrupted—to add to an elaborate series of lewd pencil drawings graffitied on every surface of the bathroom. The photos and the video depict a young, inexhaustible libido, a hunger.

There is, of course, a continuum. Many of the photographs are simultaneously masterful and ad hoc—and they are happening alongside a mass-grieving event. Their beauty amidst horror is hallucinogenic. "Our hunger will evaporate like money!" says Marlon Riggs in *Tongues Untied*, his 1994 film tracking the experience of Black gay men through the swell of AIDS, as well as the melancholy and play at the heart of the '90s. This tonality—a moodiness, a sass—is imprinted in the Blue Series. If Rivera's initial capture was spontaneous and unstrategic, his later images and their gathering into a series is intentional and aims to address stigma, to upend the predominant representation (specifically) of gay Latino male sexuality as macho and hardcore. Rivera's subjects, many of them photographed at the height of the AIDS epidemic, are presented neither as predator nor prey, but in more human terms of love, lust, and longing, The idea is to usefully deobjectify his subjects, often otherwise treated as expendable.

*

In her 1972 introduction to Lisette Model's first monograph, Berenice Abbott describes photographers ("a new breed") as strange people, whose oeuvres should not be understood in light of their lives. For Abbott, the photographs tell us everything we need to know; they are "naked" before us, revealing the photographer's worldview, aesthetic, and taste. Model's book, which Rivera pointed me to recently, comprises images shot in France in 1937, in New York in 1945, and some taken in the early 1970s, still in the US. They are not organized chronologically but the WWII-sized gap is palpable and the photographer's place—geographically, in relation to the war, but also physically, in relation to her subjects (many pictures are at the vantage point of feet)—conveys a sense of permanent displacement. Rivera and Model may be situated in very different eras and scenes, but their work shares qualities: their beaming use of light; their portraits with direct, penetrating stares; and the blurred lines of a subject or situation in motion that convey that the people and places are adamantly alive, and whether temporary or not, in the photographer's life too. "Concerned with Art, the subject is lost," Abbott concludes in her preface. "Concerned with the subject, Art is found."

It can be tricky to situate the subject in a Rivera photograph. There is the situation he captured, yes, but also his own position and state of mind when he took the photo. "Sometimes when it's in focus, it's wrong," Rivera raises to me one late night recently under the red glow of a rented darkroom downtown. It's really about the image, not about the technical know-how. Through dim rooms and blurry movements, Rivera captures the momentum and underlying drama of a scene. In terms of story, the negatives and prints also carry other histories, damage that indexes the passage of other events and time: the years a print was pinned to the wall, the burn scars on negatives almost destroyed by fire, some outsider's mishandling. These traces are valued by Rivera, who prints the cut, scratched, and seared celluloid with intrigue, reveling in the swirling abstract corners of his compositions. The distinction between "ephemera" and "art" is deliberately blurred, and Rivera focuses instead on where the story is being told. This indistinct line makes it harder to historicize the work, to institutionalize it—or at least harder for others, since Rivera playfully identifies new threads, series, and pairings as he goes, retitling or reprinting editions with a new tonality, irreverent toward the record. In this sense, the work is permanently in progress, in motion, ongoingly being defined.

Sorting through Rivera's archive is a process of excavation. This body of work is an archeological dig of his life's most intimate stories. Many of these photographs and negatives lived in a box, were never meant to be categorized, and their dates were never recorded. Some were printed decades later, carrying with them two time stamps (time shot, time printed). Intentionally, each photograph in this book is dated loosely: "I want them to live in a nebulous space, a different sense of time," Rivera says, "like most queer life was—undated for fear of being found." For privacy and intimacy, the photographs are titled only after their subjects' first names (often pet names, stage names, or pseudonyms) and, because place too is vital, for where they were shot. Sometimes, the same setting recurs with different scenes, different lovers. And when the subjects or locations are unknown, the titles are pared down even further.

In Chris Kraus's seminal biographical essay on Rivera, written for his first monograph, *Provisional Notes for a Disappeared City*, she conveys his process of photographing as a stilling of time—a way of dealing with a life that had, especially in childhood, very few bearings and controls. Rivera often rejects the mantle of "the documentary" —whether that is assigned to the places, scenes, or people he captured—because it implies some larger view and sense of responsibility in the act of photographing, and the images in *Provisional Notes* were not initially made as art or archive. Rivera didn't have an expectations about their worth and where they would be shown. This "blue" body of work acted that way too, yet many of these photographs were even more practical; they involved self-use and acted as mementos. What gives these images their power is the abandon they portray and with which they were taken: a willingness to expend what you have (youth, energy, love, your body) while you have it. But considering now that that youthful decadence and sense of invincibility was set amid a plague and a changing city, there are palpable politics to that abandon too. And there is an obvious politics to making visible what was marginalized, but this was a much later consideration for Rivera, who only recently recognized, in retrospect, that there was a pivot point for him in the midnineties. That is when he began photographing in queer clubs—performers on stage, and the privileged intimacy of the backstage. The performers he would photograph would sometimes disappear before he could give them their prints. He understood the precarity of their lives, and the value of documenting their stories. This is when he began to take seriously being a witness to his time, even in its most intimate of moments. And while all Rivera's work tells his personal story, he recently distinguished the Blue Series he is shaping now from his other photos: "Usually, my work is about how people want to be seen, but this body of work is about how I see them."

In the darkroom again, Rivera mulls over the way his art has been received over time: "It seemed like in the '90s nothing was reliable unless it quoted others: it was about being a synthesizer." Rivera found that back then, talking about his own experience was frowned upon, dismissed as unscholarly and valueless. Today, lived experience and first-person narratives are prevalent. They are so much of what compels audiences. Self-documenting is commonplace, and candid photography is unhesitatingly shared with strangers. This body of work—intent for privacy—feels more voracious, more reckless, because it was made outside of this time and yet now lives in it. Between the moments the photographs were taken and the moment they are now collected into a book, they have evolved from documenting a life to documenting an era, though always through individual stories. And it is through stories that Rivera organizes his work. He is both a phenomenal storyteller and an unreliable narrator—the kind who shifts the emotional pitch of a tale, alters it for each telling, and retelling, to a new audience, imprinting it with a new tenor.

*

While we are gathering the images for this book, Rivera has an exhibition at Reena Spaulings Fine Art in LA, titled *Ya no me quieres*. In the vast white square of the gallery, he improvises diptychs from the Blue Series, creating new couplings between the pictures. *Erotic* as a noun is also "a 'doctrine' or 'science' of love," and Rivera is, and has been, circling around his conception of love. This book is

one manner of achieving that—images of love nascent, consumed, lost, gripped, groped at like one might try to hold sand. As he describes it, one's relationship to love is "the thing no one can take away from you, this inner core." A foundational imprint. In that sense, this is also a book about disclosures, about what we divulge to (and about) each other, about how much of ourselves is in anything we make. It's what we tell each contributing writer when we ask them for a "blue" text: something revealing, a first-person account, a performance for one. "This book is about beginnings and endings," Rivera tells me, though I don't remember where or when.

One evening, as the book is slowly taking shape, Hedi throws a party. I introduce Rivera to a documentary filmmaker on the patio. The idea is that Rivera's life would make a great film, or series. Each character—cousin Tricia, Monika, Craig, Steven, Bianco—could be an episode. Sometimes during our walks, we dedicate our time to a single person, a chapter of his life, and he recounts their story cinematically, with great flair and a sophisticated sense of pace. But instead of getting some advice from the director, I find him hours later, locked in a conversation about longing with the director's boyfriend. *We talked about the cell phone as a new site of desire,* he tells me when we get back in the car, *akin to once waiting by the phone, but the pressure is heightened when the contact is meant to be instantaneous—the images can be extra enticing, and the silence particularly intentional.* Or something like that, about desire in one's pocket and our newish relationship to availability. Then Rivera says he's considering *Tissue Hunger* as a title for this book, because it is a recovery term for the craving a dry alcoholic feels on her skin, in her cells, when she is thirsty. A kind of longing. I'm listening but only about half because it's late, and my mind is drifting to the overlapping vocabularies of desire and addiction.

There is more.

Derek Jarman's 1993 film *Blue* consists of an eighty-minute, fully immersive screen-fill picture of solid blue. A voice-over, delivered by the filmmaker, overlaid by bits of Foley (the outside world in sound only, etc.), describes, in the first person, the experience of a young man dying of AIDS and losing his sight. The voice is reflexive, literary, metaphysical, and occasionally interrupted by a medical exam ("look down, look left, look up, look right"). The hour-plus experience is charged and effectively blinding. The screen's blue color was synthesized in a lab (it was not photographed) and is therefore purely abstract. Jarman's idea, or one of them, was to "show" the world through the eyes of the prematurely aged body of a sick young man, as opposed to much art and advocacy at the time, which would show the sick body itself. Jarman has often, in journals and interviews, described his form of cinema as "an archaeology of the soul"—a darkened interior space plumbed for the sake of the self and society.

Blue is darkness made visible. ...

In the pandemonium of image
I present you with the universal blue
Blue, an open door to soul
An infinite possibility
Becoming tangible

Here I am again in the waiting room.
Hell on earth is a waiting room.

*

In 1997—let's call it the halfway point of this series—Rivera is hospitalized at Cedars-Sinai after a suicide attempt. He captures it on film: Set over one of Chavela Vargas's operatic *rancheras*, Rivera's camera, strapped to a tripod facing his bed, records him swiftly cutting his arm open with a razor blade. He screams a gritty, blood-curdling growl and quickly steps out of the frame, asking his sister Martine for help. "Why did you do that?" she lilts off-screen. And as they call a friend and hustle down to the hospital, the camera keeps rolling for an impossibly long time—steadily documenting the now-empty bed as the music finishes and the curtains billow silently, framing a window looking out onto the daylight of the street. At the hospital, Rivera does group therapy and recalls a woman telling her story: "She was in her late sixties, maybe seventy, an old hippie, she had been with a man for forty years, and she was like, 'You know, I went day by day, month by month, year by year, thinking that in the future we're going to have a house, a great life, and vacations—and I kept thinking, *You know, in the future this is going to be great.* And one day, I was sitting in the kitchen, and I had this realization that this *is* the future. This is the day. This is it. This is what things turned out to be.'" During this stint, Rivera describes being diagnosed with "melancholia related to living in the past": his doctor felt that his attempt to capture everything was like a psychosis. It was suggested, Rivera recalls, that his

photographs were retriggering his anxiety. "There are these photos on the walls, and all the while the people in them were dying." He took everything down and essentially stopped photographing for twenty years.

*

In *Carla, Echo Park* (1997), a woman is standing in the foreground. She looks securely at the camera, her hands resting on her lower back, elbows bent, hips tilted forward, chin down. In the background, she is doubled in a mirror. The curves of her pose are emphasized in her reflection, which offers the additional view of her legs—one is seductively bent, the other usefully straight. She is wearing strappy black wedge heels, save for which she is naked. The edge of a bed is visible in the mirror. There is a closet door ajar behind her. A small white towel hangs on its knob. A belt or robe hangs over its side. Across the room, in the corner, there is a piece of a desk and its matching chair. Their dark wood arcs gracefully, matching the round edges of Carla's shoulders as they draw forward into an affected shrug. Against the wall, there is a large television, turned off. It's a black hole in the image, velvety and opaque (a "black without end that lurks behind the blue sky," Jarman once wrote of his own scenes), in which only careful and intense scrutiny will reveal Rivera's elbows—light-colored blobs turned inward as he trains his camera on Carla. She does not seem to be angling to seduce him but rather to look seductive. Desire here resides in self-fulfillment, self-image. On the TV rest two large antennas, protruding insect-like; a glass sculpture (an hourglass?); and a remote. And above still, on the wall, is a portrait of a man (*Bianco, Echo Park* [ca. 1992]). Fully frontal and resonating with Carla's direct stare, he faces his photographer, confidently. Other than his open leather jacket, he is nude. The room is flooded with light from a fixture above and a single bulb behind Carla that blows out one side of her face, dissolving the edges of her features. Her reflection is in focus. Carla's mirror leans on the wall from the ground; a broom rests on it, doubled, too. Beside them, broom and mirror, is an open door that reveals a piece of hallway. A Persian runner, and two paintings hung flatly on a white wall. The possibility of someone else walking in.

In his 1966 chapter-length ekphrasis of Velázquez's most famous painting—*Las Meninas*—Michel Foucault methodically inventories its component parts: a dark room, lit from above by a beam of natural light; nine figures and a dog, looking intently ahead; the back of a large canvas cutting the edge of the picture like a portal; and a painter (Velázquez himself) leaning back, paintbrush in hand, as if midcapture. What the protagonists are all facing is presumably the central focus of the scene, the painter's subject, but it lives in the imaginary space outside of the canvas—a space beyond the painting's physics—where the viewers (we, I) stand. In the background of the image a mirror divulges the painting's "real" subjects—a king and a queen. Their regal scale is stunted by the distance of their reflection. Beside the mirror, an open door reveals a piece of hallway. A person is walking in.

Foucault's list makes the argument that the painting is not about its contents but rather about representation itself, and the subjectivities that construct it. In *Las Meninas*, the viewer is being watched in the act of looking. The painting is about both, the painter painting (or in our case, the photographer photographing) and the viewer viewing; it stresses our complicity in completing the image. Through a series of stares and positions, Velázquez's painting, like a Rivera photograph, decenters its subject. And when an image is no longer simply about what is depicted, when it transcends both the artist and his subject, it speaks to something larger, more metaphysical, apart from individual lives and questions of consent.

After Foucault's death, in 1984, his friend the writer Hervé Guibert gained notoriety partly for outing the philosopher. This was the nonconsensual aftereffect of a friendship—after death, the intimacies shared remain in the possession of one, no longer two, and social contracts expire. Guibert was dying too, and in his diaries, he recorded his messy, voracious, unprecious hunger to write as much as possible, with abandon. Illness had accelerated time, and as it ran out, the dying writer no longer wanted to modulate disclosure or gossip. *To Write As If Already Dead*, Kate Zambreno titles her study of Guibert, which is also about running out of time. A similar irreverence pulses through Rivera's early work—though it fades in his more mature oeuvre, where time seems to slow. "When I was younger, everyone thought I would be the first to go because I was so wild. Yet they're all dead and I'm still here." His later works are quieter, single individuals mostly, save for a few couples. Photography, Rivera muses again, is inherently about nostalgia, and "the world tasted better ten minutes ago." The witness is the last one standing, left to hold and testify to the flavor of a scene and the people who comprised it.

Some—many—condemned Guibert's indiscretion as self-serving. The publisher Jérôme Lindon turned down the book of Guibert's that contained the most explicit and revelatory details, supposedly to preserve the philosopher's privacy. But others, like Lindon's son, Mathieu, understood that outing Foucault after death was also a tribute: it was about making him whole, restoring the parts of himself he had hidden from society. Guibert was also a photographer and he documented his friend's apartment—bed, papers, and windows—after he died, as well as Foucault himself prior to death. In her book, Zambreno writes about the disorienting flatness of the person Guibert captured on film, which I recognize and feel also about Rivera's subjects, who are similarly divorced from themselves, estranged from the live people these images were intent on preserving as they are alchemized into print. A photograph's subject is fixed in a singular situation and mood state: the image loses the multiplicity of the person's life, their "multiple selves, within a singular self," as artist-writer Gregg Bordowitz puts it. In a photograph, a pensive gaze doesn't contain the moment of laughter, or the throb of lingering pain, that follows the shutter's release. Rivera is a custodian of these moments, a teller of other people's stories as they become image—larger than themselves, more akin to myth, a version of history Rivera shapes and releases with purpose.

Does expertise emerge from the devotional qualities and shared time of a friendship—and relatedly, is friendship a kind of expertise? A book like this one is the result of a series of influences. Friends and lovers, family and others. Along with the question of consent is the question of who gets to historicize this material, with what voice and in what form? Whom does it belong to? This is a book composed of scenes that were intent on being seen, scenes that weren't, and of the very moments at which one makes that decision. To betray, or to alchemize.

*

"Blue" because it evokes a variety of the lewd, the illicit, the pornographic, but also blue blood, blue lips, blue balls, blue poems, the film *Blue*, *Blue Movie*, a room of engulfing blackness lit by a few small flashlights shining blue, a bruise, and the very alive, much documented raw, tender feeling: blue.

SEMIOTEXT(E) image & text series
Edited by Hedi El Kholti & Lauren Mackler

All photographs © 2025 by Reynaldo Rivera
All texts © 2025 by the authors
This edition © 2025 by Semiotext(e)

All rights reserved. No part of this book may be
reproduced, stored in a retrieval system, or transmitted
by any means, electronic, mechanical, photocopying,
recording, or otherwise, without prior permission of the
publisher.

Published by **SEMIOTEXT(E)**
PO Box 629
South Pasadena, CA 91031
www.semiotexte.com

Designed by Lauren Mackler
Proofreading by Robert Dewhurst
Scanning and image processing by Alejandro Rico-Gomez
Archiving by Andréa Nieto and Emiliana Vázquez

"Sight" by Gil Cuadros was originally published in *City of
God* (1994), and is included here with permission from the
Estate of Gil Cuadros.

"I've Listened to This Breakup Song a Million Times" was
first published in *The New York Times Magazine* on
August 1, 2023, with the subhead "Why does it feel so
good to cry this hard?"

Special thanks to Marisol Aynat, Connie Butler,
Becky Elmquist, Daniel Gaby, Kat Herriman, Lucy Hunter,
Ruba Katrib, John Kelsey, Jackie T. Kennedy,
Kevin J. Martin, Jack Ramunni, Kari Rittenbach,
Cathy Rivera, Amy Scholder, Joseph Stuart,
Emily Sundblad, and Bedros Yeretzian

Funded in part by the Institute for Studies on Latin
American Art (ISLAA)

Printed in Italy by Conti Tipocolor
Via Guido Guinizzelli, 20
50041 Calenzano
Florence

ISBN: 978-1-63590-242-6

10 9 8 7 6 5 4 3 2 1

Distributed by the MIT Press, Cambridge, MA
and London, England

Polaroid   B03915A22076

FRONT COVER: *Reynaldo, Bianco, Echo Park*, ca. 1991
JACKET: *Bianco, Echo Park*, ca. 1995

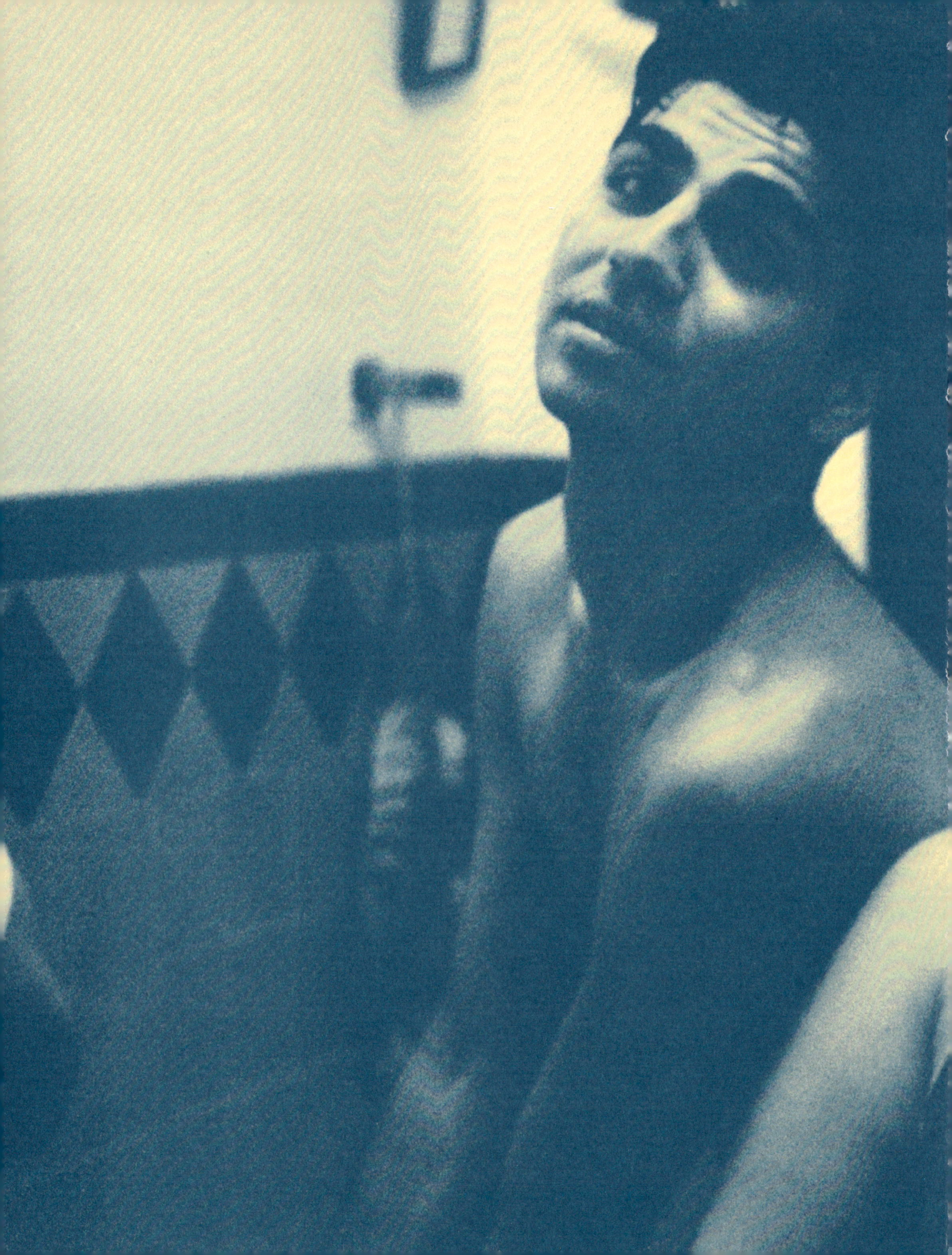